The Human Journey

The Human Journey

A Concise Introduction to World History

Volume 2: 1450 to Present

KEVIN REILLY

ROWMAN & LITTLEFIELD PUBLISHERS, INC.
Lanham • Boulder • New York • Toronto • Plymouth, UK

Published by Rowman & Littlefield Publishers, Inc.
A wholly owned subsidiary of The Rowman & Littlefield Publishing Group, Inc.
4501 Forbes Boulevard, Suite 200, Lanham, Maryland 20706
http://www.rowmanlittlefield.com

Estover Road, Plymouth PL6 7PY, United Kingdom

British Library Cataloguing in Publication Information Available

Library of Congress Cataloging-in-Publication Data
Reilly, Kevin
   The human journey : a concise introduction to world history / Kevin Reilly.
      p. cm.
   Includes bibliographical references and index.
   ISBN 978-1-4422-1352-4 (cloth : alk. paper) — ISBN 978-1-4422-1353-1 (pbk. : alk. paper) —
   ISBN 978-1-4422-1354-8 (electronic) — ISBN 978-1-4422-1384-5 (cloth v. 1 : alk. paper) —
   ISBN 978-1-4422-1385-2 (paper v. 1 : alk. paper) — ISBN 978-1-4422-1386-9 (electronic v. 1) —
   ISBN 978-1-4422-1387-6 (cloth v. 2 : alk. paper) — ISBN 978-1-4422-1388-3 (paper v. 2 : alk. paper) —
   ISBN 978-1-4422-1398-0 (electronic v. 2) 1. World history—Textbooks. I. Title.
D21.R379 2013
909—dc23   2011030048

∞™ The paper used in this publication meets the minimum requirements of American National
Standard for Information Sciences—Permanence of Paper for Printed Library Materials, ANSI/NISO
Z39.48-1992.

Printed in the United States of America

For Pearl

Brief Contents

Contents

Illustrations

Tables

Preface

OVER THE years that I have been teaching world history, I have frequently been asked, "How are you able to cover everything?" My answer—after "of course you can't cover *everything*"—is that you have to broaden your focus. Just as a photographer switches to a wide-angle lens to capture a landscape, we must survey larger patterns of change to understand the history of the world. This means rethinking what is important, rather than cutting parts of the old story. When I was a college student and the course was "Western Civilization," instructors solved the problem of coverage, as each passing year made their subject longer and larger, by calving off much of ancient and recent history. Thus, we began with the Roman Empire and barely got to World War II. More recently, those who designed the first Advanced Placement world history course decided to view everything before the year 1000 as prelude. These are arbitrary cuts, not solutions to the problem of understanding the human story. In fact, that problem requires us to dig deeper into the past than we are used to, so that we can understand the formative stage of human development. And it also requires that we try to understand the recent past not only as a chain of important events, but also as the continuation of long-term processes. Thus, while twelve chapters might seem a spare space to describe *The Human Journey*, I have devoted the first chapter to what historians have often dismissed as "prehistory" and used the last two chapters to locate the present—on the surface and in depth. Consequently, the remaining nine chapters—the centerpiece of the story—take on greater meaning: the rise of states and empires as a consequence of the Agricultural Revolution, the classical age that shapes even our own, the development and spread of the universal religions that dominate our world, the stages of globalization from "southernization" to westernization, and the impact of industrialization and democratization.

Too many people to name have made this book possible. In addition to the scholars I have read, only a small fraction of whom are cited here, there were dozens of others who advised me or reviewed parts of this work, many anonymously. I am extraordinarily lucky to count many of them as good friends. It is regrettably impossible to thank the late Jerry Bentley, but Ross Dunn was also an early supporter. Steve Gosch, Sue Gronewold, Marilyn

Hitchens, David Kalivas, Lauren Ristvet, and George Sussman also read all or parts of the manuscript. Discussions with David Christian, Marc Gilbert, Craig Lockard, Heather Streets-Salter, John McNeill, and Adam McKeown helped me as well. Finally, my good friend Bob Strayer played a far greater role than he would allow, from first suggesting the project to contributing at every stage.

At Rowman & Littlefield I am enormously grateful to my editor Susan McEachern. In addition, I'd like to thank Carrie Broadwell-Tkach, Grace Baumgartner, and Karie Simpson in Acquisitions and Alden Perkins in Production.

7

Empires and Encounters
in the Early Modern Era
1450–1750

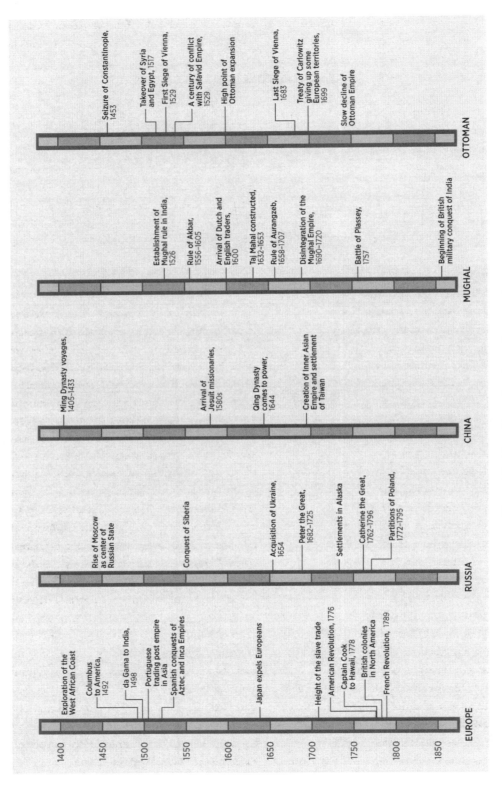

Figure 7.1 Time Line of early modern empires.

THE SINGLE most important historical fact memorized by generations of
students not too long ago was "in four-
teen hundred ninety-two, Columbus sailed
the ocean blue." Today, the name "Columbus"
may not ring as loudly as it did then. We have
learned to substitute words like "encounter"
for "discovery," and no one imagines anymore
that American Indians were lost (or that they
came from India). But 1492 is still the date to
remember—or 1500 or thereabouts: because it
was in the wake of Columbus and other European voyagers to the Western Hemisphere that
the world became one. In bridging the ocean
barriers that had long separated large segments
of humankind, Europe's "discoveries" had profound consequences for world history. Some
were bleak: the decimation of American Indians
and the enslavement of millions of Africans in
the Western Hemisphere. And some neutral
or positive: the construction of whole new societies in the Americas, the modern growth in
world population, and, indirectly, the industrial
revolution. European oceanic voyages marked
the initiation of a genuinely global network of
communication and exchange and the beginning of the densely connected world that we
commonly define as "modern." Thus, historians often refer to the early centuries of this
era, roughly from 1450 to 1750, as the "early
modern" period of world history.

We will pick up the European part of the
story in the next chapter, but first we must set
it in a larger context. To put it simply, that context is that the fragmented world of the Middle
Ages was rapidly becoming unified in other regions around 1500, before and after Columbus
and other Europeans set sail across the Atlantic
and the Pacific and joined the two together.
Even before the European maritime voyages
began, Chinese ships had sailed as far as Africa,
and large land empires were established across

much of Asia and sub-Saharan Africa. In short,
the modern world began before—and outside
of—Europe.

Common Patterns across the World

Europe expanded after 1500 into a world that
was already coming together into a few large
empires. Without them European expansion
would have been meaningless; in fact, it probably would not have happened.

Patterns of Expansion

Premodern Connections. Nor were European countries the first expansive societies.
Polynesians had been sailing and settling the
wide Pacific for at least 1,000 years. The huge
Roman, Arab, and Mongol empires had earlier
brought together very diverse populations.
Merchants and monks had traded across the
Eurasian "silk roads," the Sahara Desert, and
the Indian Ocean since the time of the Romans. Buddhism, Christianity, and Islam had
spread far beyond their places of origin. Islam
in particular gave rise to a world civilization
that joined parts of Asia, Africa, and Europe in
a single zone of communication and exchange.
Technologies such as papermaking, gunpowder, and the compass; foods such as processed
sugar, bananas, and citrus fruits; and diseases
such as the plague, or Black Death—all these
had diffused widely, generally moving from
the eastern end of the Eurasian network to the
west. So Europeans did not begin the process
of joining the world's separate peoples and
civilizations. Their maritime voyages and empires marked another stage in a long history
of cross-cultural encounter and deepening
interactions of a shrinking world.

Early Modern Empires. Furthermore, at the same time that Europeans ventured overseas, other empires were also taking shape. During much of the sixteenth and seventeenth centuries, for example, while Europeans were taking the initiative in the Atlantic, they were very much on the defensive to the east, where the powerful Ottoman Empire was vigorously expanding its territory and spreading Islam. At the same time, yet another Muslim power, the Mughal Empire, was bringing most of India under Islamic rule, while the Songay Empire briefly unified a large part of West Africa in a state dominated by Muslim elites. Farther east, in the fifteenth century, the Chinese sent into the Indian Ocean fleets of treasure ships that dwarfed the slightly later European caravels. By the eighteenth century, China was constructing a huge inner Asian empire, doubling its territory in the process, and had extensively settled the neighboring island of Taiwan. Russians, beginning around 1550, were building the world's largest empire across Siberia to the Pacific.

For native peoples and cultures, these empires were like bulldozers. Few had the weapons or disease immunities to resist. Native Americans were not the only people to be decimated by European diseases and conquest. The native peoples of Siberia suffered something similar at the hands of invading Russians, while native Taiwanese were numerically, culturally, and economically overwhelmed by massive Chinese settlement on their island. And the Japanese state was expanding into the northern island of Hokkaido, incorporating the native Ainu people. In the process, the Ainu, according to a modern historian, "degenerated from a relatively autonomous people . . . to a miserably dependent people plagued by dislocation and epidemic disease."[1]

Gunpowder Revolution. The creation of these larger states and empires owed something to the spread of gunpowder technology, which allowed those who controlled it to batter down previously impregnable fortifications and to dominate peoples without gunpowder weapons. Originating in China, this technology was incorporated in the arsenals of China, Japan, India, the Ottoman Empire, and various European states by the sixteenth century. But this military revolution played out differently in various parts of the world. In Japan, for example, gunpowder weapons played an important role in unifying the country by around 1600 after centuries of civil war. But then the new rulers of the country, known as the Tokugawa shogunate, deliberately turned away from the new technology, banning handguns. Internal peace and external isolation for two centuries made the gunpowder weapons seem unnecessary and even dangerous. It was within European states, with their intensely competitive relationships with one another, where this military revolution developed most fully. Shipboard cannon gave European fleets a decisive edge over other navies, and the practice of close-order drill—enabling large numbers of soldiers to move as a single unit—gave their armies a growing advantages on land. Here was the beginning of a European military superiority that became increasingly pronounced in the eighteenth and nineteenth centuries.[2]

Patterns of Internal Change

Population Growth. The great agrarian civilizations of the early modern era were growing internally as well as expanding into empires. Population doubled from roughly 450 million in 1500 to 900 million by 1800. But it was a highly uneven process. The populations of Europe, India, Japan, and China grew substantially. China in particular quadrupled its numbers between 1400 and 1800, from 75 million to around 320 million people, then about one-third of the world's population. One cause of this population growth was due to the European Atlantic empire: the spread of American crops such as corn and potatoes greatly increased the world's food supply. On the other hand, indigenous populations in the Americas dropped catastrophically in the wake of European conquest and disease, while those of Africa grew very little as the slave trade drained millions from the continent.

Empires and growing populations also meant vast environmental change as forests, wetlands, and grasslands gave way to cultivated fields. In several places, such as Japan and the British Isles, shortages of firewood and its rising price represented a kind of energy crisis by the eighteenth century. Japan responded to these pressures by sharply limiting its population growth during the eighteenth century, by propagating an ideology of restrained consumption, and by a remarkable program of forest conservation and the replanting of trees. The British response to a similar set of environmental pressures was quite different. Far from seeking to limit growth, the British increasingly shifted from scarce wood to plentiful coal as a source of energy and aggressively sought new resources in its worldwide trading connections and colonial empire.[3]

Market-Based Economies. Another widespread pattern in many parts of the early modern world lay in a substantial increase in trade, production for the market, and wage labor, a process known generally as commercialization. China, India, Japan, and Europe all experienced this kind of economic change. When China in the 1570s imposed

taxes payable in silver, millions of Chinese were required to sell either their products or their labor to get the silver necessary for paying taxes. This spurt of commercialization stimulated international trade throughout East and Southeast Asia. In India, high-quality cotton textiles, produced in rural villages, found markets all across the Eastern Hemisphere. At the other end of Eurasia, a more well known process of commercialization took shape in the Atlantic Basin and in western European societies as transatlantic commerce boomed in the wake of European "discoveries" in the Americas. Europeans in North America and Russians in Siberia stripped the forests of fur-bearing animals in a voracious search for pelts that brought a good price on world markets. Although Europeans were becoming more prominent in global commerce, the center of gravity for the world economy remained generally in Asia and especially in China throughout the early modern era. Eighteenth-century China achieved the remarkable feat of adding some 200 million people to its society while raising its standards of living to levels "almost unmatched elsewhere in the world."[4]

European merchants and bankers hitched a ride on this Eurasian trade network, eventually gaining greater power in European societies than did their trading partners in Asia. As a consequence, European states, though smaller than those of Asia, became more commercialized, their governments more dependent on the class of money people, and their lives more determined by markets. Some historians have labeled these changes, especially as they developed in the city-states of Italy and in Dutch Flanders in the fifteenth century, as the beginning of market-based or capitalist societies.

Cities. Urbanization also accompanied the growth of populations, economies, and commerce. Cities, of course, have been central to all agrarian civilizations since ancient times. But the burgeoning of international commerce in the early modern era stimulated the growth of the port cities of East and Southeast Asia as well as in western Europe during the fifteenth and sixteenth centuries. India, now unified under the Mughal Empire, generated at least three cities with populations of half a million people and a substantial percentage of its total population in urban areas. Japan was probably the most urbanized region of the early modern world with the city of Edo (modern Tokyo) boasting more than a million residents in 1720, probably the largest city in the world and double the size of Paris at the time.

Religious and Intellectual Ferment. These social and economic changes provoked some thinkers all across Eurasia to question the received wisdom of their cultural traditions.[5] Perhaps the most far reaching of these challenges to the old order occurred in Europe. There, Renaissance artists and writers broke with long-established conventions inherited from the Middle Ages, the sixteenth-century Protestant Reformation challenged both the authority and the teachings of the Catholic Church, and the scientific revolution of the seventeenth century projected a whole new approach to knowledge based on human rationality rather than religious revelation and painted a very different picture of the cosmos. We turn to these developments in the next chapter.

But new thinking was not confined to Europe. The Chinese philosopher Wang Yangming (1472–1529) won numerous Confucians to a more meditative or Buddhist "neo-Confucianism" that was similar to Martin Luther's challenge to the Catholic Church. Early modern India also witnessed serious challenges to established religions. A traditionally educated northern Indian named Nanak (1469–1504) established a new faith known as Sikhism that combined elements of Hinduism and Islam and rejected the religious authority of the Brahmin caste. Declaring that there is "no Hindu, no Muslim, only God," Sikhism grew rapidly in northern India with a special appeal in urban areas and to women. In the late sixteenth century, the Muslim emperor of Mughal India, Akbar, actively encouraged religious toleration and sought to develop a new and more inclusive tradition that he labeled the "divine faith," drawing on the truths of India's many religions.

Continuities. Thus, we can find early signs across much of Eurasia of a transformation that later generations called "modernity"— deepening connections among human societies, more powerful states, economic growth, rising populations, more market exchange, substantial urban development, and challenges to established cultural traditions. But nowhere was there a breakthrough to that most distinctive feature of modern life—industrialization. Most people continued to work in agricultural settings, to live in male-dominated rural communities, to produce most of the necessities of life for themselves, and to think about the big questions of life in religious terms. The primary sources of energy remained human, animal, wind, and water power, and technological change continued to be slow and limited. Traditional elites—royal families, landowning aristocracies, political officials, military men, and tribal chiefs—dominated the world's major societies. Not until the nineteenth century did the industrial revolution, quite unexpectedly, give birth to more fully modern societies with rapid and sustained economic growth based on continuing technological innovation, first in Great Britain and then in western Europe, eastern North America, Japan, and Russia.

These shared processes all across Eurasia remind us that the European stamp on modernity was hardly apparent when Columbus set sail in 1492. Nor was it obvious in 1750, when China was still the world's largest economy, Japan the most urbanized society, Russia the largest empire, and Islam the most widespread religion. This chapter, then, highlights the varying historical trajectories of early modern societies in three major regions of the Afro-Eurasian world—the Islamic world, China, and Russia—as the many peoples of the world came into increasing contact with one another. The next chapter focuses the historical spotlight on the eruption of western Europeans onto the world stage and the beginning of genuine "globalization." How might we compare Islamic, Chinese, Russian, and western European patterns of expansion? How and why did the relationship among them change over time? How did European expansion achieve a global reach while the others remained regional in scope?

Islamic Expansion: Second Wave

For almost 1,000 years before Europeans ventured far into the Atlantic, the Islamic Middle East was the main crossroads linking African, European, and Asian societies. For several centuries (roughly 650–950 CE), a Muslim empire stretched from Spain in the west to the borders of India and China in the east. Even after this empire fragmented into separate political units, the religion of Islam and the Arabic language provided some coherence for an enormous and diverse civilization. The language and culture of the Arabian Peninsula became dominant in much of North Africa and the Middle East. And Islam took root well beyond the boundaries of Arab culture, penetrating

the West African interior, the East African coast, and parts of Central and Southeast Asia, China, and India. Within this vast region, a distinctly Islamic civilization emerged that drew on, exchanged, and blended the products, practices, and cultures of Europe, Africa, the Middle East, and Asia. Pilgrims, scholars, officials, traders, and holy men from throughout the region traveled the length and breadth of this "abode of Islam." Thus, the religion of Islam, wrote a leading historian, "came closer than any had ever come to uniting all mankind under its ideals."[6]

Islamic expansion persisted into the early modern centuries. What changed around 1500 was the creation of several large and powerful empires that brought a measure of political unity and stability to an Islamic world that had been sharply fragmented for at least 500 years: the Ottoman Empire in the Middle East, the Safavid Empire in Persia (present-day Iran), and the Mughal Empire in India. All of them were created by Turkish-speaking invaders from central Asia, all made use of new gunpowder weapons and built huge armies, and all boasted rich and culturally sophisticated court life, flourishing economies, and impressive bureaucracies. Together they brought about a "second flowering" of Islamic power and culture, comparable only to the early centuries of Islamic civilization.[7]

The Ottoman Empire

Chief among these expanding states was the Ottoman Empire. From the fourteenth through the sixteenth century, the Ottoman Turks advanced from their base in Anatolia, or Asia Minor, to incorporate much of southeastern Europe, North Africa, and the Middle East. Lasting into the early twentieth century, the Ottoman Empire began as a regime of

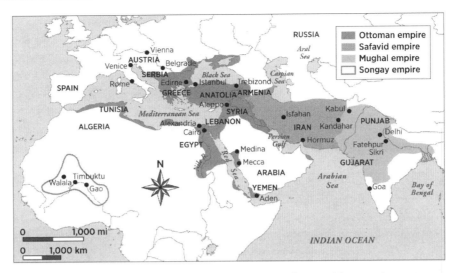

Map 7.1 The Islamic world in the early modern era featured four major states or empires: Ottoman, Safavid, Mughal, and Songay.

conquest that sometimes took the form of frontier raids and skirmishes by military bands called *ghazis*, inspired by the warrior culture of central Asian nomads. Later, formal imperial campaigns mobilized huge armies whose disciplined elite military units, the *janissaries*, actively adopted the new technology of gunpowder into their arsenals and were probably unmatched as a fighting force at the time. Both forms of Ottoman expansion were justified in terms of spreading Islam, and together they produced an empire almost continually at war between the mid-fifteenth and the early seventeenth century.

Ottomans and the Arabs. In the process of these enormous conquests, the Ottoman Turks, relative newcomers to Islam, came to occupy a leading position within the vast community of Muslim societies. Their victories against Christian powers and especially the taking of Constantinople in 1453 gave them a growing prestige in the Islamic world that eased the expansion of the empire. Most

notably, the Ottoman Empire incorporated much of the Arab world, where the faith had originated, including the Islamic holy places of Mecca and Medina. In an age when religious identity was more important than ethnicity, the Ottoman Empire was widely viewed as the protector of Muslims—the strong sword of Islam—rather than as Turks who conquered Arabs. Muslims in Spain, Egypt, central Asia, and elsewhere appealed to the Ottoman state for support—both military and political—in their various struggles against infidels and one another.

Ottomans and the Persians. But in one part of the Islamic world, the Ottoman Empire came into prolonged conflict with fellow Muslims, for to its eastern border lay the rising Safavid Empire, governing the ancient lands of Persia. With traditions of imperial rule going back 2,000 years, Persia was in many ways the cultural center of the Islamic world. Its language, poetry, architecture, and painting had spread widely within the lands of

Figure 7.2 The janissaries were the elite military unit of the Ottoman Empire. *The Granger Collection, New York.*

Islam. Beginning in 1500, the Safavid dynasty, Turkish in origin, now ruled this ancient land. Its most famous leader, Shah Abbas I (1587–1629) turned the country into another prosperous and confident center of Islamic power. A new capital of Isfahan became a metropolis of 500,000 people with elaborate gardens and homes for the wealthy, public charities for the poor, dozens of mosques, religious colleges, public baths, and hundreds of inns for traveling merchants.

The Ottoman–Safavid rivalry was largely a struggle for influence and territorial control over the lands that lay between them (modern Iraq), but it also reflected sharp religious differences. The Ottoman Empire adhered to the Sunni version of Islam, practiced by most Muslims, but the Safavid Empire had embraced the Shi'ite variant of the faith. This division in the Islamic world originated in early disputes over the rightful succession to Muhammad and came to include disagreements about doctrine, ritual, and law. Periodic military conflicts erupted for over a century (1534–1639) and led to violent purges of suspected religious dissidents in both empires. These religious conflicts within the Islamic world paralleled similar struggles within Christian Europe as Catholic and Protestant rulers battled one another over issues of theology and territory in the Thirty Years' War (1618–1648).

Ottomans and the West. In conquering much of the Arab world and in extended military confrontation with the Safavid Empire, the Ottoman Empire encountered other Muslim societies. But its expansion into southeastern Europe represented a cultural encounter of a different kind—the continuation of a long rivalry between the world of Islam and Christian European civilization. In 1453, the Ottomans seized Constantinople, the ancient capital of the Eastern Roman, or Byzantine, Empire, and by 1529 their armies had advanced to the gates of Vienna in the heart of central Europe, led by Suleiman (r. 1520–1566), the most famous of all Ottoman rulers. All southeastern Europe now lay under Muslim control, including Greece, the heartland of classical Western culture. Furthermore, the Ottoman Empire controlled the North African coast and battled Europeans to a naval stalemate in the Mediterranean Sea. Here was an external military and cultural threat to Christian Europe that resembled the much later threat of communism in the twentieth century. In both cases, an alien ideology backed by a powerful state generated great anxiety in the West. One European ambassador to the Ottoman court in the mid-sixteenth century summed up the situation in fearful terms:

> It makes me shudder to think of what the result of a struggle between such different systems must be; one of us must prevail and the other be destroyed. . . . On their side is the vast wealth of their empire, unimpaired resources, experience and practice in arms, a veteran soldiery,

an uninterrupted series of victories, readiness to endure hardships, union, order, discipline, thrift and watchfulness. On ours are found an empty exchequer, luxurious habits, exhausted resources, broken spirits, a raw and insubordinate soldiery, and greedy quarrels; . . . and worst of all, the enemy are accustomed to victory, we to defeat.[8]

Even in distant England, the writer Richard Knolles in 1603 referred to "the glorious empire of the Turks, the present terror of the world." The Islamic threat in the east was one of the factors that impelled Europeans westward into the Atlantic in their continuing search for the riches of Asia.

But not all was conflict across the cultural divide of Christendom and the Islamic world. Within the Ottoman Empire, Christians and other religious minorities were largely left to govern themselves, and little attempt was made to force Islam on them. Balkan peasants commonly observed that Turkish rule was less oppressive than that of their earlier Christian masters. Furthermore, politics and greed sometimes overcame religious antagonism. Christian France frequently allied with the Ottoman Empire against their common enemy, the Austrian Habsburg Empire, and not a few Christian merchants sold weapons to the Turks, knowing full well that these would be used against fellow Christians.

The Mughal Empire

If the Ottoman Empire brought a part of Christian Europe under Muslim control, the Mughal Empire incorporated most of India's ancient and complex Hindu civilization within the Islamic world. Established in 1526 by yet another central Asian Turkish group, the Mughal Empire continued a 500-year-old Muslim presence on the South Asian peninsula; created a prosperous, powerful, and sophisticated state; and deepened the long encounter between Islamic and Hindu civilizations. For 150 years (1550–1700), successive Mughal emperors repeatedly went to war until they had conquered all but the southern tip of a normally fragmented subcontinent, ruling some 100 million people. In doing so, they laid the foundations for a united India that was later taken over by the British and after 1947 by the independent states of India and Pakistan.

Muslims and Hindus. The Mughal Empire represented a remarkable experiment in multicultural state building. Even more than their Ottoman counterpart, the Mughal Empire governed a primarily non-Muslim population and went to considerable lengths to accommodate its Hindu subjects. Its most famous emperor, Akbar (1556–1605), encouraged intermarriage between the Mughal aristocracy and leading Hindu families, ended discriminatory taxes on non-Muslims, patronized Hindu temples and festivals, and promoted Hindus into prominent government positions. He sought to solidify the empire by creating a cosmopolitan Indian Islamic culture that would transcend the many sectarian conflicts of Indian society rather than promoting an exclusively Muslim identity. As a part of this effort, Akbar invited leading intellectuals from many traditions to court for serious philosophical discussions that he introduced with this speech:

> I perceive that there are varying customs and beliefs of varying religious paths. . . . But the followers of each religion regard . . . their own religion as better than those of any other. Not only

so, but they strive to convert the rest to their own way of belief. If these refuse to be converted, they not only despise them, but also regard them as . . . enemies. And this caused me to feel many serious doubts and scruples. Wherefore I desire that on appointed days the books of all the religious laws be brought forward, and the doctors meet and hold discussions, so that I may hear them, and that each one may determine which is the truest and mightiest religion.[9]

Thus, Mughal India witnessed no single or officially prescribed Muslim culture such as existed in the Safavid Empire. Rather, a wide variety of Islamic practices competed with each other, and many of them received support from the state. Furthermore, elements of Islamic and Hindu/Buddhist culture blended in distinctly Indian patterns—in architecture, painting, poetry, and literature. Such blending was apparent in popular culture as well. Adherents of the Hindu devotional tradition known as bhakti and Islamic mystics known as sufis practiced similar forms of worship and blurred the otherwise sharp distinction between Islam and Hinduism. Hindus and Muslims sometimes venerated the same saints and shrines. Some Muslims even found a place in a Hindu-based caste system.

But this policy of accommodation and cultural blending incurred the opposition of some Muslim leaders who felt that Akbar and his immediate successors had betrayed the duties of a Muslim ruler and compromised the unique revelation granted to Muhammad. That opposition found expression during the reign of Aurangzeb (1658–1707), who reversed the conciliation of Hindus and sought to govern in a more distinctly Islamic fashion. Hindu officials were dismissed, some Hindu temples destroyed, and discriminatory taxes reimposed on non-Muslims. These actions weakened the tradition of religious toleration that had earlier balanced the multiple communities of the empire. Internal rebellion flared, pitting "Hindu" against Muslim, and regional power centers became more prominent as the central state lost power. Thus, the Mughal Empire, like the Ottoman, featured a significant cultural encounter with reverberations that have lasted into the twenty-first century.

An Expanding Economy. Mughal India's experiment in multicultural state building was underwritten by impressive economic expansion. Its participation in the world of Islam fostered trade, and Indian merchants, perhaps 35,000 of them, conducted business in the major cities and some of the rural areas of Iran, Afghanistan, central Asia, and Russia.[10] It was a commercial network fully as sophisticated as and much more extensive than those that Europeans created in Asia. At home, the Mughal Empire became a highly commercialized society, for its demand that peasants pay their land taxes in imperial coin rather than in produce required them to sell agricultural products on the market and to buy salt, iron, and other commodities. As late as 1750, India accounted for 25 percent of world manufacturing output, and its high-quality cotton textile industry dominated the markets of the world.

The Songay Empire

Yet a further center of Islamic political power lay in West Africa, where the Songay Empire took shape in the late 1400s around the bend of the Niger River and extended deep into the Sahara Desert. It was the latest and the largest of a series of West African empires based on trade in gold and salt across the desert. Like the Mughals in India, the Songay people were

a minority ethnic group that ruled over a vast and diverse domain. The rulers and merchant elites in the cities—especially Timbuktu—were Muslim, but Islam had penetrated very little into the rural hinterlands. Therefore, Songay rulers, like the Mughals, had to constantly balance their allegiance to Islam with duties to traditional religious rituals and deities. Unlike the Mughal and Ottoman empires, Songay had not yet incorporated gunpowder weapons into its arsenals but relied on cavalry forces bearing swords and bows and arrows in which both horses and riders were protected with a thick armor of quilted cloth.

The Songay Empire was short lived, collapsing in 1591 when it was confronted with an invasion from Morocco, and dissolved into a series of smaller states. But the disappearance of large-scale political structures did little to disrupt the long-established relationships that bound sub-Saharan Africa from the Atlantic Ocean to the Red Sea to the larger world of Eurasia. Continuing trans-Saharan trade links and the slow growth of Islam tied this part of Africa solidly into the web of Eurasian interactions. A Moroccan traveler, Leo Africanus, wrote about the Songay city of Timbuktu in 1526:

> The shops of the artisans, the merchants, and especially weavers of cotton cloth are very numerous. Fabrics are also imported from Europe to Timbuktu, borne by Berber merchants. . . . The inhabitants are very rich, especially the strangers who have settled in the country. . . . There are in Timbuktu numerous judges, teachers and priests, all properly appointed by the king. He greatly honors learning. Many handwritten books imported from Barbary are also sold. There is more profit made from this commerce than from all other merchandise.[11]

Religious Vitality and Political Decline

An Islamic World. Despite its division into various and sometimes hostile states and empires, the Islamic world remained also one world, united by the bonds of faith, by common scriptures, by historical memories, by the ties of commerce, by pilgrimage to Mecca, and by the travels of learned and holy men. Scholars and scribes, prayer mats and precious books, and officials and jurists made the journey between the heartland of Islam in the Middle East and its outlying peripheries in India, Southeast Asia, southern Europe, and West Africa.

Conversion. It was certainly not a static world. Together, the Ottoman, Safavid, Mughal, and Songay empires demonstrate the political vitality and expansiveness of the Islamic world even as Europe expanded into the Atlantic and beyond. The religious vitality of Islam was apparent in the continued spread of the faith both within and beyond the major Muslim empires. The Ottomans brought Islam to Anatolia (modern Turkey), and a modest number of European Christians in the empire converted as well. So did perhaps 20 percent or so of India's population. More widespread Islamization took place in Southeast Asia, especially what is now Indonesia, and in the African savanna lands south of the Sahara. These conversions were encouraged by expanding networks of Muslim traders who carried the faith with them. Islamic mystics or holy men, known as sufis, often gained reputations for kindness, divination, protective charms, and healing and in so doing facilitated conversion. The support of Muslim governments; the material advantages of a Muslim identity, including exemption from taxes on nonbelievers; and the general prestige of the Islamic

world also attracted many into the "abode of Islam." But conversion did not always mean a complete change of religious allegiance; rather, it often involved the assimilation of bits and pieces of Islamic belief and practice into existing religious frameworks.

The incompleteness of the conversion process and the blending of Islam with other religious practices created tensions in many societies. In the eighteenth and nineteenth centuries, these tensions gave rise to movements all across the Islamic world seeking to purify the practice of the faith and to return to the original Islam of Muhammad. One of the most prominent was associated with a young Muslim theologian, Abd al-Wahhab, in mid-eighteenth-century Arabia. He called for a strict adherence to the shari'a, or the Islamic law code, and denounced the widespread veneration of sufis and of Muhammad's tomb, both of which he viewed as potentially leading to idolatry and thus as threats to the absolute monotheism of authentic Islam. Although militarily crushed by Egyptian forces loyal to the Ottoman Empire, the revivalist impulse persisted and surfaced repeatedly throughout the Islamic world during the nineteenth century, from Africa to Indonesia, sometimes directed against local deviations from prescribed Islamic practice and at other times against growing European intrusion.

Decline of Islamic Empires. The case for religious reform was strengthened by the internal decline of the great Muslim empires during the eighteenth century. During that century, the Ottoman Empire substantially weakened and lost territory in wars with the Austrian and Russian empires, the Safavid Empire collapsed altogether, and the Mughal Empire fragmented and was increasingly taken over by the British. Muslims who understood history as the triumphal march of Allah's faithful were dismayed by these setbacks, and some blamed them on a gradual process of decay and departure from the pure faith that had crept in as Islam adapted to various Asian and African cultures.

Modern historians offer other explanations. Some emphasize the declining quality of imperial leadership and internal conflicts that became more acute as opportunities for further expansion diminished. Muslim empires were also weakened by the growth of European oceanic trade routes that increasingly bypassed older land-based routes through the Middle East and deprived Islamic states of much-needed revenue. Others stress the cultural conservatism of Islamic societies. Accustomed to a near millennium of success and prominence in the Afro-Eurasian world, many elite Muslims remained uninterested in scientific and technological developments then taking place in an infidel Europe. In 1580, for example, conservative Muslims forced the Ottoman sultan to dismantle an astronomical observatory that was as sophisticated as any in Europe at the time. In 1742, they protested a recently established printing press as impious and successfully demanded its closure. An Ottoman official, Kateb Chelebi, responded with a warning against blind ignorance:

> For the man who is in charge of affairs of state, the science of geography is one of the matters of which knowledge is necessary. If he is not familiar with what the entire earth's sphere is like, he should at least know the map of the Ottoman domains and that of the states adjoining it, so that when there is a campaign and military forces have to be sent, he can proceed on the basis of knowledge. . . . Sufficient and compelling proof of the necessity for [learning] this science is the fact that the unbelievers [Christian Europeans], by their application to and their esteem for

those branches of learning, have discovered the New World and have overrun the ports of India and the East Indies.[12]

For much of the early modern era, however, the Islamic world was a dynamic place with powerful and expanding empires bringing large areas of Christian, Hindu, and African civilizations under Islamic control. These empires prospered with their merchants active participants in world trade. Sophisticated cultures produced such magnificent works as the Taj Mahal in India and the Blue Mosque in Istanbul. And the religion of Islam continued to grow throughout the Afro-Eurasian world. Clearly, Europeans had no monopoly on political or cultural expansion in the early modern world.

China Outward Bound

While expanding Muslim empires dominated the Middle East and South Asia in the early modern world, China was the engine of expansion in East Asia. Early modern China was heir to a long and distinctive civilization, a sophisticated elite culture informed by the writings of Confucius, an ethnically homogeneous population compared to India and Europe, and long periods of political unity under a succession of powerful dynasties. Headed by an autocratic emperor, these dynasties governed through a prestigious bureaucracy recruited from a landowning elite by competitive written examinations.

Early modern China, governed by the Ming (1368–1644) and Qing (1644–1912) dynasties, was an impressive place. Its state, according to one recent historian, was "arguably the strongest, most centralized, most stable of the early modern empires."[13] It presided over an economy that was able to support a fourfold increase in its population from 75 million in 1400 to 320 million in 1800 while generating standards of living, life expectancies, and nutritional levels that were among the highest in the world at the time. Achieving this remarkable record involved tripling the area of land under cultivation, developing more productive techniques of farming, and assimilating American crops, such as corn and the sweet potato. The growing population also pushed forward the long-term process of internal colonization in which Chinese settlers occupied sparsely populated and often hilly lands south of the Yangtze River. This in turn provoked frequent hostility from non-Chinese groups in the south, such as the Miao, Yao, and Yi peoples, who were increasingly assimilated into Chinese culture.

China and the World

While often depicted as a separate and even isolated civilization, China had long interacted with a wider world. During its early Han dynasty (202 BCE–220 CE), China was the eastern terminus of the trans-Eurasian Silk Road trading network. Buddhism initially penetrated China during these centuries and became a major cultural force in the country. Furthermore, the enormous presence and attractiveness of Chinese culture ensured that elements of that civilization—Confucianism, Buddhism, artistic and architectural styles, administrative systems, and elite culture—spread to adjacent regions such as Japan, Korea, and Vietnam. Chinese armies invaded Korea and Vietnam and fought repeatedly with the nomadic peoples to the north and west who had

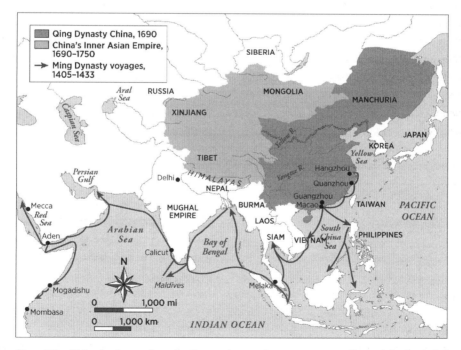

Map 7.2 China's dynamism in the early modern era was reflected in its brief maritime voyages, its empire-building activities in inner Asia, and its settlement of Taiwan.

long represented the chief threat to China's security. The Mongols under Genghis Khan were the most successful of these northwestern nomads, conquering Peiking (Beijing) in 1215. Mongols ruled all of China for almost a century (1279–1368). Chinese merchants established themselves in many of the ports of East and Southeast Asia. Chinese influence (and sometimes political control) penetrated westward into central Asia and north of the Great Wall into the lands of various nomadic peoples. And Chinese products, such as silk and ceramics, and technologies, such as papermaking, printing, and gunpowder, spread widely beyond China itself.

The Tribute System. Thus, an interacting world in eastern Asia, centered on China, paralleled an interacting Islamic world centered on the Middle East. What normally held it together, however, was not a common religious tradition but the so-called tribute system, in which the non-Chinese participants ritually acknowledged the superiority of China and their own dependent status by sending tribute to the emperor and "kowtowing" before him. In return, they received lavish gifts and much-desired trading opportunities within China. It was clear to everyone that this was no equal relationship.

New Forms of Chinese Expansion. Much of this persisted into the early modern era, but Chinese patterns of expansion also took new shape in three new ways. First, in the early fifteenth century, China undertook a series of massive though short-lived maritime voyages into the South China Sea and the Indian Ocean. Second, in the late seventeenth and eighteenth centuries, China vastly extended its territorial reach to the north and west, bringing a variety of peoples under Chinese colonial rule and roughly doubling the size of the Chinese state in the process. Finally,

China incorporated the large offshore island of Taiwan, settling it with many thousands of Chinese immigrants. All this marks China as a major center of expansion in the early modern era and invites comparisons with similar processes in the Islamic and European worlds.

A Maritime Empire Refused: The Ming Dynasty Voyages

In the fall of 1405, a fleet of some 317 vessels departed Nanjing, then the capital of Ming dynasty China, bound for Calicut on the west coast of India. The largest, called "treasure ships," measured some 400 feet in length and 160 feet wide and carried 24 cannon and a variety of gunpowder weapons. The crew of this enormous fleet numbered over 27,000, about half of them seamen and soldiers but including also military commanders, ambassadors and administrators of various ranks, medical officers and pharmacologists, translators, astrologers, ritual experts, and skilled workmen. This was the first of seven such expeditions between 1405 and 1433 that visited major ports in Southeast Asia, southern India, the Arabian Peninsula, and the East African coast, projecting Chinese power and influence throughout the South China Sea and the Indian Ocean basin. And then, quite abruptly, the voyages stopped. The building of large ships ended, and the Chinese fleet declined sharply. In 1525, an imperial edict ordered the destruction of all oceangoing ships. Even the official records of the earlier maritime voyages disappeared. "In less than a hundred years," wrote a recent historian of these voyages, "the greatest navy the world had ever known had ordered itself into extinction."[14]

A Road Not Taken. The Ming dynasty voyages pose one of the most intriguing "what-if" questions of modern world history. Clearly, fifteenth-century China had the capacity to create an enormous maritime empire in the Indian Ocean and beyond and to dominate its rich commercial potential. What would have happened if this formidable Chinese navy had encountered the far smaller Portuguese expeditions that entered the Indian Ocean in the early sixteenth century? Had the Chinese rounded the southern tip of Africa, entered the Atlantic Ocean, and made contact with the Americas, a China-centered economy or empire of global dimensions was surely possible, and an entirely different direction to modern world history would have been likely. This kind of speculation invites a comparison between Chinese maritime expansion and the early phases of European, mostly Portuguese and Spanish, oceanic "discoveries." These European voyagers had crept down the West African coast in the fifteenth century, traversed the Atlantic with Columbus in 1492, entered the Indian Ocean with Vasco da Gama in 1497, and penetrated the Pacific with Magellan in 1520. How did these voyages differ from the Chinese maritime expeditions?

Comparing Chinese and European Voyages

The most obvious differences were of size and scale. Columbus's first transatlantic voyage contained but three ships, each no more than 100 feet in length, less than a quarter the size of Chinese treasure ships, and a total crew of 90 men. The largest fleet which the Portuguese ever assembled in Asia contained just 43 ships. Clearly, the Chinese possessed a degree of wealth, manpower, and material resources that far surpassed that of the Europeans.[15] But the Chinese were entering known and charted waters in which long-distance commercial shipping had been long practiced, while the

Europeans, particularly in the Atlantic basin, had little idea where they were going and no predecessors to guide them.

Power and Religion. A further difference lay in the conduct of the expeditions. The Portuguese in the Indian Ocean frequently resorted to violence, attempted to monopolize trade, and established armed fortifications where they could, and the Spanish in the New World soon turned to outright conquest, carving out a huge empire in the Caribbean, Mexico, and the Andean highlands. Inspired by the spirit of the crusades, Europeans sought to implant their own religion wherever possible. The Chinese, by contrast, seldom used force; they did not construct forts, conquer territory, or establish colonies. Perhaps their huge numbers, obvious military potential, and enormous wealth provided an incentive for cooperation that the weaker and poorer Europeans lacked. The Chinese sought rather to incorporate maritime Asia and Africa within the tribute system, and this required an acknowledgment of Chinese authority and superiority in return for commercial access to China. The fourth voyage, for example, brought back the envoys of 30 separate states or cities to pay homage to the Chinese emperor. Nor did the Chinese voyages have a religious mission. The admiral of these voyages, Zheng He, was a Muslim, and on one of his visits to Ceylon, he erected a tablet honoring alike the Buddha, a Hindu deity, and Allah. It would be difficult to imagine a Spanish or Portuguese monarch of the same era entrusting his ships to a Muslim sea captain or any European ruler practicing such religious toleration.

Differing Motives. The impulse behind these voyages differed as well. In Europe, a highly competitive state system sustained exploration and oceanic voyaging over several centuries, and various groups had an interest in overseas expansion. Revenue-hungry monarchs anxious to best their rivals, competing merchants desperate to find a direct route to Asian riches, rival religious orders eager to convert the "heathen" and confront Islamic power, and impoverished nobles seeking a quick route to status and position—all of these contributed to the outward impulse of a European civilization vaguely aware of its own marginality in the world. In China, by contrast, the Ming dynasty voyages were the project of a single unusually visionary emperor, eager to cement his legitimacy and China's international prestige after a bitter civil war. His primary supporters were a small cadre of eunuchs, such as Zheng He, with official positions at the court. Most Chinese merchants already had access to whatever foreign goods they needed through long-established ties to Southeast Asia and from foreign traders more than willing to come to China. And the powerful scholar-gentry class, which staffed the official bureaucracy, generally opposed the voyages, believing them a wasteful and unnecessary diversion of resources from more pressing tasks. In their view, China was the Middle Kingdom, the self-sufficient center of the world with little need for foreign curiosities. After the death of the emperor Yongle, who had initiated these voyages, these more traditional voices prevailed. A single centralized authority made it possible to order an end to official maritime voyaging, while in the West the endless rivalries of competing states drove European expansion to the ends of the earth. Thus, the Chinese state turned its back to the sea, focusing on the more customary threat of nomadic incursions north of the Great Wall.

Differing Legacies. Despite their unprecedented size and power, Chinese voyages made little lasting impression on the societies they visited. And back at home, the memory of his achievements was deliberately suppressed, and even the records of his journeys were destroyed. This was very different from Europe's celebration of men like Columbus and Magellan, who achieved the status of folk heroes. But the cessation of Zheng He's voyages did not mean the end of a Chinese commercial presence in Southeast Asia, for private Chinese traders and craftsmen in the sixteenth and seventeenth centuries, especially from the southern province of Fujian, often settled in East and Southeast Asia. Sizable Chinese communities emerged in Japan, the Philippines, Taiwan, Vietnam, Cambodia, Thailand, the Malay Peninsula, and throughout the Indonesian archipelago, where they proved useful to local authorities and to intruding Europeans in brokering commerce with China. While Europeans were developing a huge maritime market in the Atlantic basin, the Chinese had created one in East and Southeast Asia.

But China's maritime world altogether lacked the protection and support of the Chinese state. When the Spanish in the Philippines massacred some 20,000 Chinese in 1603, the Chinese government did nothing to assist or avenge them. Thus, Chinese official maritime voyages, private settlement abroad, and an impressive entrepreneurial presence throughout Southeast Asia did not lead to an expanding Chinese empire. In this respect, China differed sharply from European governments, which licensed and supported their overseas merchants and settlers as a foundation for a growing imperial presence in the Americas and in Asia.

China's Inner Asian Empire

Manchus Move West. If China declined to create a maritime empire in Southeast Asia and beyond, it actively pursued a land-based empire in inner Asia, to the north and west of heartland China—from where the Mongols had come to conquer in the thirteenth century. During the late seventeenth and eighteenth centuries, China's Manchu or Qing dynasty rulers brought Mongolia, Xinjiang, and Tibet under direct Chinese control. These were huge dry areas, sparsely populated by largely no-madic peoples practicing Islam, Buddhism, or ancient animistic religions. While they had long interacted with China through commerce, war-fare, and tribute missions, they had normally remained outside formal control of the Chinese state. But the new Qing dynasty (1644–1911), itself of non-Chinese origins from the northeast in Manchuria, felt threatened by a potential al-liance of Mongol tribes and Tibet and by grow-ing Russian encroachment along the Amur River valley. This sense of threat motivated a prolonged series of military and diplomatic ef-forts, lasting well over a century, that brought these areas under sustained and direct Chinese rule for the first time. In the process, China became more than ever an empire, ruling over a variety of non-Chinese people.

Empires of Many Nations. This new Chi-nese Empire broadly resembled the European empires under construction in the Americas and elsewhere at roughly the same time. Like their European counterparts, the Qing dynasty took advantage of divisions among subject peoples, allying with some of them and gov-erning indirectly through a variety of native elites, local nobilities, and religious leaders. Furthermore, the central Chinese government administered these new territories separately from the rest of the country through a new bureaucratic office called the Lifan Yuan, simi-lar to the Colonial Office, which later ran the British Empire. Chinese authorities also limited immigration into these areas. Such ef-forts to keep the new territories separate from

China proper contrast with policies toward non-Chinese peoples to the south, where the climate and geography made a Chinese style of agriculture possible. There, assimilation was the goal with Chinese officials operating through the normal provincial administra-tion, establishing schools to promote Chinese culture, forbidding men to wear traditional clothing, and encouraging both immigration and intermarriage.[16]

But the early modern Chinese Empire also differed from its European counterparts in important ways. Most obviously, it was a land-based empire, like the Ottoman Empire, gov-erning adjacent territories rather than those separated by vast oceans. This gave the Chinese central state somewhat greater control over its newly subjected regions than Europeans who often had to wait months or years to communi-cate with the colonies, at least before the advent of the steamship and telegraph. Furthermore, the Qing dynasty governed areas with which China had some cultural similarities and his-torical relationships, whereas the Europeans felt little in common with their American, African, or Asian possessions and had almost no prior direct contact with them. This may have contributed something to the sharper sense of difference between colonizers and the colonized that characterized European relation-ships with subject peoples. Qing rulers, unlike Europeans in America, generally tolerated local cultures, trusting that the evident superiority of Chinese civilization would win the allegiance of local people. One emperor, Qianlong, even took a Xinjiang Muslim woman as a concubine, permitted her to maintain strict religious and dietary practices, and inscribed her tomb with passages from the Quran in Arabic. No Euro-pean ruler would have practiced such toleration.

Consequences of Empire. Qing dynasty empire building had lasting consequences.

Together with Russian imperial expansion across Siberia, it finally put an end to the independent power of central Asian nomadic peoples who had for 2,000 years both connected and threatened the agrarian civilizations of outer Eurasia. Without easy access to gunpowder weapons, these peoples were incorporated within one or another of the great early modern empires. An ancient way of life was passing into history. Furthermore, the simultaneous growth of the Chinese and Russian empires meant the division of central Asia between them and the beginning of a long and often contentious relationship that even the common experience of twentieth-century communism did not overcome. And by transforming China into a multinational empire, although one with an overwhelmingly Chinese population, the Qing dynasty set in motion tensions that would plague China in the twentieth century and beyond. As the potent force of modern nationalism penetrated China in the late nineteenth century, it undermined the legitimacy of the non-Chinese Qing dynasty itself and set the stage for the Chinese revolution of 1911, which both overthrew that dynasty and ended China's dynastic history altogether. But it also worked on the consciousness of those non-Chinese peoples newly incorporated into the Chinese Empire. It is surely no accident that efforts to achieve autonomy or independence from China in the early twenty-first century derive from those areas incorporated into the empire during Qing times—Tibet and Xinjiang in particular.

China and Taiwan

A third focus of Chinese expansion in early modern times took shape on the island of Taiwan, about 100 miles off the coast of southern China.[17] The native peoples of Taiwan, ethnically and linguistically quite distinct from those of China, had long lived independently in agricultural villages while exporting deerskins to their giant neighbor and providing occasional refuge for Chinese and Japanese pirates. In the early seventeenth century, the island came briefly under Dutch control as Europeans sought offshore bases from which to take part in lucrative Asian trade. In order to make the island self-sufficient in rice, Dutch authorities invited Chinese immigrants to settle there, a process that only intensified after China expelled the Dutch in 1661 and took control of the island. During the eighteenth century, Chinese migration to Taiwan boomed, particularly from the densely populated regions of coastal South China, and the native Taiwanese soon found themselves greatly outnumbered by the recent immigrants.

Unlike native peoples in Siberia or the Americas, indigenous Taiwanese did not suffer from imported diseases; their earlier connections with the mainland provided them with immunities to standard Chinese maladies. And the Chinese state generally required their settlers to respect the land rights of the native peoples. But the overwhelming numbers of Chinese settlers gradually undermined the economic basis of Taiwanese life. The trade in deerskins on which many had depended largely collapsed by the mid-eighteenth century as overhunting and the loss of habitat to agriculture greatly reduced the deer herds. By the early nineteenth century, many Taiwanese were well on their way to becoming Chinese as they took on the Chinese language, names, modes of dress, medicine, and religious practice. It was a process more similar to China's internal colonization than to the creation of its inner Asian empire or its short-lived maritime expeditions in the Indian Ocean.

Collectively, these three forms of Chinese expansion, together with its highly productive economy, powerful state, growing population, and sophisticated culture, remind us that early modern China was a dynamic and expanding society. It was very much in motion on its own trajectory when it encountered an outward-bound Europe in the sixteenth century and beyond.

The Making of a Russian Empire

Paralleling both Islamic and Chinese expansion in the early modern era and intersecting with them was a rapidly growing Russian Empire. It was an unlikely story. In the mid-fifteenth century, a small, quarrelsome Russian state, centered on the city of Moscow and embracing the Eastern Orthodox variant of Christianity, had emerged on the remote, cold, and heavily forested eastern periphery of Europe after 200 years of Mongol domination and exploitation. That state and the society it embraced evolved in quite distinctive ways during the early modern centuries.

Mother Russia

In western Europe, rulers generally respected the property rights of their subjects while negotiating with them over political power. But Russian tsars, following the Mongol model, claimed total authority over both the territory and the people of their country. While these claims were never fully realized, the Russian state came to exercise greater authority over individuals and society than was the case in western Europe. A long and bloody struggle removed the nobility as an obstacle to royal authority and required them to render service to the tsar in return for their estates and the right to exploit their peasants. Urban merchants, few in number and far removed from the main routes of international commerce,

had learned that "the path to wealth lay not in fighting the authorities but in collaborating with them."[18] And while the Catholic Church in western Europe resisted state authority, Russia's Orthodox Church was closely identified with and controlled by the government.

As the nobility, the bourgeoisie, and the Orthodox Church came under the control of an increasingly powerful state, so too were the ancient privileges of the peasantry undermined. From early times, Russian peasants had been tenants, free to move from one landlord to another. But when, in the sixteenth and seventeenth centuries large numbers of them took advantage of this right to move into the recently conquered and fertile "black soil" region south of Moscow, the state acted to enserf them and to forbid their leaving the estates of their landlords. There serfs had a measure of autonomy over their own internal affairs but were subject to harsh and frequent discipline by their owners, usually severe floggings with a birch rod. Serfdom was created in Russia just as it was declining in western Europe.

But the most striking feature of early modern Russia was its relentless expansion. Despite its unpromising location on the interior margins of major European and Asian societies, Russia became the world's largest territorial empire, stretching from Poland to the Pacific and from the Arctic Ocean to the northern borders of the Ottoman and Chinese empires to encompass roughly one-sixth of the world's land area. Russian empire building paralleled the overseas expansion of Portugal, Spain, and England on Europe's western periphery but proved more enduring than any of them.

"Soft Gold": An Empire of Furs

The greatest part of Russia's emerging empire lay to the east of the Ural Mountains in that

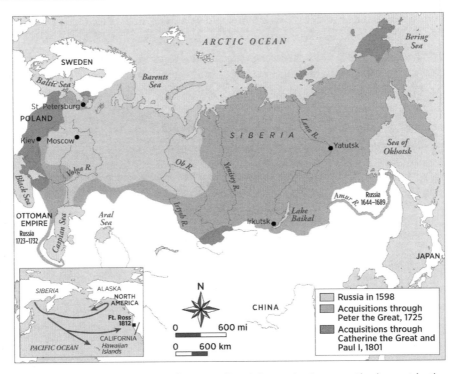

Map 7.3   During the early modern era, Russia's empire became the largest in the world.

vast territory of frozen swampland, endless forests, and spacious grasslands known as Siberia. Sparsely inhabited by various hunting, fishing, and pastoral peoples, most of them without state structures or gunpowder weapons, Siberia hosted societies organized in kinship groups or clans, frequently on the move and worshipping a pantheon of nature gods. The way to Siberia opened up only after Moscow brought other Russian principalities under its control and especially after defeating the Muslim state of Kazan, a fragment of the earlier Mongol Empire. Then, in the 1580s, Siberia stretched before them some 3,000 miles, largely unknown, populated by only about 200,000 people, and possessed, many believed, of great wealth. In less than a century, Russians penetrated to the Pacific Ocean across some

of the world's most difficult terrain; subdued dozens of Siberian peoples; erected a line of fortifications, trading posts, and towns; and claimed all of northern Asia for their tsar. In its continental dimensions, Russian expansion resembled that of the United States as it moved westward toward the Pacific, though it occurred much more rapidly. The early nineteenth-century French writer Alexis de Tocqueville noticed the similarity when he observed that these two countries seemed "marked out by the will of heaven to sway the destinies of half the globe."[19]

Siberia and Beyond. The Russian Empire was a military and bureaucratic project of the Russian state, but it was undertaken by a variety of private interests. A wealthy merchant family, the Stroganovs, led the way into

Kazan and Siberia. Their shock troops were hired Cossacks made up of former peasants, criminals, and vagabonds who had escaped the bonds of serfdom. They were fiercely independent, egalitarian, and ready to turn bandit or sell their formidable military skills to the highest bidder. Like the small groups of conquistadores who pioneered Spanish conquests in the Americas, Cossack troops with firearms overwhelmed, often brutally, the far more numerous Siberians armed only with bows and arrows. Trappers and hunters followed in the wake of conquest, as did a growing number of Russian peasants who could escape the bonds of serfdom by migrating to Siberia. Priests and missionaries of the Russian Orthodox Church likewise accompanied the advance of empire. Siberia became as well a place to dump Russia's undesirables—convicted criminals, political prisoners, and religious dissidents. Thus, the Russian population of Siberia grew rapidly over the centuries: in 1700, they numbered about 300,000; by 1800, 900,000; and by 1900, more than 5 million. In 1911, the indigenous people of Siberia, overwhelmed by the newcomers, represented little more than 10 percent of its total population.[20]

Nor was Siberia the end of Russian ambitions to the east. Tsar Peter I (known to history as Peter the Great) set in motion plans for extending Russian power and colonization to another continent across the Bering Sea to the northwestern corner of the Americas. Beginning in the mid-eighteenth century, Russian explorers and merchants established a Russian presence in Alaska, pushed down the west coast of Canada to northern California, and penetrated the Pacific Ocean as far as Hawaii, where they briefly established a fort and dreamed of a Russian West Indies. But a permanent Russian presence in the New World proved untenable, the victim of enormously long supply lines, American and British opposition, and more attractive opportunities in China and central Asia. The end of the American venture came in 1867 when Russia finally sold Alaska to the United States.

The Impact of Empire. Siberia, however, remained a permanent and fully integrated part of Russia and exercised a profound impact on the emerging Russian state. It was a source of great wealth, initially in the form of animal furs—sables, black foxes, sea otters, and others. Europe's growing wealth in early modern times, derived in part from the profits of its own empires, created a huge market for these furs and rendered them extremely valuable. China too became a market for Russian furs. The quest for furs—often called "soft gold"—pulled the Russians across Siberia and onto the North American continent in a fashion similar to the French fur-trading empire in Canada. Russian hunters and trappers rapaciously reaped this natural harvest to the point of exhaustion and then moved on to fresh territory. The native peoples of Siberia suffered tremendously from this Russian "fur fever" as they were forced to hand over large quantities of pelts as tribute and had to endure bitter punishment if they failed to do so. Russians also brought new diseases that substantially reduced their numbers, new goods that rendered them dependent on Russians, and alcohol and tobacco, to which many became addicted. As in the Americas, the cost of incorporation into the network of agrarian empires was high indeed.

What was a grievous loss to native Siberians was a great gain for the Russian state, which by 1700 acquired about 10 percent of its revenue from taxes on the fur trade. In addition to fur, western Siberia provided high-quality iron ore for its industries and armies and turned Russia by the mid-eighteenth

Figure 7.3 This woodcut shows hunting sable, a kind of weasel, for its valuable fur in Siberia. *The Granger Collection, New York.*

century into a major exporter of that metal. Siberian copper, gold, and silver likewise enriched the empire. In short, the resources of Siberia played a major role in transforming Russia into one of the great powers of Europe during the eighteenth century. Its oil, gas, timber, and mineral resources did the same for the Soviet Union in the twentieth.

Siberia also turned Russia into an Asian power as it came to dominate the northern region of that continent. Its subsequent expansion into central Asia during the nineteenth century only enhanced its Asian presence. In the process, Russia came into contact—both military and commercial—with China, with ancient Muslim societies of central Asia, and with the Ottoman Empire. As it incorporated large numbers of Muslims, Buddhists, and other non-Christian people into its empire, Russia also developed something of an identity

problem, felt most acutely by its intellectuals in the nineteenth century and after. With an empire that stretched from Poland to the Pacific, was Russia really a European society shaped by its Christian heritage and developing along western lines, or was it an Asian power shaped by its Siberian empire and its Mongol heritage with a different, distinctly Russian pattern of development? The famous Russian writer Dostoyevsky had one answer to the question: "In Europe," he wrote, "we were hangers-on and slaves, whereas in Asia we shall go as masters."[21]

Russia and Europe

Dostoyevsky's statement highlights the difference between Russian empire building in Asia and its less extensive but equally important expansion to the west in Europe. Russians generally approached Asia with a sense of superiority and confidence, believing that they were bringing Christianity to the heathen, agriculture to backward peoples, and European culture to barbarians. But in relationship to Europe, Russian elites were aware of their marginal status and often felt insecure and inferior. Far removed from major trade routes and only recently emerged from two centuries of Mongol domination, early modern Russia was weaker than many European states and clearly less developed both economically and politically. That weakness had been demonstrated on the field of battle with Russian defeats at the hands of both Poland and Sweden, then major regional powers. Thus, unlike its expansion in Siberia, where Russia faced no major competitors, its movement to the west occurred in the context of great power rivalries and military threat.

Looking Westward. Between the seventeenth and early nineteenth centuries, Russia absorbed Ukraine, much of Poland, the Baltic coast, and Finland. It also pushed southward into the Caucasus to offer protection to the Christian societies of Georgia and Armenia, then under Muslim control. Some of these regions, such as Ukraine, were extensively integrated into the Russian Empire both administratively and culturally, while others, such as Poland with its large Jewish community and Finland, retained more of their separate identities.

Russia's engagement with the West also stimulated a major effort to overcome its weakness by imitating certain aspects of European life. Thus, Russia was among the first of the world's major societies to perceive itself as backward in comparison to the West. How to catch up with Europe, enhance Russian power, and yet protect the position of its ruling elite—these issues posed the central

dilemma of modern Russian history. How much of Western culture should be absorbed, and what aspects of Russian culture should be discarded? In the nineteenth century and later, similar questions assumed great prominence in the affairs of China, the Ottoman Empire, Japan, and many other societies on the receiving end of European aggression.

Peter the Great. The first major effort to cope with the dilemma is associated with Tsar Peter the Great, who reigned from 1689 to 1725. An extended trip to western Europe early in his reign convinced Peter of the backwardness and barbarity of almost everything Russian and of its need for European institutions, experts, and practices. A huge energetic man, Peter determined to haul Russia into the modern world by creating a state based on the European model, one that could mobilize the country's energies and resources.

Even a short list of Peter's reforms conveys something of their enormous scope. Much of this effort was aimed at increasing Russia's military strength. He created a huge professional standing army for the first time, complete with uniforms, modern muskets and artillery, and imported European officers. A new and more efficient administrative system, based on written documents, required more serious educational preparation. Thus, Peter established a variety of new, largely technical schools and tried to require at least five years of education for the sons of nobles. A decree of 1714 forbade noblemen to marry until they could demonstrate competence in arithmetic and geometry. To staff the new bureaucracy and the army, Peter bound every nobleman to life service to the state and actively recruited commoners as well. State power and compulsion were also applied to the economy. Aware of the backwardness of Russia's merchants and entrepreneurs, Peter established 200 or more manufacturing enterprises, particularly in metallurgy, mining, and textiles, with the government providing overall direction, some of the capital, and serf labor.

In cultural matters, Peter and his successors, especially Catherine the Great (r. 1762–1796), tried vigorously to foster Western manners, dress, and social customs. A decree of 1701 required upper-class men to wear French or Saxon clothing on the top and German clothing below the waist. Women were to wear Western dresses and underwear. Finally, he built a wholly new capital, St. Petersburg, in the far north of the country on the Gulf of Finland. European in its architecture, the city was to serve as Peter's "window on the West," the place where Europe's culture would penetrate the darkness of Russian backwardness.

The Cost of Reform. During Peter's reign, Russia became one of the major military powers of Europe, though it remained economically and socially far behind Western Europe. But the price of this transformation was high. Growing government revenues placed an enormous burden on an already impoverished peasantry. Later tsars required the landlords to collect the taxes, thus increasing their control over the serfs, who were little more than slaves. By promoting Western education and culture so vigorously, Peter fostered an elite class largely cut off from its own people. The educated nobility spoke French, were familiar with European literature and philosophy, and often held Russian culture in contempt. Under the influence of Western liberal ideas, some of this group came also to oppose the regime itself, giving rise to a revolutionary movement that ultimately brought the tsarist system to an end.

Others opposed Peter's reforms from a conservative point of view. One critic, an eighteenth-century aristocrat Mikhail Shcherbatov, pointed to what he saw as the many negative outcomes of Peter's policies:

> We have hastened to corrupt our morals. . . . [F]aith and God's laws have been extinguished from our hearts. . . . Children have no respect for parents and are not ashamed to flout their will openly. . . . There is no genuine love between husbands and wives, who are often coolly indifferent to each other's adulteries. . . . [E]ach lives for himself. . . . [W]omen, previously unaware of their own beauty, began to realize its power; they began to try to enhance it with suitable clothes, and used far more luxury in their adornments than their ancestors.[22]

Despite the sometimes violent opposition, Peter imposed his reforms ruthlessly. Forcing members of the nobility to shave their beards became a hated symbol of this effort at westernization. Punishments for resistance to Peter's regime included dismemberment, beheading, mutilation, flogging, banishment, and hard labor. Whereas Europe's economic development was largely a matter of private initiative percolating up from below, in Russia only the state had the capacity and the motivation to undertake the apparently necessary but painful work of social and economic transformation. This pattern of state-directed modernization continued under later tsars and under communist officials in the twentieth century.

But Peter's efforts at "westernization" were highly selective. He had little interest in promoting free or wage labor on a large scale, preferring to tighten the obligations of serfs to their masters. A harsh Russian serfdom in fact lasted until 1861. Representative government also held little appeal for tsars committed to autocracy. And there was little effort to encourage a large private merchant class or to foster westernization beyond a small elite.

Russia and the World

The Russian Empire encountered many of the other centers of early modern expansion. It sparred repeatedly with the Ottoman Empire over territorial claims in the Balkans and the Caucasus and incorporated many Muslims within the Russian domain. It ran up against Chinese expansion in the Amur River valley and retreated in the face of Chinese power while trading its furs and skins for Chinese cotton cloth, silk, tea, and rhubarb root during the eighteenth century. It was deflected from a New World presence by European and American power and was stimulated to great internal change by the threat of that growing power.

While Russia's empire shared much with these other imperial societies, it was also distinctive. Unlike European empires in which the mother country and colonies were quite separate, in Russia that distinction hardly existed as newly conquered areas generally became integrated politically and, at least for the elites, culturally as well into the larger Russian state. Nonetheless, by the end of the nineteenth century, relentless Russian expansion had made Russians a minority in their own empire. That empire also had a distinct psychology. The enormous scope of the empire testified to its aggressive features, and its subject peoples, such as native Siberians, had painful evidence of Russian brutality. Yet many Russians perceived themselves as victims of other peoples' aggression, remembering the devastating Mongol invasion, the threat of nomadic raids from the steppe, and the growing danger from powerful European countries. Russians were warriors, but they often felt like victims. Finally, Russia's empire

had a unique duration. While Europe's American empires dissolved in the late eighteenth and early nineteenth centuries and its subsequent Afro-Asian empires collapsed after World War II, the Russian Empire, under Soviet communist auspices since the revolution of 1917, continued intact until 1991, and the greater part of it (namely, Siberia) remains still under Russian control.

Parallel Worlds

By the beginning of the early modern era, around 1450, four quite separate "worlds," or big interacting regions, had taken shape on the planet. By far, the largest was the world of Europe, Asia, and parts of Africa. With perhaps 75 to 80 percent of the earth's population, various Afro-Eurasian societies had long interacted with one another and in doing so had generated the largest and most expansive civilizations, the most productive agricultures, the most highly developed technologies, and all the world's literary traditions. Islamic, Chinese, and Russian expansion in the early modern era took place within this Afro-Eurasian world and continued its long-established connections while deepening the web of relationships that bound its peoples together. But beyond this vast region lay three other smaller "worlds" that had developed independently before their brutal incorporation into the "one world" born of Europe's global expansion.

The World of Inner Africa

Much of the northern third of the African continent participated in the religious and commercial networks of Afro-Eurasia. So too did much of eastern Africa, home to the ancient Christian kingdom of Ethiopia and, farther south, to the Islamic Swahili civilization along the coast of East Africa, where dozens of commercially oriented city-states had for centuries shared actively in the world of Indian Ocean trade. However, the rest of the continent—inner Africa—was only marginally connected to this larger system.

By 1450, most of inner Africa was organized in small-scale, iron-using agricultural or pastoral societies. In many places, these societies had evolved into states or kingdoms. One cluster of complex states had emerged in the area surrounding Lake Victoria by the sixteenth century. The largest of them was Bunyoro, the king of which controlled large herds of cattle that he redistributed to his followers. In the grasslands south of the Congo River basin, a series of loosely connected states emerged about the same time and created a zone of interaction from the Atlantic Ocean to the Indian Ocean across southern Africa. In southeastern Africa, the kingdom of Zimbabwe generated a substantial urban center of 15,000 to 18,000 people at its height in the fourteenth century, erected intricate huge stone enclosures, and channeled its ivory and gold to Swahili traders on the coast. Here the world of inner Africa and the larger world of Indian Ocean commerce had a modest meeting. Yet another cluster of states, towns, and cities emerged in what is now Nigeria, including the kingdoms of Igala, Nupe, and Benin and the city-states of the Yoruba people. Trade in kola nuts, food products, horses, copper, and manufactured goods linked these areas to one another and to the larger savanna kingdoms farther north.

Elsewhere, African peoples structured their societies on the basis of kinship or lineage principles without state organizations. These societies too had long absorbed people, borrowed ideas and techniques, shared artistic styles, and exchanged goods with neighboring peoples. When the pastoral Masaai came into contact with the agricultural Kikuyu in the highlands of central Kenya around 1750, they engaged in frequent military conflict that the Masaai most often won. As a result, the Kikuyu adopted from the Masaai age-based military regiments and related customs, such as the use of ostrich-feather headdresses for warriors and the drinking of cow's milk before battle.

Some institutions or practices spread quite widely. Bananas, first domesticated in Southeast Asia, found their way to Africa, where they spread widely in the eastern region of the continent. The position of a medicine man specializing in war magic was found in the northern savanna, the forest areas of equatorial Africa, and also in the southern savanna among peoples who are otherwise culturally very different. "They all apparently wanted more effective war magic," writes historian Jan Vansina, "and so borrowed their neighbors' way of getting it."[23] Inner Africa, an interacting world of its own before 1450, would soon be rudely integrated into the larger world system via the Atlantic slave trade, a subject explored in greater detail in the next chapter.

The Amerindian World

Yet another self-contained "world" was that of the Americas, or the Western Hemisphere, home to perhaps 40 to 100 million people. Here two major centers of dense population, sophisticated cultural and artistic traditions, and urban-based civilizations had emerged over the centuries. The Aztec Empire, founded in the mid 1300s by the Mexica people, drew on long-established civilizations in Mesoamerica. Its capital city of Tenochtitlan with a population of perhaps 250,000 awed the Spanish

Figure 7.4   Located high in the Andes Mountains, the Inca city of Machu Picchu was constructed in the fifteenth century.

invaders with its elaborate markets, its high-quality crafts, its sophisticated agriculture, and its specialized group of long-distance traders called *pochteca*. One European observer wrote, "Some of our soldiers who had been in many parts of the world, in Constantinople, in Rome, and all over Italy, said that they had never seen a market so well laid out, so large, so orderly, and so full of people."[24] But Mexica society also appalled them with its pervasive human sacrifices, drawn largely from the ranks of conquered peoples. This sharp division between the dominant Mexica and their many subject and tribute-paying peoples was among the factors that facilitated Spanish conquest in the early sixteenth century.

The Inca Empire, established only in 1440, covered a far larger territory than its Aztec counterpart. With an impressive network of roads, amazing cities high in the mountains,

and a state-controlled economy, the Inca Empire stretched some 2,500 miles along the western coast of South America, incorporating dozens of conquered peoples and creating a huge zone of interaction and cultural blending. The latest in a long series of Andean civilizations, the Inca state, while no less a product of conquest than the Aztec Empire, attempted actively to integrate its enormous realm. Unlike the Aztec Empire, the Inca authorities encouraged the spread of their Quechua language; a remarkable communication system, using a series of knotted strings called quipus, enabled the central government to keep track of the population and of the tribute and labor owed by subject peoples; Quechua speakers were settled in various parts of the empire; and a system of runners and way stations made possible rapid communication throughout the realm.

But these two centers of urban-based civilization were probably unaware of one another and had no direct contacts. Writing, developed earlier among the Maya of Mesoamerica, never spread to the Andes, and the domestication of the llama, guinea pig, and potato in the Andean highlands did not penetrate farther north. Mexican maize, or corn, did spread slowly through much of North America, and there is evidence for considerable trade among the various peoples of the Mississippi valley and the eastern woodlands in what is now the United States. The arrival of Mexican corn apparently stimulated the development of small cities centered on huge pyramid-like earthen mounds, similar to those of Mesoamerica. The largest of these cities, Cahokia near present-day St. Louis, probably had a population of 20,000 to 25,000 people at its height in the twelfth century, roughly similar to that of London at the time.

Nonetheless, the network of relationships among the various societies of the Americas was much more limited than among those in the Afro-Eurasian world. This in turn limited the agricultural, technological, and political development in the Americas in comparison with the more frequent and stimulating encounters of Afro-Eurasian societies. Thus, many peoples of the Americas practiced a relatively simple form of agriculture, hunting-gathering styles of life also persisted in places such as California, Afro-Eurasian forms of metallurgy were unknown, and the absence of pack animals (apart from the llama in the Andes) put the burden of trade on human shoulders. Despite evidence suggesting sporadic contacts across the Atlantic or Pacific Oceans, no sustained interaction beyond the hemisphere broke the isolation of the Americas until the fateful arrival of Columbus in 1492.

The World of Oceania

Finally, the "world" of Oceania, including Australia and the islands of the central and western Pacific, represented another major region that had few sustained connections to either the American or the Afro-Eurasian world. But within Oceania, the many separate hunting-gathering societies of the huge Australian landmass encountered one another and exchanged foods, oyster shell jewelry, tools, skins, and furs. And the island peoples of Polynesia, who had earlier navigated the vast Pacific to populate these lands, developed sophisticated agricultural societies and highly stratified states and chiefdoms. In some places, such as Tonga, Fiji, and Samoa, people on nearby islands kept in regular touch with one another through trade and intermarriage. The history of Oceanic peoples also took a sharp turn when Europeans intruded violently into their domain in the eighteenth century.

Conclusion: Durability of Empire

Empires dominated the early modern world, as they did much of the ancient world. Their strengths are obvious: large, well-organized military forces; transportation and communication networks that reinforced unity and control; and some degree of cultural conformity. Variations abounded. We have noticed that some allowed a greater diversity of religion, some were more mercantile, and others were more military. But they all proved adept at controlling large populations over long periods of time. Why, then, have they all disappeared? Did empires suffer from a particular fault that made them ultimately untenable?

Two weaknesses are easy to diagnose. One is the problem of legitimacy, and the other is succession or transition. They are related, of course. An empire's legitimacy was based on its exercise of unchallenged power. That concentration of power in the hands of a single ruler was not easily transferable on the emperor's death. Mongol and Turkic rulers had a tradition of allowing claimants to fight each other for rule, thus ensuring that the strongest would govern and that possible challengers would be neutralized. But this system resulted in heavy militarization and in a civil war with each passing ruler. In the Mughal Empire, it became almost common for a son to challenge his brother or father for succession.

The modern world has replaced empires with nation-states. The ideology of nationalism provides a firmer legitimacy than the exercise of brute force, especially when joined to a representative or democratic political process. The roots of the modern national and democratic revolutions grew in different terrain than that of the great empires. Nationalism and representative democracy took root in small states and city-states on the border of great empires. Such states were often controlled by merchants rather than landed aristocracies or military leaders. Scattered along oceans and seas, they breathed salt rather than dust. The maritime trading centers of Italy and the North Atlantic were particularly important in this process. It was not the great Habsburg Empire, which combined Spain and Germany, but the tiny cities of the Netherlands, England, and Italy—more prosperous than powerful—that were to nurture the successful politics of the modern world.

Suggested Readings

Bushkovitch, Paul. *Peter the Great*. Lanham, MD: Rowman & Littlefield, 2001. An up-to-date and readable biography of Russia's modernizing tsar.

Goffman, Daniel. *The Ottoman Empire and Early Modern Europe*. New York: Cambridge University Press, 2002. An account of the Ottoman Empire that attacks Western perceptions of it as exotic and wholly different.

Levathes, Louise. *When China Ruled the Seas*. New York: Simon and Schuster, 1994. A fascinating and detailed account of China's maritime voyages during the Ming dynasty.

Richards, John F. *The Mughal Empire*. Cambridge: Cambridge University Press, 1993. A brief account of the rise and decline of the Mughal Empire with a vivid account of Akbar's reign.

———. *The Unending Frontier: An Environmental History of the Early Modern World*. Berkeley: University of California Press, 2003. Examines on a global basis how expanding societies affected the environment.

Tracy, James D., ed. *The Rise of Merchant Empires: Long-Distance Trade in the Early Modern World, 1350–1750*. New York: Cambridge University Press, 1990. An examination of global commerce stressing the equivalence of Western and Asian contributions.

Wills, John E., Jr. *1688: A Global History*. New York: Norton, 2001. A fascinating tour of the world in 1688 with a focus on ordinary life.

Notes

1. Brett L. Walker, *The Conquest of Ainu Lands: Ecology and Culture in Japanese Expansion* (Berkeley: University of California Press, 2001), 11.

2. William H. McNeill, "The Age of Gunpowder Empires," in *Islamic and European Expansion*, ed. Michael Adas (Philadelphia: Temple University Press, 1993), 103–40.

3. John Richards, *The Unending Frontier: An Environmental History of the Early Modern World* (Berkeley: University of California Press, 2003).

4. Jack A. Goldstone, "Efflorescences and Economic Growth in World History," *Journal of World History* 13, no. 2 (Fall 2002): 351.

5. For this idea, see J. R. McNeill and William H. McNeill, *The Human Web* (New York: Norton, 2003), 181–84.

6. Marshall G. S. Hodgson, *The Venture of Islam*, vol. 1 (Chicago: University of Chicago Press, 1974), 71.

7. Marshall G. S. Hodgson, *The Venture of Islam*, vol. 3 (Chicago: University of Chicago Press, 1974).

8. Quoted in C. T. Forster and F. H. B. Daniell, eds., *The Life and Letters of Ogier Ghiselin de Busbecq*, vol. 1 (London: Kegan Paul, 1881).

9. Athar Abbas Rizvi, *Religious and Intellectual History of the Muslims in Akbar's Reign* (New Delhi: Munshiram Manoharlal Publishers, 1975), 126–31.

10. Scott Levi, *The Indian Diaspora in Central Asia and Its Trade, 1500–1900* (Leiden: Brill Academic Publishers, 2002).

11. Leo Africanus, *History and Description of Africa*, trans. John Pory (London: Hakluyt Society, 1896). Originally published in 1600. Available online at http://www.learnnc.org/lp/editions/nchist-colonial/1982.

12. Quoted in Norman Iztkowitz, *Ottoman Empire and Islamic Tradition* (New York: Knopf, 1972), 106.

13. Richards, *The Unending Frontier*, p. 118.

14. Louise Levathes, *When China Ruled the Seas* (New York: Simon and Schuster, 1994), 175.

15. Robert Finlay, "The Treasure Ships of Zheng He: Chinese Maritime Imperialism in the Age of Discovery," in *The Global Opportunity*, ed. Felipe Fernandez-Armesto (Brookfield, VT: Ashgate, 1995), 96.

16. Nicola Di Cosmo, "Qing Colonial Administration in Inner Asia," *International History Review* 20, no. 2 (June 1998): 287–309.

17. This section is based on Richards, *The Unending Frontiers*, chap. 3.

18. Richard Pipes, *Russia under the Old Regime* (New York: Scribners, 1974), 220.

19. Alexis de Tocqueville, *Democracy in America*, vol. 1 (1835; reprint, New York: Vintage Books, 1945), 452.

20. James Forsyth, *A History of the Peoples of Siberia* (Cambridge: Cambridge University Press, 1992), 115.

21. Quoted in Dominic Lieven, *Empire: The Russian Empire and Its Rivals* (London: John Murray, 2000), 220.

22. M. M. Shcherbatov, *On the Corruption of Morals in Russia* (Cambridge: Cambridge University Press, 1969).

23. Philip Curtin et al., *African History* (Boston: Little, Brown, 1978), 274.

24. Bernal Diaz, *The Conquest of New Spain*, trans. J. M. Cohen (London: Penguin, 1963).

8

The Roots of Globalization

1450–1750

"GLOBALIZATION" SEEMS so twenty-first century. But that process of building a dense web of relationships across the boundaries of oceans, nations, regions, and civilizations actually had its roots in the early modern era of world history. We have seen how the empires of Eurasia stretched the web of contacts and trade between 1500 and 1800. What Europeans did in this period was to integrate the previously unknown Western Hemisphere into that emerging global network.

This network was new in at least four major ways. First, it was genuinely global, encompassing all the inhabited areas of the world, while earlier networks had been limited to particular regions. Second, this new global network came to have a single dominating center—western Europe. This was quite different from the earlier Afro-Eurasian web in which various peoples and societies participated on a more equal basis. Third, this new global system worked far more profound changes on many of its participants than had earlier transregional encounters. The twin tragedies of the early modern world—the decimation of Native America peoples and the Atlantic slave trade—vividly illustrate this unprecedented impact.

Finally, globalization was driven by the relentless expansionism and quest for profits associated with modern capitalism. Earlier patterns of expansion had been motivated by population pressures, dynastic and military rivalries, religious conversion, and the search for exotic or high-prestige goods—gold, silk, pottery, and ostrich feathers—that conveyed status. Much of this continued after 1500, but at the heart of modern globalization lay the endless acquisitiveness of corporate capitalism. The European empires of the early modern era were increasing driven by the quest for profits. Religion played a role in the early stages of the Spanish conquest of the Americas and the colonial conflicts of the Protestant Reformation. But from Columbus's efforts to raise money for his voyages to the granting of corporate charters to entities like the Massachusetts Bay Company, the European settlement of the Americas was an endeavor of capitalists as well as kings. The hallmarks of European expansion were the great commercial trading companies such as the British East Indies Company, the plantation economies of the New World, and the slave, silver, and spice trades. By the nineteenth century, industrial capitalism, with its voracious need for materials and markets, supplied the central driving force of globalization. And in the twentieth century, especially its second half, giant transnational corporations—like Boeing, Exxon, Mitsubishi, and Microsoft—became primary players in the drama of globalization.

At the starting line of this new globalizing process were the peoples of western Europe—the Portuguese, Spanish, English, French, and Dutch. Through exploration, commerce, conquest, and settlement, they set in motion a vast process of change that embraced most of the world.

In initiating this enormous process, Europeans bore the advantages common to many Afro-Eurasian societies. Their food production capacity, based on a variety of protein-rich grains, was far greater than that of the Americas, which had a much more limited range of food crops. Afro-Eurasians enjoyed a virtual monopoly on large domesticated animals providing protein, power, and manure. They were also relatively more immune to a wider range of diseases and possessed more sophisticated technologies, including metallurgy, gunpowder, and means of harnessing wind and water power. Many of these advantages derived from their larger and more intensely interacting populations which could learn from one another. Finally, Eurasians had more powerful states with literate elites able to mobilize their societies' resources on a large scale.[1] On the basis of these advantages, Europeans colonized the Americas, extracted millions of slaves from Africa and, somewhat later, penetrated Oceania as well.

They also created new layers of linkages—both commercial and cultural—among the already interacting societies of Afro-Eurasia. Here, however, they confronted peoples that enjoyed many of the same advantages that gave Europeans such an edge in their encounter with Native Americans. Thus, throughout the early modern era, they were generally unable to exercise in Asia and Africa the kind of political, military, and economic domination that came with such relative ease in the Americas and Oceania. Not until the industrial revolution of the nineteenth century dramatically altered the balance of power within Afro-Eurasia did this situation change.

The European Explosion

No Martian would have predicted Europe's explosion onto the global stage after 1500. Since the end of the Roman Empire around 500 CE, the European world had lost much of its claim

to "civilization" as city life, literacy, long-distance trade, and land under cultivation all declined sharply along with any semblance of centralized political authority or stability. For many centuries, Europe was a backwater in world affairs. Even when Europeans began to rebuild the institutions of civilized life after 1000 CE, they long remained on the periphery of Afro-Eurasian interaction, clearly less developed, less unified, and less influential than the older centers of civilization in China, India, or the Islamic world. Why, then, should western Europe, rather than some other part of Afro-Eurasia, have led the way to the "one world" of modern times?

Europe Outward Bound

Momentum. One answer is momentum. European societies, like those of the Islamic world and China, had a long tradition of expansion. Memories of the great Roman Empire lingered despite its collapse many centuries earlier. And various European peoples had long been expanding internally, creating larger states, growing populations, and wealthier societies since around 1000 CE. Scandinavian Vikings had sailed the North Atlantic and established briefly a colony in Newfoundland. Military conquest and missionary activity brought Slavic peoples in the Baltic region into Christian European civilization, and Catholic missionaries had reached both India and China. European Christian Crusaders of the eleventh to thirteenth centuries launched massive expeditions to reclaim the Holy Lands for Christendom. The Spanish adventure into the Atlantic followed on the heels of the Spanish Christian conquest of the Iberian Peninsula and the expulsion of Muslims and Jews—not incidentally in 1492.

Opportunity. Another factor was opportunity, both geographical and technological.

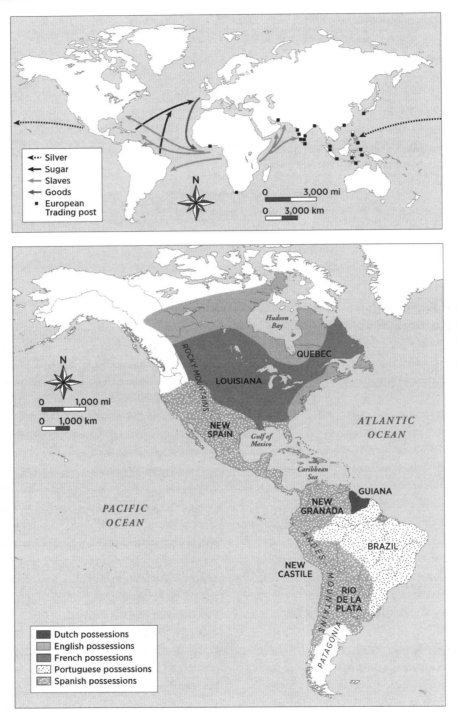

Map 8.1   European expansion and global integration, 1450–1750.

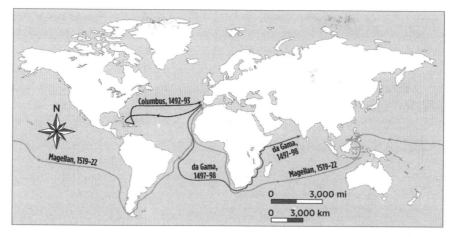

Map 8.1   *Continued.*

Europe was simply closer to the Americas than any other center of maritime voyaging, and its primary potential competitor, China, had voluntarily withdrawn from oceangoing ventures in the fifteenth century. West African societies, equally close to the Americas, had long oriented their commerce northward across the Sahara toward the Islamic world rather than seaward. Technologically, Europeans could draw on a long tradition of Mediterranean and North Atlantic voyaging and on their ability to borrow various navigational and shipbuilding techniques from China and the Islamic world. By the fifteenth century, these pieces had come together in a particular technology, the caravel—an efficient, full-rigged, oceangoing sailing ship, outfitted with naval guns and a compass to calculate its location with reasonable accuracy. It was of little use against major land-based empires, like those of the Turks, Chinese, or Russians, but it was fast and maneuverable on the open sea and able to carry heavy cannon.

Motivation. Once naval technology made it possible, many European groups and individuals found overseas expansion an attractive proposition. European society was in fact distinguished by a widespread support for overseas expansion in contrast to the very limited enthusiasm for it in China. For some, it was the militant crusading tradition with its fierce antagonism toward Islam that motivated expansion. One goal of the Portuguese voyages around Africa was to join forces with a legendary Christian kingdom of "Prester John," located vaguely somewhere in Africa or central Asia, and to fight Muslims together. Religious hostility to Islam was only compounded by the frustrating need to rely on Muslim intermediaries for access to Asian spices and luxury goods, such as nutmeg, ginger, pepper, and cloves, which wealthy Europeans so highly prized.

A further source of support for overseas expansion came from a growing merchant class, benefiting from western Europe's increasingly active commercial life. They easily imagined vast profits if direct access to these treasures could be achieved, and Italian merchants in particular generously funded Portuguese overseas expeditions. In some parts of western Europe, such as England and the

Netherlands, such men of commerce and business acquired a social prestige and political influence unknown in most other societies, which were socially dominated by landowning aristocracies. Furthermore, European monarchs, perpetually short of revenue to run their kingdoms and fight their wars, saw a taxable overseas trade very much in their interests. Their endless competition with one another, so different from the single centralized empire of China, also provided a motor for continuous expansion once the process got under way. And impoverished members of the landowning nobility needed new sources of wealth, for declining income from feudal payments was eroding their economic base. This was particularly true in a small country such as Portugal with little room for internal expansion.

Beyond these particular sources of support for overseas expansion, Europe's economy as a whole was running short of gold needed to finance its growing internal trade and to pay for spices, jewels, and other Asian luxuries for its wealthy elite. The initial motive for the Portuguese voyages was to gain direct access not to Asian spices but to West African gold fields, long monopolized by North African Muslim middlemen. And Europe's agriculture, based on wheat and livestock, could expand only by adding territory, whereas the more intensive rice agriculture of Asia could grow by the application of more labor. Thus, the increasing desire in Europe for wheat, sugar, meat, and fish meant that Europeans needed new lands to support the growth of their economies.[2]

Behind all these motives lay the perception of many Europeans that the "East" held the promise of great wealth. It was an acknowledgment that theirs was a relatively "underdeveloped" society. Europeans, after all, were seeking routes to Asia; few Asians were looking for ways to get to Europe.

A Changing Europe

Europe's overseas expansion drew strength and energy from an unusually wide range of internal changes. It was the youngest of the world's major civilizations, having taken shape only after 1000 CE, and it proved willing to borrow from the more established civilizations of Asia and the Islamic world. It was recovering from the disruption of the Black Death of the fourteenth century, which had reduced its population by perhaps one-third. As population grew again, new and stronger states, such as England, France, and Spain, were gaining a greater capacity to mobilize the resources of their societies. A growing economy was developing the institutions of an early capitalism, such as banks, insurance companies, stock exchanges, joint stock companies, and a wealthy merchant class.

The European Renaissance. At the same time, Europeans began to think in less religious and more secular terms about their place in the world. The Renaissance, a flowering of urban culture between the fourteenth and sixteenth centuries, reflected this new consciousness. Artists and writers sought inspiration in the non-Christian literature of classical Greece and Rome. Princes patronized artists, such as Michelangelo, Leonardo da Vinci, and Raphael, whose paintings and sculptures were far more naturalistic, especially in portraying the human body, than their medieval counterparts. Europeans read humanistic scholars who argued that Christians could legitimately involve themselves in the real world of marriage, business, and politics rather than withdrawing into the secluded life of monasteries.

The Reformation. The Protestant Reformation likewise challenged older patterns of thought. It began in 1517 when the German monk Martin Luther raised a public protest against the abuses of the Catholic Church (such as selling indulgences said to remove the penalties for sin) and against some of its doctrines as well. To Luther, the source of religious belief was no longer the pope or the Church hierarchy but the Bible alone, interpreted by the individual's conscience. These protests shattered the unity of the Catholic Church, which had for the previous 1,000 years provided the cultural and organizational foundation of Western civilization. Now a proliferation of "protestant" churches, all rejecting the authority of the pope, called into question the answers to life's big questions that the Catholic Church had long provided and encouraged a skeptical attitude toward authority and tradition.

The Scientific Revolution. Europe's overseas expansion also coincided with its scientific revolution. From the time of Nicolaus Copernicus (1473–1543) to that of Isaac Newton (1642–1727), the view of the universe held by educated Europeans fundamentally changed. Instead of an earth centered under a canopy of heavenly orbs, propelled by angels and spirits, scientists began to see their planet as one of many in an infinite space. Yet the sun and innumerable stars seemed to be governed by the same principles as life on the earth, and these principles were discoverable by systematic observation, measurement, and theorizing. Highly polished Dutch lenses were turned on distant stars and previously invisible life on Earth to reveal regularities of motion, mass, and matter. The gravity that held us to our planet was the same as the force that kept the planets on their paths and prevented the objects of the earth from flying apart.

Certainly, the Renaissance, the Reformation, and the scientific revolution did not cause Europe's overseas thrust, but in their challenge to conventional thinking and in their emphasis on the power of individuals, these movements created a cultural environment that supported those who ventured abroad and contributed to Europe's vigorous response to these new opportunities.

The Making of an Atlantic World

The most significant outcome of Europe's early modern expansion was the creation of an Atlantic world—a network of communication and exchange involving Europe, Africa, and North and South America. Germs, plants, animals, people, cultures, ideas, products, and money—all this circulated across the Atlantic world, linking forever four continents. While Islamic, Chinese, and Russian expansion continued older patterns of world history, Europe's Atlantic imperialism gave rise to something wholly new and with genuinely global reverberations.

When the Spanish monarchs Isabella and Ferdinand sent the Genoese Christopher Columbus west to find the East, both they and he anticipated the development of trading connections with the richer civilizations of Asia. From their perspective, the discovery of America was an "immense disappointment, a heart-breaking obstacle on the hoped for route to the East."[3] The technologically simple societies inhabiting the Caribbean and the eastern coast of the Americas provided few trading opportunities. But it soon became apparent that other possibilities were at hand—vast expanses of fertile land, a potential native labor force, and heartening rumors of abundant gold and silver. From these possibilities, the Spanish and Portuguese—and later the British and French—fashioned empires in the Americas quite different from Islamic, Chinese, or Russian empires.

American Differences

Conquest. The rapid pace of conquest was the first important difference. Attracted by the promise of precious metals, the Spanish led the way, transferring to the Americas many of the patterns of conquest, conversion, and colonization that they had pioneered during centuries of struggle against the Muslim rulers of Spain itself. The speed and sweep of Spanish conquest in the Americas resembled only the previous conquests of early Islam. Within 50 years, most of what was to be known as the Americas had been claimed for the Spanish crown. These conquests included the sophisticated empires of the Aztecs and the Incas as well as the Indians of North America and the much of the Caribbean.

While they encountered stiff resistance in many places, the Spanish—and later the other imperial powers—were able in the long run to dominate native peoples who proved fatally vulnerable to European weapons, European diseases, and their own internal divisions.

The collapse of the Aztec Empire provides a telling example. In just two years (1519–1521), this expanding and prosperous state was suddenly and devastatingly overwhelmed. A small Spanish force, led by Hernando Cortes and joined by thousands of hostile subjects of the Aztec Empire, decisively defeated the Aztec defenders. The capital city of Tenochtitlan was left in ruins. The last Aztec emperor, Cuahtemoc, surrendered and, in a face-to-face meeting with Cortes, placed his hand on the Spaniard's dagger and begged to be killed, "for you have already destroyed my city and killed my people."[4] While the former subjects of the Aztec Empire, from whom captives had long been seized for human sacrifice, may have rejoiced at their liberation, for the dominant Mexica people all was lamentation,

as reflected in this poem composed shortly after conquest:

Broken spears lie in the roads;
we have torn our hair in our grief.
The houses are roofless now, and their
    walls
are red with blood.
Worms are swarming in the streets and
    plazas,
and the walls are splattered with gore.
The water has turned red, as if it were
    dyed,
and when we drink it,
it has the taste of brine.
We have pounded our hands in despair
against the adobe walls,
for our inheritance, our city, is lost and
    dead.
The shields of our warriors were its
    defense,
but they could not save it.
We have chewed dry twigs and salt
    grasses;
we have filled our mouths with dust and
    bits of adobe;
we have eaten lizards, rats, and worms.[5]

Disease and Disaster. Isolated for thousands of years from the world of Afro-Eurasia, the inhabitants of the Americas lacked immunity to common diseases on the other side of the Atlantic. Smallpox, measles, yellow fever, and malaria swept into oblivion both millions of individuals and many entire peoples in the Americas. The native population of the Caribbean, estimated at several million in 1492, numbered only several thousand by the 1540s. A densely populated Mexico with perhaps 14 million people declined by 90 percent or more within a century of Cortes's arrival in 1519. Far more than Spanish conquistadores or

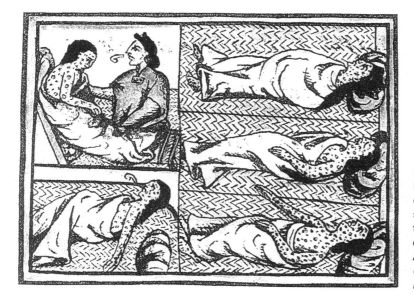

Figure 8.1 Devastating epidemics such as smallpox facilitated the European conquest of the Americas. *The Granger Collection, New York.*

missionaries, the germs of Europe and Africa shaped the transatlantic encounter.

The deadly impact of disease was only exacerbated by the brutality of European rule. A young sixteenth-century priest, Bartolome de Las Casas, wrote an eyewitness account of Spanish behavior on the Caribbean island of Hispaniola:

> Into this land of meek outcasts there came some Spaniards who immediately behaved like ravening wild beasts . . . that had been starved for many days. And the Spaniards behaved in no other way during the past 40 years . . . , for they are still . . . killing, terrorizing, torturing, and destroying the native peoples, doing all this with the strangest and most varied new methods of cruelty, never seen or heard of before. . . . After the wars and killings had ended . . . , the survivors were distributed among the Christians to be slaves . . . to send the men to the mines to dig for gold, which is intolerable labor, and to send the women into the fields of the big ranches to hoe and till the land. . . . And the men died in the

mines and the women died on the ranches from the same causes, exhaustion and hunger. And thus was depopulated that island which had been densely populated.[6]

From this combination of disease and brutality emerged a demographic catastrophe of genocidal proportions, albeit largely unintentional. Nothing of this magnitude accompanied Chinese or Islamic expansion that operated within a common disease environment; it was a distinctive and horrifying feature in the making of the Atlantic world and one that was replicated in parts of Oceania in the nineteenth century. It was, however, similar to the fate of many other isolated peoples in earlier times when they were incorporated into urban-based civilizations bearing new and deadly diseases.

Plants and Animals. Accompanying Europeans in their conquest of the Americas were not only their pathogens but also their plants and animals, which likewise contributed enormously to transforming the Western Hemisphere and its peoples. The introduction of sugarcane gave rise to plantation econo- mies and the massive use of African slaves, thus shaping the entire social structure of the Americas. The importation of cows and horses produced ranching economies and cowboy culture in both North and South America and transformed the societies of numerous Native American peoples. The Pawnee of the North American Great Plains, for example, had lived as settled farmers in sedentary villages, hunt- ing bison only on a seasonal basis. But with the adoption of the horse, hunting bison became a year-round occupation, temporary tepees replaced permanent houses, and the economic role of women diminished as a male-domi- nated hunting and warrior culture emerged. European imports like sheep, cattle, goats, and especially pigs, together with grapes, wheat, and various European vegetables, also flour- ished in the Americas and made possible the reproduction of major elements of European ways of life in a new setting. After all, the first conquistadores wondered, how was it possible to live in a country without bread and wine?

Migrations. The demographic disaster that accompanied European conquest of the Amer- icas created not only human suffering on an epic scale but also an enormous labor short- age that opened the way to massive European and African migration in the four centuries following the arrival of Columbus. It was the largest and most rapid population transfer in world history. The infusion of these new populations gave European empires in the Americas their most distinctive quality. Until the nineteenth century, African slaves were far more numerous than European immigrants, with more than 6 million arriving in the eigh- teenth century alone. After that, the slave trade gradually diminished, and the flood tide of European migration took over with some 55 million people leaving Europe between 1820

and 1930, the vast majority of them headed for the Americas.[7]

Colonial Societies in the Americas

Africans, Europeans, and Native Americans mixed and mingled in various ways, depend- ing on the extent of the demographic disaster, on the policies of various colonial powers, and on the economies that the newcomers erected. Out of this vast process of cultural transplan- tation and blending emerged several distinct kinds of colonial societies in the Americas. What they had in common was their novelty. While the Ottoman, Mughal, and Chinese empires largely incorporated existing societies and changed them only modestly, the Eu- ropean empires in the Americas gave rise to wholly new societies.

Settler Colonies. In the northern colo- nies of Britain and France, such as those in New England and Quebec, settlement colonies developed, largely without slaves, in which Europeans constituted the great majority of the population. By the late eighteenth cen- tury, people of European descent comprised about 80 percent of the population of British North America, far higher than in any of the Latin American colonies, where Europeans were generally a distinct minority. In this respect, North America resembled Siberia, where Russians and Russian culture likewise overwhelmed the indigenous people. British settlers sought both to escape the religious, political, and social restrictions of England and to transplant many elements of European culture in what was to them a New World. Authorities in Virginia wanted to limit horse racing to "men of the better sort," while laws in Massachusetts forbade ordinary people from wearing fine clothes that implied a higher so- cial status. But the vastness of the territory and the easy availability of land gradually eroded sharp class distinctions and created a more flexible and fluid society with more individualism and opportunity for social mobility than had existed in the "mother country."

"Mixed-Race Colonies." A second kind of colonial society developed in the highland areas of Mexico and Peru, home to the Aztec and Inca empires. In these areas of great wealth and more concentrated population, Spanish colonizers merely replaced the existing hierarchy with their own authoritarian rulers, who made use of various forms of forced labor in extracting mineral wealth, in agricultural production, and in workshops. These native laborers, often grossly abused and exploited, made possible the great highland estates, some producing for export, others providing cattle and grain to sustain the cities and mining

areas. Other Indian laborers toiled to premature death in grueling mines, such as those at Guanajuato in north-central Mexico and Potosi in present-day Bolivia, where the enormous output of silver fueled much of the emerging world economy. Such miners were sometimes kept underground from Monday to Saturday evening, with their wives bringing them food. When wage labor began to replace forced labor in the seventeenth century, perpetual indebtedness and high taxes kept native workers in low-paying jobs, often living little better than slaves. In these regions, a substantial minority of white settlers, primarily male, ruled a large Native American population and intermarried with them to produce a mixed-race group known as mestizos.

Plantation Colonies. Perhaps the most novel of all colonial societies grew up around

Figure 8.2 The plantation economy depended on slavery, and slavery depended on brutality.
bpk, Berlin/Art Resource, NY.

the plantation economies in the tropical low-lands of the Americas. This kind of agricultural production, organized in large-scale units and worked by slaves, had been pioneered in the Mediterranean as Europeans learned about sugarcane from Arabs during the Crusades and created plantations to produce this very labor-intensive product. As they moved out into the Atlantic in the fifteenth century, they established sugar producing plantations on offshore islands such as Madeira, the Canaries, and Sao Tome and from there transferred them to the Americas, especially the Caribbean, Brazil, Ecuador, Venezuela, and Guatemala and in the southern colonies of British North America. Producing sugar initially and then coffee, tobacco, indigo, rice, and cotton, the plantations themselves operated largely with African slave labor supervised by a relatively small group of white owners and managers. Thus, a wholly immigrant society emerged in which Africans vastly outnumbered Europeans, while Native Americans in these areas had largely died out or been pushed out. The extremely harsh conditions under which the slaves worked made it difficult to form stable families or even to survive very long. Brazilian slave owners coldly calculated a slave's life expectancy at only seven years. This meant that slave populations, except in North America, rarely became self-reproducing, requiring plantation owners to buy new slaves on a regular basis. And unlike the original sugar plantations in the Mediterranean, where slaves came from many places, including Muslim North Africa and Slavic-speaking regions around the Black Sea, in the Americas slavery took on its unique exclusive association with Africa.

American plantation societies were novel as well in their highly internationalized system of production. Europeans from Spain, Portugal, England, France, and the Netherlands supplied the capital and managerial expertise, exercised complete political control, and reaped the profits of the system. Africa supplied the workers in return for European manufactured goods. The plantations themselves were specialized units that operated in an almost industrial pattern of highly disciplined work; they produced, for the first time in world history, for a mass market in Europe; they imported much of their food and supplies; and they relied heavily on the use of credit to keep this vast network of international transactions going. In these ways, the plantation system pioneered major elements of a modern globalized economy, even while maintaining the ancient pattern of slavery as the basis for the entire enterprise.

North American Differences. Within the world of Atlantic plantations, those in the southern colonies of British North America were unique in several ways. First, a far smaller number of slaves were imported into North American colonies, about 6 percent of the total compared to 40 percent to the Caribbean, 37 percent to Brazil, and 15 percent to mainland Spanish America. Thus, unlike many Latin American territories, people of African descent remained a minority in most North American plantation societies. But slaves there became self-reproducing as they did not in most of Latin America, thus requiring the importation of fewer new slaves. Some historians have suggested that this may have diluted the African cultural heritage of slave communities in North America and rendered them less likely to rebel or run away compared to their Latin American counterparts. Finally, North American plantation societies, despite considerable racial mixing, never developed the various "mixed-race" categories and distinctions that were widely recognized elsewhere in the Americas. The children of Thomas Jefferson and his enslaved mistress Sally Hemmings were regarded as black rather than mestizo. The racial divide was sharper in North America, and the white antipathy toward Africans as black people, not just as slaves, was more pronounced.

The colonies that became the United States evolved differently than those of Spanish America. They were founded a century later and in a region that lacked the dense native populations, great empires, large cities, and precious metals that seemed to give the Spanish colonies such initial advantages. Indeed, when the British constructed their first buildings in Jamestown in 1607, the Spanish had already established nearly a dozen major cities, two great viceroyalties in Mexico and Peru, many universities, hundreds of churches and missions, and a sophisticated network of regulated commerce. Throughout the seventeenth and eighteenth centuries, the North American colonies by contrast were widely regarded as something of a backwater in terms of population, commercial potential, and their role in the world economy. Yet precisely these "backward" colonies became the wealthy, politically stable, global superpower of the twentieth century, while the former Spanish and Portuguese colonies long remained divided, impoverished, and politically volatile.

The Impact of Empire

Whatever their particular features, all of these American empires had a far more profound impact on indigenous societies than did the Ottoman, Mughal, Chinese, or West African empires. Part of this difference is reflected in the brutal facts of rapid conquest and in catastrophic population declines. Furthermore, the export economies of the Americas, producing precious metals and agricultural goods for a European market, led to extensive demands for land and labor that dispossessed millions and thoroughly disrupted traditional societies. This disruption contributed much to the wide acceptance of Christianity, which was force-fed to the dispirited Native American populations, especially in Spanish America. Many no doubt felt that their own gods had deserted them as did the Mexica poet who asked plaintively after the Spanish conquest, "Have you grown weary of your servants? Are you angry with your servants, O Giver of Life?"[8] Neither the Ottomans in Europe nor the Mughals in India nor the Chinese in inner Asia made such a concerted effort to bring a new religion to their subject peoples. But as Christianity was adopted, it was also modified as native peoples interpreted it through the lens of their own beliefs. The cross, for example, was similar to the Mayan tree of life and to the prayer sticks of the Pueblo, and while Christian churches were built on the remains of destroyed temples, American Indians assimilated Christian saints and feast days into their traditional gods and celebrations.

The environmental impact of European intrusion into the Americas was likewise remarkable. Fur trappers in North America largely eliminated beavers and drastically thinned the herds of deer. The walrus and the bowhead whale largely vanished from the North Atlantic in the wake of European fishing, while still-abundant codfish diminished in size. Settlers and plantation owners began the deforestation of the Western Hemisphere and plowed its prairies for the first time. In the absence of natural predators, the animals of Europe—sheep, goats, cattle, horses, and pigs—reproduced spectacularly both in domesticated settings and in the wild. Their arrival and the dramatic increase in their numbers, coinciding with the sharp decline in the native human population, marked a dramatic change in the ecology of the Americas. European plant life—both crops and weeds—colonized the Americas along with their human carriers. When Charles Darwin visited Argentina and Chile in the 1830s, he was amazed at the spread of the wild artichoke. "I doubt," he wrote, "whether any case is on record of an invasion on so grand a scale of one plant over the aborigines."[9]

Africa and the Atlantic World

The making of an Atlantic world occasioned two of the great tragedies of modern world history—the destruction of Native American populations and the Atlantic slave trade. The second of these processes deeply engaged African societies, particularly along the western coast of the continent during the four centuries between roughly 1450 and 1850. African individuals were the chief victims of this horrendous traffic, some 11 million of whom were shipped to the Americas and uncounted millions more who died in the process of capture and during the horrors of the Middle Passage.[10] But African societies, unlike those in the Americas, were not subject to European conquest or colonial rule in early modern times. They retained their political independence, and their political and economic elites were active participants in the slave trade. This tragedy unfolded quite differently from that which befell Native Americans.

Origins of the Atlantic Slave Trade

Demand. As a relationship of commerce rather than conquest, the slave trade had its origins in a unique combination of demand and supply. The demand, of course, came from the European plantation economies in the Americas desperately in search of workers and seeking to imitate the slave labor solution pioneered on earlier plantations in the Mediterranean and Atlantic islands. Native Americans died in appalling numbers, creating the labor shortage, while Europeans, initially employed as indentured servants, could increasingly claim that being "white" or Christian should exempt them from forced labor. Africans were attractive candidates to fill the void because they were skilled farmers, herders, and miners and because they possessed substantial immunity to both European and tropical diseases. They were also, relatively speaking, close to the Americas, and European seafaring technology made their transportation across the Atlantic economical.

Supply. They were also available. This question of supply is perhaps more difficult to understand than that of demand. Why would African societies willingly sell their own people to strangers? One answer is that, for the most part, they did not perceive the question in this way. In the early modern era, no common identity as Africans existed on the continent. The West and central African region targeted by the slave trade was divided among several larger kingdoms, such as Benin and the Kongo; many "microstates" or chiefdoms; and a large number of lineage-based societies without any state structure at all. Dozens—even hundreds—of languages were spoken, though trade, migration, intermarriage, and warfare had created substantial connections among these diverse peoples. Those individuals funneled into the slave trade were in general outsiders or marginal to their societies—prisoners of war, criminals, impoverished folks "pawned" by their families in times of debt, or desperate people fleeing famine or oppression. These were people without the protection of a lineage or kinship group, which formed the basis of most African societies.

African Slavery. Furthermore, slavery was a long-established institution in most African societies, just as it had been in many other agricultural civilizations in the Mediterranean, the Islamic world, Russia, China, and elsewhere. For centuries, a small number of slaves had been sent across the Sahara to North Africa and across the Indian Ocean to various Middle Eastern and South Asian destinations. Most African slaves, however, remained in Africa. They worked the estates of kings and other wealthy people. Most were treated as members of their master's family or lineage. As such, they or their descendants might become people of influence as court officials, soldiers, or traders. Their lives were very different from what was to become the fate of slaves in the Americas. They did not work on plantations or mines; they had protected places in a society that they knew and understood.

At first, Europeans bought Africans who were already slaves. But as the European demand for slave labor in the Americas increased, fewer were available for purchase. As the price of slaves increased fivefold between 1680 and 1840, African slave traders hunted farther inland and militarized coastal states mounted expeditions for the express purpose of capturing slaves for sale to America. Long accustomed to market transactions involving products and people, African elites—both official and private—proved willing and able to supply the external demand for slaves on the basis of their own economic and political interests.

The Slave Trade in Operation

The actual operation of the slave trade was broadly similar to that of the spice trade in Asia. European merchants established competing trading posts along the West African coast, from Senegal in the north to Angola in the

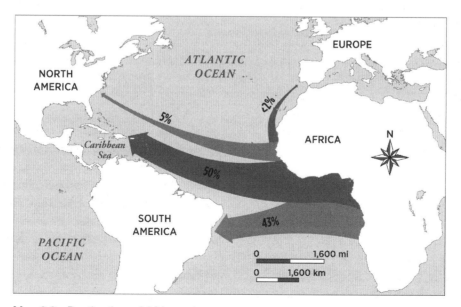

Map 8.2   Destination of African slaves.

Table 8.1   Chronology of the Slave Trade

	Number of Slaves Arriving in Americas	*Total*
1450–1600	367,000	3%
1601–1700	1,868,000	16%
1701–1800	6,133,000	52%
1801–1900	3,300,000	28%

Source: John Iliffe, *Africa: A History* (Cambridge: Cambridge University Press, 1995), 131.

south. Some of these trading posts were fortified, others were merely a few buildings to store goods and to keep slaves waiting for transshipment, and elsewhere still, Europeans simply traded from their ships anchored offshore.

Europeans exercised even less political control in Africa than they did in Asia. There was little existing oceanic trade to capture and control, as they tried to do in the Indian Ocean. Fortifications along the West African coast provided protection from European rivals rather than from African adversaries. Where Europeans established permanent trading stations or "factories," it was with the permission of local African rulers and usually involved the payment of rent, tariffs, and fees of various kinds.

An assault of an African by a European could be treated harshly. In one such case in the 1680s, a British agent tried to defend such an assault. He went to explain what happened to the king of Niumi, who was sitting under a tree surrounded by his slave bodyguards. Evidently, the king wanted an apology, not a debate:

One of the grandees [slave-bodyguards of the king], by name Sambalama, taught him better manners by reaching him a box on the ears, which beat off his hat, and a few thumps on the back, and seizing him, disarmed him together with the rest of his attendance . . . and several others, who together with the agent were taken and put into the kings pound and stayed there

three or four days till their ransom was brought, value five hundred bars.[11]

The inland trade, involving the capture, provisioning, and transporting of slaves to the coast, was almost entirely in the hands of African political and social elites, who were often in bitter competition with one another for the trade goods—textiles, metalware, firearms, decorative items, alcohol, and tobacco—that Europeans offered in exchange for human merchandise. With the exception of a vague Portuguese control over Angola, nowhere in Africa did the trade in slaves lead to the kind of territorial empires common in the Americas. And with the exception of a small Dutch outpost in South Africa, nowhere in Africa did Europeans settle in large numbers as they did in the Western Hemisphere.

Counting the Cost

Lost People. The impact of the Atlantic slave trade in Africa was both profound and uneven. Demographically, it removed millions of people, mostly men in their prime working years, and severely retarded the normal growth of African populations at a time when European and Asian populations were beginning their modern growth spurt. And it introduced a number of new diseases, though without the catastrophic impact experienced in the more isolated Americas. On the other hand, new American crops, especially maize and cassava, probably increased the food supply and partially offset the population losses from disease and export.[12]

Political Variations. The participation of African societies in the slave trade and its impact on them varied greatly depending on their social and economic organization, proximity to inland trade routes, the local political condition, population density, and other factors. Some small societies, targeted for extensive slave raiding, were virtually destroyed. Large kingdoms, such as the Kongo, were torn apart as outlying provinces and ambitious individuals established their own trading connections with European merchants. In 1526, the king of the Kongo, Nzinga Mbemba, wrote a pleading letter to the king of Portugal, describing the damage which the slave trade was inflicting on his kingdom:

> Many of our people, keenly desirous as they are of the wares and things of your Kingdom, which are brought here by your people, and in order to satisfy their voracious appetite, seize many of our people, freed and exempt men, and very often it happens that they kidnap even noblemen and the sons of noblemen, and our relatives, and take them to be sold to the white men who are in our Kingdom. . . . And as soon as they are taken by the white men they are immediately ironed and branded with fire. . . . To avoid such a great error and inconvenience . . . we beg of you to be agreeable and kind enough to send us two physicians and two apothecaries and one surgeon, so that they may come with their drugstores and all the necessary things to stay in our kingdoms.[13]

Other states, such as Asante and Dahomey, arose in reaction to the slave trade and tried to take advantage of its economic possibilities

while protecting their own people from its ravages. The Kingdom of Benin was unique in its relatively successful efforts to avoid a deep involvement in the slave trade and to diversify the exports with which it purchased European firearms and other goods.

In some cases, participation was brief. Along the coast of Sierra Leone, for example, a series of wars in the mid-sixteenth century produced a large number of slaves for sale, but when political stability returned, trade focused much more heavily on local products such as beeswax, camwood, ivory, and gold. Elsewhere, extensive and prolonged involvement produced major social changes. Along the delta of the Niger River, societies of fishing villages organized on lineage principles were transformed into small monarchies in which extended family groups assimilated large numbers of slaves and became powerful "houses" with extensive commercial networks. Drawing on sources of slaves among the Igbo in the immediate interior, these transformed societies of the Niger River delta became the largest slave exporters in eighteenth-century West Africa.

Economic Impact. From an economic viewpoint, the slave trade increasingly oriented West Africa commerce toward the Atlantic and growing integration within the emerging European-centered world economy and away from its earlier focus northward across the Sahara. Except on the coast, this new trade had little impact on African domestic industries as local textile and iron producers found continued demand for their products. But neither did it stimulate any real economic development. "The total impact of the trade," a leading historian of the slave trade wrote, "has to be measured not by what actually happened but against the might-have-been if Africa's creative energy had been turned instead to some other end than that of building a commercial system capable of capturing and exporting some eighty thousand people a year."[14]

The African Diaspora. In a global perspective, the major outcome of the slave trade lay in a vast spread of African peoples across the Atlantic world, a process commonly known as the African diaspora. Africans by the millions were deposited in the Americas, where they functioned both as laborers and as bearers of culture. As fieldworkers, domestic servants, or skilled artisans, slaves constituted a coerced and cheap labor force whose ruthless exploitation contributed greatly to the wealth of the American colonies and their European homelands. And despite the horrors of the Middle Passage across the Atlantic, Africans brought their cultures with them. Their languages, religious ideas, foods, music, social patterns, and aesthetic standards all contributed to the making of African American cultures, which in turn influenced Euro-American cultures as well. Foods such as corn mush, gumbo, fritters, cooked greens, and batter-fried chicken all had African origins. Syncretic or blended religions, such as Vodou in Haiti, Santeria in Cuba, and Candomble in Brazil, mixed Christian beliefs and practices such as church attendance, the search for salvation, and the use of candles and statues with African elements including drumming, dancing, animal sacrifice, and spirit possession.

Slaves also played a political role in colonial America, especially when their actions threatened the social order. By 1650, hundreds of runaway slave communities had been established throughout the Americas. They ranged from small villages of 50 to 200 people to more centralized states with many thousands of inhabitants, such as Palmares in Brazil. Such communities interacted with Native American societies who often sheltered them and had to contend with European settlers who sought to destroy them. Even more threatening to Europeans were slave rebellions. The largest and most successful of these occurred in the French colony of Saint-Dominique (modern Haiti) in the 1790s. It was stimulated by the liberating ideas of the French Revolution, and it gave rise to the second independent state in the Americas and the first to be ruled by people of African descent. Its violent attacks on white planters contributed much to the conservatism of later Latin American independence movements whose elite leaders feared triggering further revolutionary upheavals and challenges to white control.

The Slave Trade and Racism. A further legacy of the slave trade was racism. Europeans were better able to tolerate their brutal exploitation of Africans by imagining that these Africans were an inferior race or, better still, not even human. Lasting far longer than the slave trade itself, a racism that denigrated people of African descent served to justify the later colonial takeover of Africa and structured social life in African colonies. It found its fullest expression in the apartheid system of South Africa, which attempted to separate blacks and whites in every conceivable way while exploiting black labor in the economy. In the Americas, the abolition of slavery in the 1800s, far from ending racism, probably made it worse, for now the former slaves could exercise, at least potentially, a certain amount of economic and political influence. In the United States, the outcome was a racially inspired segregation, pervasive discrimination, and publicly sanctioned outbursts of violence against African Americans, poisoning the social life of the country into the twenty-first century.

Europe and Asia

European expansion in early modern times was unique in its genuinely global scope, encompassing in various ways the Americas,

Africa, and Asia. But while Europeans dominated the Atlantic, conquering and ruling the Americas and extracting millions of slaves from Africa, their entry into Asian waters was quite different and produced a generally far more modest impact on Asian societies.

Commerce and Coercion

Portuguese in the Indian Ocean. The Portuguese were the first. Once Vasco da Gama showed the way around Africa to India in 1498, the Portuguese, with their efficient sailing ships and powerful onboard cannon, smashed into an ancient and complex maritime trading system that included Arab, Indian, Malay, and Chinese merchants and extended from East Africa to East Asia. Had they wanted only to trade, the Portuguese could have competed freely in this open commercial network. But far from home and with limited resources, fired by a militant Christianity, and schooled in the ruthless rivalries of European warfare, the Portuguese sought to control by force of arms the enormously valuable trade in spices, which had drawn them to the East. The total absence of armed ships in the Indian Ocean following the Chinese withdrawal and the relative lack of interest of the major land powers meant that the Portuguese were able to seize and fortify major transfer points for the Indian Ocean trade—Kilwa and Mombasa on the East African coast, Hormuz at the mouth of the Persian Gulf, Goa in western India, Malacca on the west coast of the Malay Peninsula, and Ternate in the Spice Islands of Indonesia. In East Asia, where the Portuguese encountered the powerful Chinese and Japanese states, they established trade relations and small settlements only with the permission of local authorities.

Competitors. Here was a "trading-post empire," designed to control commerce rather than large populations or land areas. It was similar to the kind of control Europeans sought to exercise along the West African coast during the slave trade rather than the territorial and settlement empires they constructed in the Americas. By the seventeenth century, this Portuguese trading-post empire, overextended in Asia and without a strong base in Europe, confronted vigorous competition from the Dutch and English. Operating through private commercial East India companies rather than direct state control, these rising northern European merchants established their own parallel and competing trading-post empires, with the Dutch focusing on what is now Indonesia and the British on India.

Limitations of Empire. The impact of these European intrusions on Asian societies was important but modest. Political control was generally confined to small and divided coastal societies where European military resources, often numbering only a dozen or so ships and several hundred men, could be effective. Beyond their coastal trading posts, Europeans established real control only in parts of the Philippines and Indonesia, island chains where the Spanish and Dutch, respectively, faced politically fragmented peoples who were unprotected by their larger neighbors on the mainland of Asia. These larger Asian powers—the Ottoman Empire, Safavid Persia, Mughal India, China, and Japan—were little threatened by the modest military forces of seagoing Europeans, far from their bases of supply. Europeans could be useful to these societies in various ways, but throughout the early modern era, the great Asian powers generally established the rules of the game. As late as 1795 the Chinese emperor Ch'ien Lung decisively rejected a British request for additional trading privileges in a famous letter to King George III that reflected China's view of the world:

Our Celestial Empire possesses all things in prolific abundance and lacks no product within its own borders. There was therefore no need to import the manufactures of outside barbarians in exchange for our own produce. But as the silk, tea, and porcelain which the Celestial Empire produces are absolute necessities to European nations and to yourselves, we permitted as a signal mark of favor, that foreign *hongs* [companies] should be established at Canton, so that your wants may be supplied and your country thus participate in our beneficence. But your ambassador has now put forward new requests. . . . I do not forget the lonely remoteness of your island, cut off from the world by intervening wastes of sea, nor do I overlook your excusable ignorance of the usages of Our Celestial Empire. I have consequently commanded my Ministers to enlighten your ambassador on the subject, and have ordered the departure of the mission.[15]

The Economic Impact. The European trading-post empires shaped Asian economies in more extensive though still circumscribed ways. During the sixteenth century, the Portuguese managed to partially block the traditional Red Sea route by which spices had made their way to Europe and to carry about half of the spice trade to the West around the Cape of Good Hope, making handsome profits in the process. They also developed something of a "protection racket" by which they sold passes and charged duties to all kinds of Asian merchants, permitting them to trade in the Indian Ocean and enforcing the system with Portuguese warships. The Dutch in Indonesia succeeded in controlling not just the shipping but also the production of nutmeg and cloves by seizing several of the Spice Islands in Indonesia and using force to prevent the growing of these spices elsewhere. An enforced monoculture thus made these islands wholly dependent on the import of food and clothing. A twentieth-century Dutch historian described the results: "the economic system of the Moluccas [Spice Islands] was ruined and the population reduced to poverty."[16] The British exercised such a tremendous demand for popular Indian textiles that hundreds of villages came to specialize in export production and became dependent on it. Europeans also became heavily involved in shipping Asian goods to Asian ports, using the profits from this "carrying trade" to buy spices and other Asian products.

The Silver Trade. Among the most important goods carried on European ships was silver, which was in great demand in Asia. This was fortunate for westerners, who had little else to exchange for the Asian spices, silks, porcelain, and other products that they so ardently desired. China in particular became an enormous market for silver as this gigantic and flourishing economy, supporting 20 to 25 percent of the world's population, was transforming its currency and taxation system to a silver base and drove the price of this precious metal to double its world price in the early seventeenth century. Thus silver flowed into China in enormous quantities, much of it from rich Spanish American mines in Mexico and Peru. From Acapulco on Mexico's west coast, annual Spanish fleets carried tons of the precious metal to Manila in the Spanish Philippines, where it was exchanged for Chinese-manufactured goods. Still more tons flowed eastward through Europe to China and other Asian destinations. European ships also carried Japanese silver to China. The immense profits from the silver trade considerably financed Spain's American empire and its many European wars, indirectly underwrote the slave trade, and enriched Europe generally. But these profits occurred as Europeans participated in a vast and sophisticated Asian commercial network, suggesting that "the economic impact of China on the West was far greater than any European influence on Asia in the early modern period."[17]

American Crops in Asia. The silver trade and the slave trade marked the beginning of a genuinely global economy involving the Americas, Europe, Africa, and Asia in a single integrated network of economic transactions. Another sign of this global network lay in the impact of American food crops introduced by Europeans into Africa and Asia as well as into Europe itself. In China, for example, as rice cultivation reached its limit, New World dryland food crops, such as peanuts, corn, sweet potatoes, and white potatoes, contributed greatly to the growth of Chinese food production. They sustained China's huge and rapidly growing population in recent centuries. In the mid-1990s, some 37 percent of the food consumed in China originated in the Americas, and that country had become the world's largest producer of sweet potatoes and its second-largest producer of corn.

Europeans exploited products, routes, and techniques that had been pioneered by Asian traders, but they were not able to eliminate them. The Portuguese failed to monopolize the spice trade as they had hoped. Chinese, Indian, and Arab shipping continued to ply Asian waters as they had for centuries. Despite growing Dutch control of Indonesia, Chinese merchants handled most of the spice trade to China. Europeans entered long-established Asian trade routes as shippers, carrying goods between Japan and China, for example, but they neither created nor destroyed these routes. Large-scale trade within the Ottoman Empire, India, and China and

the land-based trade among them remained wholly in Asian hands.

Missionaries in East Asia

Jesuits in China. The cultural impact of the European intruders in Asia was likewise modest. Unlike the Americas, where elements of Christian belief and practice were widely accepted, the considerable missionary effort in Asia won far fewer converts. Jesuit missionaries in China, armed with the latest in European scientific and technological developments, initially won considerable respect among the learned elite, particularly as the Jesuits had mastered the Chinese language and Confucian culture. They proved useful to the Chinese court in constructing calendars, clocks, and canon. But when the papacy and rival missionary orders became critical of Chinese culture, forbidding Chinese Christians to venerate their ancestors, the court lost interest, and the Jesuits' plan to convert China from the top down proved a failure.

Japan and European Missionaries. Japan's encounter with Christianity was even more dramatic. A politically fragmented Japan, chronically engaged in civil war in the sixteenth century, welcomed Western traders and missionaries, as various parties in these conflicts found the firearms and trade goods that the Europeans brought with them useful. A sizable Christian community, numbering perhaps 300,000 by the early 1600s, emerged from the missionaries' efforts. But by that time, Japan had overcome its earlier conflicts and unified under the Tokugawa shogunate. These new rulers of a more unified Japan, viewing Christians as potential dissidents and a threat to Japan's largely Buddhist culture, brutally suppressed the embryonic Christian movement and executed large numbers of its followers. They drove the missionaries out and

Figure 8.3 Early missionaries—mostly Jesuits—won acceptance in official circles in China because they conformed to Chinese dress and culture and because they were useful in predicting eclipses and constructing calendars. *Left: Art Resource, NY. The New York Public Library, New York, NY, USA. Right: Snark/Art Resource, NY. Bibliotheque Nationale, Paris, France.*

restricted contact with Europeans to a small island near Nagasaki, where only Dutch traders were permitted to operate. In all of Asia, Christianity developed deep roots only in the Spanish Philippines, which remained under direct European control.

Europeans in Oceania

A final indication of the limited European role in early modern Asia involves its penetration of Oceania, the large and small islands of the Pacific basin. European exploration of the vast Pacific Ocean began with Magellan's famous circumnavigation of the world between 1519 and 1522 and continued with Dutch explorer Abel Tasman's mapping of parts of Australia, New Zealand, Fiji, and Tonga in the seventeenth century. But not until the voyages of the English captain James Cook (1768–1780) did Europeans begin to affect the previously isolated world of Oceania. During most of the three centuries of the early modern era, it remained a separate world. But once European merchants, missionaries, settlers, and colonial officials descended on these societies, beginning in the late eighteenth century, the impact was devastating, resembling the demographic disasters in the Americas. A Hawaiian population of perhaps 500,000 in 1778, when Captain Cook happened on the islands, was reduced to less than 60,000 a century later.

The Fruits of Empire

Europe itself was transformed by its empire. Neither Ottoman, Chinese, or Russian expansion so fundamentally changed their own core societies. In large part, this is because Europe became the hub of a wholly new network of global communication and exchange that brought together a variety of already established regional networks into a single worldwide system. As Europe moved rapidly from a marginal position in Afro-Eurasia to a central position in this new world system, it accumulated unprecedented power, wealth, and information, greatly transforming European society.

A World Economy

Above all, Western expansion created a global economic network centered on Europe. The Dutch of the seventeenth century provide a telling example:

> Everything was grist for the Dutch mill. Who could fail to be surprised that wheat grown . . . in South Africa was shipped to Amsterdam? Or that Amsterdam became a market for cowrie shells brought back from Ceylon and Bengal, which found enthusiastic customers, including the English, who used them for trade with black Africa or for the purchase of slaves destined for America? Or that sugar from China, Bengal, sometimes Siam . . . was alternately in demand or out of it in Amsterdam, depending on whether the price could compete in Europe with sugar from Brazil or the West Indies?[18]

Eastern Europe in the World Economy. But not all parts of Europe were affected in the same way or to the same extent by this new world economy. Eastern Europe, especially Poland, was one of the first areas to be connected to the new global commercial system, largely through the export of rye and wheat to western Europe in exchange for herring, salt, silk, wines, and other manufactured goods. The strong demand for grain in western Europe encouraged a powerful landlord class in eastern Europe to produce for this market. In doing so, these landlords found it profitable to reduce their relatively free peasantry to serf laborers. The absence of both strong monarchs and an independent merchant class gave the landlords the political clout necessary to accomplish this "second serfdom." Thus, the new world economy pushed eastern Europe into a subordinate and dependent position and gave rise to a quite different kind of society from that of a dynamic and modernizing western Europe.

Spain and Portugal in the World Economy. Even in western Europe, there were differences. The early leaders of Europe's outward thrust— the Iberian powers Spain and Portugal—were not as substantially transformed as the Dutch, British, and French who followed a century later. Aztec and Inca treasure and vast quantities of silver and gold from the forced labor of Indians in American mines floated Spanish and Portuguese prosperity throughout the sixteenth century. But landed aristocrats (hidalgos), conquistadores, and priests ran Iberian society. The precious metals of the Americas paid for foreign luxuries, conquests, and conversions, not investment in domestic industry. Spanish gold found its way to the new money class on the borders of Iberia in Amsterdam and northern Europe. While the hidalgo class voiced contempt for enterprise, the new middle class of lenders, merchants, and producers flexed its muscles. It was not Portugal or Spain that was to direct the seventeenth century but the mercantile countries of northern Europe, beginning with the 17 lowland provinces of the Spanish Empire that were to fashion themselves the Dutch Republic, or the Netherlands.

Northwestern Europe in the World Economy. In Britain, France, and the Netherlands, the profits and products of empire worked their most transforming effects. Merchants, enriched by the profits of empire, gained a social and political prominence unknown elsewhere. They developed new mechanisms for accumulating capital, notably joint stock companies such as the British and Dutch East India Companies, which did so much to energize European commerce in Asia by allowing individual investors to pool their funds for a common purpose. Market relationships based on supply and demand became more deeply entrenched throughout society. In short, more thoroughly capitalist societies were emerging in this part of Europe. And in the late eighteenth century, the most dynamic, innovative, and globally expansive of these societies, Great Britain, gave rise to the industrial revolution, which initiated an unprecedented and revolutionary transformation of human society. "The wealth of the New World was not the only cause of the Industrial Revolution," wrote historian Alfred Crosby, "but it is difficult to see how it could have happened when and as rapidly as it did without stimulus from the Americas."[19]

Changing Diets. The European empire also transformed the way that Europeans—and eventually the rest of the world—ate. The long-established European diet, based on wheat, barley, oats, and rye, was vastly enriched by the addition of numerous American foods: corn (maize), white and sweet potatoes, tomatoes, lima beans, peanuts, manioc, squashes,

pumpkins, avocado, pineapple, chili peppers, and more. Corn and potatoes especially furnished more calories per acre, grew more rapidly, and could be stored more easily than traditional grains. By the eighteenth century, their use had spread widely in Europe, particularly as a food for the poor. So dependent had Irish peasants become on the potato that when the crop failed because of disease in 1845, about 1 million people died, and hundreds of thousands fled to the New World from which the potato had originated. Cod, found in great abundance in North Atlantic fishing grounds, provided inexpensive protein.

Population Growth. These foods played a major role in sustaining Europe's rapidly growing population, which rose from 105 million in 1605 to 390 million by 1900. They had a similar impact in much of Asia, especially China, and in general provided an important part of the nutritional foundation for the world's modern population explosion. These productive and inexpensive foods also contributed much to the diets of poorly paid factory workers as Europe's industrial revolution got under way in the nineteenth century. One prominent historian has suggested, with only a little exaggeration, that the potato made the industrial revolution possible.[20]

Coffee, Tea, and Chocolate. Plants from abroad provided not only nutrition but also stimulation. Europeans found chocolate in Mexico, tea in China, coffee and sugar in the Arab world, opium in India, and tobacco in the Americas. All of them became increasingly popular in the seventeenth and eighteenth centuries and were produced for a mass market in various colonial settings, usually with slave labor. Tea was an exception, as China largely monopolized its production until the nineteenth century. Beginning often as luxuries for the rich, these drug foods became

Figure 8.4   Smoking tobacco was among the ways that European life changed as a result of American empires. *Boyer/Getty Images.*

part of middle-class culture and then, as their prices dropped, became available to the poor as well.

These addictive foods became a profitable staple of the emerging world economy, widely used all across Europe, the Middle East, and Asia by 1800. They made millions for European merchants and their governments while causing misery for those who produced them. New forms and places of leisure emerged for their enjoyment, such as opium parlors in China and coffeehouses in Europe and the Ottoman Empire. Coffeehouses became popular and sometimes politically subversive meeting places, but they illustrated the more densely connected world that was being born. "The coffeehouse was the world economy in miniature . . . joining coffee from Java, Yemen, or the Americas, tea from China, sugar and rum from Africa's Atlantic islands or the Caribbean, and tobacco from North America or Brazil."[21]

New Knowledge

The global network was a conduit not only for foods, drugs, products, labor, and capital but also for information, and most of this too wound up in Europe. In the 1570s, the Italian mathematician and physician Girolamo

Cardano wrote about how extraordinary it was to be born in a century "in which the whole world became known; whereas the ancients were familiar with but a little more than a third of it." He worried, however, that this would mean that "certainties would be exchanged for uncertainties."[22]

The sheer immensity of the new information and the speed with which it was acquired was staggering. Entire new continents; vast oceans; wholly unknown plants, animals, and geographical features; peoples of the most varying descriptions; magnificent cities; unusual sexual practices; and religions that were neither Muslim nor Jewish and certainly not Christian—knowledge of all this and much more came flooding into Europe in the several centuries following the earliest Iberian voyages, provoking much debate and controversy. Movable-type printing and the growth of a publishing industry made this new knowledge much cheaper and more widely accessible than the older system of hand-copied manuscripts. European intellectuals tried to organize this torrent of data by drawing new maps; by classifying the new plants, animals, and cultures that came to their attention; and by inventing whole new fields, such as botany, zoology, and geology.

This accumulation of unsettling new knowledge surely contributed to Europe's seventeenth-century scientific revolution, which transformed so dramatically the view of the world held by educated Europeans. Clearly, many factors played a role in this complex intellectual change—the inadequacies of older models of the universe; new data from careful observation of the heavens; the secularism of the European Renaissance; the stimulus of Islamic learning; the growth of independent universities teaching astronomy, mathematics, and physics; and the printing press, which allowed easy dissemination of new ideas. But it is arguable that new knowledge born of European expansion produced "uncertainties," as Cardano had predicted; undermined long-held views of the world; and thus opened the way to a novel scientific understanding of the universe and human life.

The First World Wars

Europe's overseas expansion was a highly competitive process that reflected the long rivalry of Europe's various "great powers." Global empire and global commerce projected these rivalries abroad and led to a series of conflicts that might be considered the earliest global wars. Spain and Portugal, the first European states to venture abroad, managed to avoid outright conflict by negotiating a treaty dividing the newly discovered world between them in 1494. But no such division was possible once other European powers joined the fray. In the sixteenth and seventeenth centuries, the English, French, and Dutch vigorously contested Spain's imperial monopoly in the Americas and Portugal's trading-post empire in the Indian Ocean. The pirates, merchants, and navies of these newcomers to empire challenged the Iberians all across the colonial world. In the late sixteenth century, the English sent more than 70 expeditions to attack Spanish outposts in the Atlantic and the Caribbean, while the Dutch forces ousted Portuguese merchants from much of Southeast Asia.

As Spanish and Portuguese power declined, the British and French took their place. In the mid-eighteenth century, their rivalry led to the Seven Years' War (1756–1763). Often referred to as "the great war for empire," this global conflict was fought in Europe, North America, the Caribbean, and India. British victories paved the way for a largely English North America, for British colonial rule in

India, and for British domination of the seas and of global commerce for the next 150 years. Warfare on a global scale did not begin in the twentieth century.

Conclusion: Empire and Globalization

The early modern era in world history can be viewed in two different ways. On the one hand, it was an age of empires—Ottoman, Mughal, Songay, Chinese, Russian, and western European. In particular, it witnessed the eruption of the previously marginal western Europeans onto the world stage. Europeans created imperial systems that bore both similarities to other empires—conquest, divide-and-rule tactics, and a sense of superiority—and strikingly new features, including new colonial societies, massive use of slave labor, and catastrophic death rates among Native Americans and Africans.

Alternatively, we might view the early modern era as a vast and quite rapid extension of human connections. With western Europeans as its primary agents, this early globalization involved destruction and creation and victims and beneficiaries. Native Americans who died in the millions, Africans unwillingly transported to Caribbean or Brazilian plantations, Indian weavers now producing for European markets, Chinese who paid their taxes in silver and ate sweet potatoes, Japanese who briefly experimented with Christianity, and Europeans who found new homes across the Atlantic—all these and many more experienced the consequences of incorporation into a new "worldwide web."[23] The making of this web contained both remarkable achievements and tragedies of immense proportions.

The Europeans who initiated the process were likewise transformed by it. The great changes of modern European history—population growth, the scientific revolution, capitalism, and industrialization—coincided with Europe's emergence at the hub of a new network of global exchange and communication. While Europe was certainly not the only center of expansion and innovation in the early modern world, it was the only one whose expansion catalyzed changes of this magnitude. This "modern transformation," together with the subsequent deepening and extension of the European-centered global network, combined to produce a new and even more revolutionary phase of world history in the nineteenth century.

Suggested Reading

Benjamin, Thomas, Timothy Hall, and David Rutherford. *The Atlantic World in the Age of Empire.* Boston: Houghton Mifflin, 2001. A set of readings from major historians on the making of an Atlantic world.

Crosby, Alfred W. *Germs, Seeds, and Animals.* Armonk, NY: M. E. Sharpe, 1994). A collection of writings on the Columbian exchange by its most well-known historian.

Gunn, Geoffrey. *First Globalization: The Eurasian Exchange, 1500–1800.* Lanham, MD: Rowman & Littlefield, 2003. Focuses on the cultural rather than economic exchange between Europe and Asia in the early modern era.

Parry, J. H. *The Establishment of European Hegemony: 1415–1715.* New York: Harper and Row, 1961. An older and classic account of the roots of European expansion.

Ringrose, David. *Expansion and Global Interaction, 1200–1700.* New York: Longman, 2001. Places European expansion in the context of other expanding societies.

Schlesinger, Roger. *In the Wake of Columbus.* Wheeling, IL: Harlan Davidson, 1996. Explores the impact of the Americas on Europe in the centuries after Columbus.

Thornton, John. *Africa and Africans in the Making of the Atlantic World, 1400–1800.* Cambridge: Cambridge University Press, 1998. A well-regarded study that views Africans as participants in as well as victims of the Atlantic slave trade.

Waley-Cohen, Joanna. *The Sextants of Beijing.* New York: Norton, 2000. Explores China's relationships with the wider world, including the West. Chapter 2 is a fascinating case study of the encounter between Jesuit missionaries and Chinese society.

Notes

1. Jared Diamond, *Guns, Germs, and Steel* (London: Vintage Books, 1998).

2. This paragraph is based on Immanuel Wallerstein, *The Modern World System: Capitalist Agriculture and the Origins of the European World Economy in the Sixteenth Century* (New York: Academic Press, 1974), chap. 1. The quote is from p. 51.

3. D. K. Fieldhouse, *The Colonial Empires from the Eighteenth Century* (New York: Dell, 1966), 6.

4. Miguel Leon-Portilla, *The Broken Spears: The Aztec Account of the Conquest of Mexico* (Boston: Beacon Press, 1992), 123.

5. Leon-Portilla, *The Broken Spears*, 137–38.

6. Bartolome de Las Casas, *The Devastation of the Indies: A Brief Account*, trans. Herma Briffault (New York: Seabury Press, 1974), 38–52.

7. Alfred W. Crosby, *Germs, Seeds, and Animals* (Armonk, NY: M. E. Sharpe, 1994), 88–93.

8. Leon-Portilla, *The Broken Spears*, 149.

9. Quoted in Alfred W. Crosby, *Ecological Imperialism* (Cambridge: Cambridge University Press, 1986), 160. See also John Richards, *The Unending Frontier: An Environmental History of the Early Modern World* (Berkeley: University of California Press, 2003).

10. For a recent summary of the debate over the numbers involved in the slave trade, see David Eltis and David Richardson, "The 'Numbers Game' and Routes to Slavery," *Slavery and Abolition* 18 (1997): 1–10.

11. Quoted in Donald R. Wright, *The World and a Very Small Place in Africa* (Armonk, NY: M. E. Sharpe, 2010), 95.

12. John Iliffe, *Africans: The History of a Continent* (Cambridge: Cambridge University Press, 1995), 137–39.

13. Quoted in Basil Davidson, *The African Past* (Boston: Little, Brown, 1964).

14. Philip Curtin et al., *African History* (Boston: Little, Brown, 1978), 248.

15. Henry Farnsworth MacNair, *Modern Chinese History: Selected Readings* (Shanghai: Commercial Press, 1923), 2–9.

16. Bernard H. M. Vlekke, *Nusantara: A History of the East India Archipelago* (Cambridge, MA: Harvard University Press, 1943), 139.

17. Dennis O. Flynn and Arturo Giraldez, "Born with a 'Silver Spoon': The Origin of World Trade in 1571," *Journal of World History* 6, no. 2 (Fall 1995): 217.

18. Fernand Braudel, *The Perspective of the World,* (New York: Harper and Row, 1984), 220.

19. Alfred W. Crosby, "The Columbian Voyages, the Columbian Exchange, and Their Historians," in *Islamic and European Expansion*, ed. Michael Adas (Philadelphia: Temple University Press, 1993), 154.

20. Crosby, *Germs, Seeds, and Animals*, 148–63.

21. Kenneth Pomeranz and Steven Topic, *The World That Trade Created* (Armonk, NY: M. E. Sharpe, 1999), 79.

22. Quoted in Crosby, "The Columbian Voyages, the Columbian Exchange, and Their Historians," 151–52.

23. J. R. McNeill and William H. McNeill, *The Human Web* (New York: Norton, 2003).

9

Breaking Out and the First Modern Societies

1750–1900

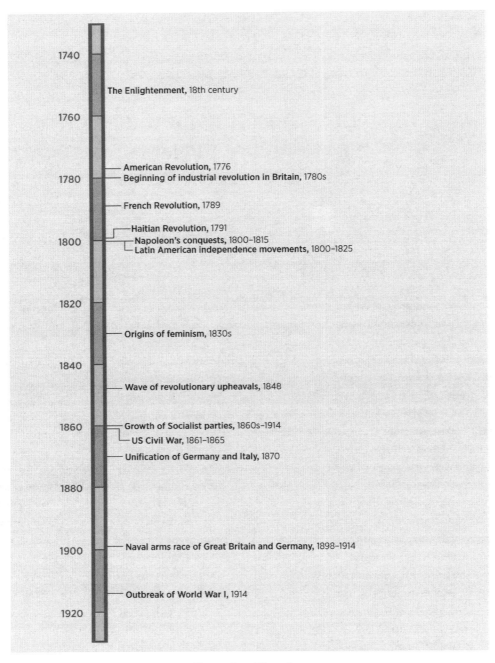

Figure 9.1   Time line.

WORLD HISTORY seldom turns sharp corners, especially in as little as a century or two. But in 150 years, roughly between 1750 and 1900, two distinct and related processes marked a decisive turn in human affairs. One was the breakthrough to distinctly "modern" societies, a process that occurred first in western Europe and derived from the English industrial revolution and from the political revolution that swept England, France, and North America. These upheavals unfolded in the second half of the eighteenth century, and their example and influence echoed in varying degrees elsewhere in Europe and the Americas, Russia, Japan, and other parts of the world in the nineteenth century and after. This modern transformation gave rise to enormous changes in virtually every aspect of life, raising some individuals, groups, and nations to dizzying heights of power and wealth while casting others, at least temporarily, into new forms of poverty and dependence. Virtually no one and nothing remained unchanged.

Nor did its influence stop at the borders of those countries that experienced it most fully, for this breakthrough to modernity clearly made possible the second major process—the unprecedented global extension of European

and North American political, economic, and cultural power over the rest of the planet. The peoples of Asia, Africa, the Middle East, and elsewhere now found themselves threatened by Europe's unsurpassed military might, increasingly drawn into economic networks centered in Europe, confronted by ideas (both secular and religious) that derived from Europe, and incorporated against their will into European colonial empires. Never before had one region of the world exercised such extensive power and influence.

In exploring the making of the first modern societies, the spotlight of world history focuses temporarily on the western tip of the Eurasian landmass, where that transformation was first experienced. Western Europe became for a time the global center of technological, economic, and cultural innovation much as other regions had played that role in earlier periods. Mesopotamia and Egypt had long ago pioneered advanced agriculture and urban civilization (around 3000–3500 BCE). The ancient Greeks developed ways of thinking and political organization that had a profound influence in the Mediterranean and Middle Eastern regions (500 BCE–200 CE). India had generated Buddhism, advanced mathematics, and numerous agricultural innovations, all of which spread widely in the first millennium CE. The Arab people gave rise to a new religion (Islam) and to an expanding and enormously creative civilization (600–1600 CE). China was clearly the global leader in technological innovation between 1000 and 1500 CE and exercised a profound influence throughout the Eurasian world.[1] All these "flowerings" produced ripples of influence and circles of interaction far beyond their points of origin. So too did the modern transformation of western European societies. Theirs was a unique but not an unprecedented process.

Why Europe?
A Historian's Debate

At the heart of the breakthrough to modernity was the industrial revolution. But why should western Europe in general and Great Britain in particular have been at the center of this enormous disturbance in human affairs? Few people living in 1700 or 1750 would have predicted that the endlessly quarrelsome societies of western Europe would soon lead the world to a wholly new kind of economy and to a greatly altered balance of global power. But in the nineteenth century, Europeans did precisely that. In doing so, they have presented historians, especially world historians, with one of their most sharply debated questions: how to explain this European breakthrough to an industrial society and the global power that followed from it. Why Europe?

Was Europe Unique?

One kind of answer lies in some unique quality—or combination of qualities—lying deep in Europe's history, society, culture, or environment that gave it a decisive advantage over all other regions and led inexorably toward the industrial revolution. For well over a century, scholars have argued about what, precisely, it might be.

A Favorable Environment? For some, the environment provided an important clue to European economic success: winters cold enough to kill infectious microorganisms that so infested Asian and African populations but warm enough to sustain a productive agriculture, plentiful and regular rainfall rather than the seasonal downpours of India and Africa, more limited exposure to natural disasters (volcanoes, earthquakes, cyclones, floods, and droughts) that afflicted less favored areas—and

coal. A rich supply of that critical fuel, so important as a source of energy as firewood became more scarce and expensive, was located close to major centers of economic activity in Great Britain and certainly facilitated the first industrial revolution, whereas in China coal fields lie deep in the interior, far removed from population concentrations and urban centers near the coast.

The Advantage of Backwardness? Other candidates for the source of the "European miracle" abound. The relative "newness" of Europe's civilization, emerging only after 1000 CE, may help explain European willingness to borrow from others—scientific treatises from the Arabs, mathematical concepts from India, the compass, gunpowder, and printing from China—while Chinese and Islamic societies, long accustomed to success and prominence in their regions, felt that they had little to learn from outsiders. It is what some historians have called the "advantages of backwardness."

The Absence of Unity? The political character of European civilization—a system of separate and competing states rather than a unified empire such as China or the Ottoman Empire—may likewise have stimulated innovation and served as "an insurance against . . . stagnation."[2] And within these newly emerging states, urban merchants had perhaps greater freedom and security of property than their counterparts in the stronger and more solidly established states of Asia and the Middle East. Frequent conflict between the Catholic pope and various European monarchs and the further divide between Protestants and Catholics only added to the pluralism of European society. Thus, Europe's "failure" to achieve consensus and uniformity in both religious and political life arguably heightened its dynamism and set it on the path to the industrial revolution.

Science and Engineering? Yet another possible internal source of Europe's uniqueness lay in its scientific revolution and a culture of inventiveness. As early as the thirteenth century, mechanical clocks were becoming widespread in Europe.[3] And in England, during the seventeenth and eighteenth centuries, scientific thinking took a distinctive form with an emphasis on precise measurements, mechanical devices, and commercial applications. The "engineering culture" that emerged among English artisans, craftsmen, and entrepreneurs helps explain the invention of the steam engine, which was so important in increasing the supply of useful energy for productive purposes.[4] While much of early science was largely theoretical with few direct applications, by the later nineteenth century, science and technology became intimately related and have remained so ever since.

Society and Religion? Other scholars have discerned European advantages in certain social patterns. A tradition of late marriages and a celibate clergy arguably restrained European population growth. With fewer people to provide for, slightly higher per capita incomes followed. In India, by contrast, nearly universal teenage marriages may have held back the accumulation of wealth. European willingness to allow women to work outside the home may have permitted their employment in early textile factories, while Chinese refusal to do so perhaps inhibited their adoption of the factory system. And some have suggested that Christianity, with its sense of linear time and its command to "subdue the earth," may have encouraged an aggressive and manipulative attitude toward nature and thus fostered technological development.

All these ideas point to internal features of European society that contributed to a long-term economic advantage. They suggest that Europe's economic lead over the rest of the world started well before the industrial revolution of the eighteenth century. Technological innovations, including the water windmill, eyeglasses, mechanical clocks, and movable-type printing; the growth of markets in land, labor, and goods; the development of capitalist institutions, such as banks offering credit and partnerships for mobilizing capital; and overall per capita wealth—in all these ways, some scholars argue, a late-developing European civilization had caught up to and gradually surpassed the older civilizations of Asia and the Middle East. These eastern regions, in this view, suffered from the arrogance of long success, which made them unwilling to learn from the upstart Europeans and from powerful states that squelched the private entrepreneurial activities of their people. Thus, the industrial revolution both grew out of and continued a long-term pattern of European advantage and advance.

Critics of Eurocentrism

"Surprising Similarities." But critics have challenged this point of view and made a serious accusation.[5] It reflects, they say, a Eurocentric understanding of the past. They argue that such an account of the origins of the industrial revolution vastly exaggerates European uniqueness. They view western Europe before 1750 or so as one of a number of advanced agricultural societies including China, India, Japan, and the Islamic Middle East. All of them enjoyed relatively free markets, growing economies, wealthy merchant communities with money to invest, widespread and highly skilled handicraft industries, and a substantial amount of agricultural production for the market. Economic similarities across Eurasia in the eighteenth century included

life expectancies, nutritional levels, wages, and overall living standards, which were generally comparable for the wealthiest core regions of China, Japan, India, and western Europe. Of course, each of these regions was unique with its particular mix of economic advantages and drawbacks, but none of them had a decisive lead, and none were poised for a major economic breakthrough.

Furthermore, features of European life, once regarded as uniquely favorable for economic growth, turn out to have counterparts in other regions. While Europeans, for example, limited their fertility through late marriages, Chinese families did so by delaying pregnancy and spacing births more widely within marriage. The growth of rural handicraft manufacturing in Europe, sometimes regarded as a precursor to industrialization, had distinct parallels in China, India, and Japan. As late as 1750, India and China alone accounted for more than 57 percent of world manufacturing output, while Europe and North America represented about 27 percent.[6] Yet this "protoindustrialization," common across much of Eurasia, was followed by an urban industrial revolution only in Europe.

And while European merchants are frequently regarded as uniquely active and independent of their state authorities, many West Africans, Arabs, Armenians, Indians, and South Chinese also operated as private merchants, often far from home. "The typical Asian port," wrote one historian, "housed Gujeratis, Fujianese, Persians, Armenians, Jews and Arabs just as European trading centers housed separate groups of Genoese, Florentine, Dutch, English, and Hanseatic merchants."[7]

Finally, China, Japan, and western Europe all experienced quite rapid rates of population growth after 1500 that put growing pressure on resources available from the land. Deforestation, erosion, and soil depletion were early signs of what some historians have seen as an approaching ecological crisis, limiting the possibilities of further economic growth. All this suggests that Europe's divergence from the main patterns of Eurasian development was late, dating from 1750 or after, and not the consequence of some centuries old and deeply rooted advantage which Europe alone possessed.

Competition from Afar But if exceptional internal features of European historical development do not fully explain the industrial revolution, what does? For some historians, the answer lies in placing industrialization in a broader global context, highlighting the ways in which Europe benefited from a variety of international linkages. One such linkage lies in the example of and competition from foreign manufacturing. For centuries, India had dominated world cotton textile production. The fine quality and bright colors of Indian cotton textiles and the example of dyeing techniques from the Ottoman Empire stimulated among British textile manufacturers a search for machinery and processes that would enable them to match these Eastern products.[8] The British government assisted the process in the late eighteenth century by levying substantial tariffs on Indian textiles, making them more expensive in the British market. Likewise in the iron industry, inexpensive imports from Sweden and Russia stimulated British technological innovation.

"The Decline of the East." Another connection involves what some historians have referred to as the "decline of the East" as major Asian and Middle Eastern societies experienced political or economic setbacks that unexpectedly opened the way for the backward but energetic societies of western Europe to achieve a greater prominence. Examples of this "decline" include the withdrawal of Chinese

maritime forces from the Indian Ocean after 1435; the weakening or collapse of the Ottoman, Mughal, and Safavid empires in the eighteenth century; a growing ecological and economic crisis in early nineteenth-century China; and perhaps a certain conservative turning inward on the part of Islamic and Chinese intellectuals. The "decline of the East," in this view, made way for the "rise of the West."[9]

The Advantages of Empire

But by far the most significant international linkage was that of the American empires that Europeans carved out after 1492. Here lies one of the most sensitive moral as well as intellectual issues involving the origins of Europe's industrial revolution. Was Europe's economic progress purchased at the direct expense of exploited peoples in Africa and the Americas? Did the resources gained from empire provide a crucial boost to Europe's industrial development?

Not all empires are alike. The Chinese, Ottoman, and Russian empires, for example, did not generate the kind of economic windfall that Europeans gained from their American colonies. In at least four ways, Europe's New World empires may have contributed to its industrial takeoff.

Gold and Silver. The first was plunder. The enormous treasures of gold and especially silver looted from Aztecs and Incas or mined with forced labor and smaller amounts seized in India finally gave Europeans something that Asians, particularly the Chinese, really wanted. It enabled backward Europeans to buy their way into lucrative Asian markets and stimulate their own economies in the process.

Markets and Profits. But colonies were markets as well, as both settlers and slaves became favored customers for Europe's manufacturing industries. England's colonial trade, for example, exploded in the eighteenth century as exports to North America and the West Indies doubled between 1750 and 1790 and those to India more than tripled. This growing demand from the colonies certainly stimulated England's capitalist economy and its emerging mechanized textile industry in particular. And the profits from the colonial trade in both products and slaves contributed to the pool of capital from which British and continental industrialists drew as they invested in new machines and factories.

Resources. Europe's American empires also provided real resources: cod, timber, grain, sugar, and rice—some of it produced by slave labor from Africa. Especially important for an industrializing England was a ready supply of cotton. Here, some have argued, was Europe's decisive difference. The resources of the New World enabled Europe alone to solve the problem, common across Eurasia, of a growing population and limited land on which to produce necessary goods. "An unparalleled share of the earth's biological resources was acquired for this one culture," writes historian E. L. Jones, "on a scale that was unprecedented and is unrepeatable."[10]

An Industrial Model. Finally, the plantation system that was at the core of European expansion in the Americas may have modeled and pioneered patterns of economic activity that became central to industrial production. Sugar plantations, for example, involved large capital investment and a highly disciplined and regimented workforce aimed at the mass production of an increasingly inexpensive commodity for a mass market. Exposure to these new patterns of production and marketing arguably assisted European businessmen in developing an industrial factory-based system that operated on similar principles.

So the argument about the "why Europe?" question shapes up as a debate between those who emphasize Europe's internal uniqueness and those who stress distinctive international circumstances, especially the bounty of empire. But the two approaches are not mutually exclusive. Even if Europe gained much of value from its overseas empire, some countries were able to make use of these resources more effectively than others. If the wealth of empire was decisive for an industrial takeoff, why were Spain and Portugal, the first beneficiaries of that bounty, among the most backward and least industrialized of European countries even into the twentieth century? And why were some parts of the world able to follow the early example of British industrialization quite rapidly (France, Germany, the United States, and Japan), while others lagged far behind. Perhaps the serfdom of eastern Europe, the Confucian culture and powerful state of China, the military despotism of the Ottoman Empire, or the frequent political upheavals of Latin America inhibited their industrialization. Did these internal features of other regions hold back their modern development? The debate continues.

The Industrial Revolution

While the origins of Europe's industrial revolution remain controversial, its significance is hardly in doubt. Its place in world history can be compared only with the agricultural revolution around 10,000 BCE. Like that earlier transformation, the industrial revolution was rooted in a series of technological breakthroughs that gave humankind a new degree of control over nature, created vast new wealth, transformed the daily economic activities of most people, and opened up unimagined possibilities for social and cultural life. But while the agricultural revolution occurred separately in a number of places over thousands of years, its industrial counterpart had a single point of origin—late eighteenth-century England—and spread from there to the far corners of the earth too quickly to allow for independent invention elsewhere. And whereas agriculture has become an almost universal and apparently permanent feature of human life, industrialization is very much an unfinished process with many parts of the world still struggling to acquire the technology, wealth, and power that it promises. Since industrialization has been under way for little more than two centuries, it remains an open question as to whether it represents a viable long-term future for the planet. Is it possible to imagine that people 500 years from now might view the industrial revolution as a temporary and unsustainable burst of human creativity that petered out after several centuries? Or will the entire planet resemble the currently most urbanized and industrialized societies?

Toward Economic Modernity

Machines and Factories. At its heart, the industrial revolution was a matter of technology. Machines now did what only men, women, and animals had done before. During the eighteenth century, innovations in the British cotton textile industry led the way, speeding up the weaving and spinning processes. But the real breakthrough was the steam engine, which provided for the first time a huge, reliable, and inanimate source of power that could replace human and animal muscles by converting heat into useful work. That power could drive textile machinery, pump water out of mines, and propel locomotives and ships. Later in the nineteenth century, electricity and

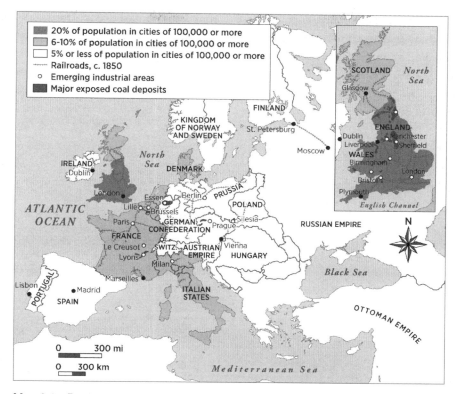

Map 9.1   By the middle of the nineteenth century, industrialization had begun to take root in western Europe.

internal combustion motors provided new power sources, while petroleum joined coal as a fuel. Industrialization began in the textile industry, but it soon spread to other fields: ironworking, railroads, and steamships by the 1840s; electrical and chemical industries a few decades later; and cars, refrigerators, radios, airplanes, and electronic products as the twentieth century accelerated the cumulative process of technological development. And beyond technology, industrialization involved dramatic changes in the organization of work, symbolized by the modern factory with its large-scale facilities, its minute division of labor in the assembly line, its dependence on wage-earning workers, and its centralized and highly disciplined management. The peasant farm or the artisan's workshop must have seemed worlds away.

New Wealth. The changes induced by the industrial revolution were neither immediate nor uniform, but over the course of a century or more, not so long in terms of world history, they fundamentally transformed the conditions of life in those societies most directly affected. The most obvious change, perhaps, lay in sustained economic growth, a continuous increase in the amount of goods that it was now possible to produce. It took traditional hand spinners in India 50,000 hours to produce 100 pounds of cotton yarn; steam-driven machinery in England in 1825 could produce the same amount in 135 hours.[11] Iron production in Britain jumped from 68,000 tons per year in 1788 to some 4 million tons in 1860, an almost 60-fold increase. So enormously productive were industrial economies that visionary thinkers, such as Karl Marx, could begin to imagine the end of poverty as a necessary condition of human society. Living standards did begin to rise, albeit unequally, and by the mid-twentieth century, many quite ordinary people in industrialized societies lived materially more abundant lives—and longer lives—than anyone could have imagined two centuries earlier.

Urbanization. The location of these manufacturing processes likewise changed. No longer scattered in numerous farmsteads or in artisans' workshops, industrial production became concentrated in urban centers that pulled millions of people into city life. In 1800, about 20 percent of Britain's population lived in sizable urban communities of 10,000 people or more; in 1900, 75 percent did. Here was the beginning of a continuing trend toward city living that by the end of the twentieth century brought fully half the world's population into urban centers. In its impersonal social relationships, its blending of different peoples, and its cultural creativity, urban life has given a distinctive flavor to modern societies.

Capitalism. The industrial revolution also extended the principle of the market—buying

Figure 9.2   High-tech metalworking with a huge steam-powered hammer illustrates the new source of power and the immense productivity of early industrial Europe. *bpk, Berlin/Art Resource, NY. Science Museum, London, Great Britain.*

Table 9.1   World Population Changes in the Modern Era

	Millions					
	1650	*1750*	*1850*	*1900*	*1950*	*2000*
Europe	100	150	263	396	532	729
United States and Canada	1	2	26	82	166	304
Australasia/Oceania	2	2	2	6	13	53
Mainly "European"	103	154	291	484	711	1086
Latin America	12	16	38	74	162	519
Africa	100	106	111	133	217	785
Asia	330	515	822	959	1,396	3,683
Mainly "non-European"	442	637	971	1,166	1,775	4,987
World total	545	791	1,262	1,650	2,486	6,073
	Percentages					
Europe	18.3%	19.1%	20.8%	24.0%	21.5%	12.0%
United States and Canada	.2	.2	2.1	5.0	6.7	5.0
Australasia/Oceania	.4	.2	.2	.3	.5	1.0
Mainly "European"	18.9	19.5	23.1	29.3	28.7	18.0
Latin America	2.2	2.0	3.0	4.5	6.5	8.5
Africa	18.3	13.0	8.8	8.1	8.7	12.9
Asia	60.6	65.0	65.1	58.1	56.1	60.6
Mainly "non-European"	81.1	80.0	76.9	70.7	71.3	82.0
World total	100.0	100.0	100.0	100.0	100.0	100.0

Source: R. R. Palmer, *A History of the Modern World* (New York: McGraw-Hill, 2002), 556.

In the nineteenth century, Europeans dramatically increased their demographic weight among the world's peoples, but in the second half of the twentieth century, their numbers returned to the proportions of 1650.

and selling based on supply and demand—to far more people and to a far greater range of goods. New urban residents had to depend on the market to provide their daily needs (food, clothing, and furniture), whereas their rural ancestors had been much more self-sufficient. Wealthy entrepreneurs wielded much of the capital that financed industrial production. As working for money wages became widespread for the first time, most people were selling their own labor on the market as well. As market relations penetrated European society more deeply, the hold of tradition, family, rulers, and the church on economic life diminished, and the values of the market—risk taking and innovation, individualism and competition, accumulation of material goods, and an acute awareness of clock time—became ever more prominent. Almost all agricultural societies had elements of the market, but Europe's industrial revolution gave rise to the world's most thoroughly commercialized societies, in which virtually everything was for sale—raw materials, finished products, land, money, and human labor. And increasingly, those who dominated the market were not individuals pursuing their own interests but large and wealthy corporations. The shorthand term for this kind of society has become "capitalism."

Death Rates and Birthrates. The revolutionary impact of industrialization also contributed much to that distinctive process of modern world history—the enormous and unprecedented growth of world population. That growth had begun well before the industrial revolution, fueled by global climate changes and the improved diet resulting from the proliferation of New World food crops. But industrial and scientific techniques applied to agriculture, accompanied by improvements in public health and sanitation, sustained and enhanced that population explosion by sharply lowering death rates. That potent combination pushed Europe's population from about 150 million in 1750 to almost 400 million by 1900, while Europe's colonies or former colonies provided opportunities for another 50 million Europeans to emigrate to the Americas, Australia, South Africa, and elsewhere. In that century and a half, people of European origin increased from about 20 percent of the world's total population to almost 30 percent.[12] But industrialization also acted, a bit later, to help stabilize the population of the more economically advanced countries, though at substantially higher levels, by encouraging lower birthrates. In urban industrial settings, children represented prolonged burdens on the family economy rather than productive members of it as they had been in more rural agricultural societies. As this logic took hold, parents acted to limit family size, making use of more readily available means of contraception.

Humanity and Nature. Growing populations in conjunction with industrial technology placed new pressures on the natural environment far beyond those associated with hunting-gathering or agricultural/pastoral societies. Those pressures became global in their implications and widely recognized by the general public only in the second half of the twentieth century, but they were apparent in more localized forms in the nineteenth. The massive extraction of nonrenewable raw materials to feed and to fuel industrial machinery—coal, iron ore, petroleum, and much more—altered the landscape in many places. Sewers and industrial waste emptied into rivers, turning them into poisonous cesspools. In 1858, the Thames River running through London smelled so bad that the British House of Commons had to suspend its session.[13] And

smoke from coal-fired industries and domestic use polluted the air in urban areas and sharply increased the incidence of respiratory illness.

Against these conditions, a number of individuals and small groups raised their voices. Romantic poets such as William Blake and William Wordsworth inveighed against the "dark satanic mills" of industrial England and nostalgically urged a return to the "green and pleasant land" of an earlier time. A few scientists promoted the scientific management of natural resources (forests in particular), while others, such as the American John Muir, pushed for the preservation of wilderness areas in national parks.[14] Although governments tried sporadically to address the problems, no widespread environmental movement surfaced until later in the twentieth century. Well into that century, many people in a heavily polluted Pittsburgh regarded industrial smoke as useful in fighting germs and a sign of progress.

Thus, the industrial revolution began to alter the relationship of humankind to the earth itself. Since the beginning of time, people had been vulnerable to the vagaries of nature—floods, drought, and storms—even as they transformed nature through farming, hunting, fires, and more. Now the balance started to change, and the earth and its many living inhabitants seemed increasingly at risk from the works of industrial humanity. It was a startling reversal of an ancient pattern.

Class and Industrial Society

Aristocrats and Peasants. Within western Europe's industrializing societies, old social groups declined and new ones arose, creating a wholly novel and distinctively modern class structure. Landowning nobles, proud bearers of Europe's ancient aristocratic traditions, lost many of their legal privileges, much of their economic power, and some of their social prestige. As the economic basis of society shifted to urban industrial property, the landed wealth of the nobility counted for less, and their disdain for commerce inhibited their adjustment to a capitalist society, increasingly dominated by the "new money" of commercial and industrial elites. Likewise, the peasantry, long representing the vast majority in all agricultural societies, now shrank as a proportion of the population as millions were pulled into industrial cities or pushed into emigration abroad. Those who remained on the land were increasingly oriented to producing for the market rather than for their own subsistence.

"Only a Weaver." Furthermore, many of Europe's artisans, who had for centuries produced their societies' manufactured goods by handicraft methods, found themselves displaced by industrial machinery. In 1820, Britain still had some 240,000 hand-loom weavers; by 1856, more than 90 percent of them were gone.[15] A nineteenth-century song lamented the fate of unemployed English weavers:[16]

> Who is that man coming up the street,
> With a weary manner and shuffling feet;
> With a face that tells of care and grief
> And in hope that seems to have lost
>   belief?
> For wickedness past he now atones,
> He's only a weaver that no one owns . . .
> Political economy now must sway
> And say when a man shall work or play.
> If he's wanted his wages may be high,
> If he isn't, why, then, he may starve
>   and die.

Other craftsmen less affected by machine competition, such as butchers, masons, and carpenters, flourished in the growing cities of industrial Europe.

"Middling Classes." The chief beneficiaries of Europe's industrial revolution were its growing and diverse "middle classes." Earlier, merchants, lawyers, and doctors, sometimes referred to as the "bourgeoisie," represented a small urban middle class occupying a social niche between the aristocratic landlords above them and artisans and peasants below them on the social scale. Industrialization greatly enlarged this class. But no single middle class emerged. At the top, wealthy industrialists and bankers might match the affluence of aristocratic magnates. Rather less exalted were small-business owners and professionals such as engineers, architects, pharmacists, and secondary school and university teachers along with older medical and legal professionals. By the end of the nineteenth century, the most advanced industrial societies had generated a whole army of clerks, salespeople, office workers, and small shopkeepers, eager to claim middle-class status and distinguish themselves from the factory workers below them.

Working Classes. These urban factory workers, dubbed the "proletariat" by Karl Marx, represented the other major new social group to emerge from the industrialization process, growing rapidly to about 30 to 40 percent of the population in the most highly industrialized countries. Unlike the artisans, who had their own tools and skilled traditions, the new working class in factories, docks, and mines entered the labor market with few skills and no tools of their own. There, they worked long hours at a pace dictated by the machines they served and subject to the instabilities of an industrial capitalist society.

The factory experience of a 19-year-old woman, recorded by an English reformer in the 1840s, illustrates the conditions in which early industrial workers had to labor:

The clock strikes half past five; the engine starts, and her day's work commences. At half past seven, and in some factories at eight, the engine slacks its pace (seldom stopping) for a short time, till the hands have cleaned the machinery, and swallowed a little food. It then goes on again, and continues full speed till twelve o'clock, when it stops for dinner. Previously to her leaving the factory, and in her dinner hour, she has her machines to clean. The distance of the factory is about five minutes' walk from her home. I noticed every day that she came in at half-past twelve or within a minute or two. The first thing she did, was to wash herself, then get her dinner (which she was seldom able to eat), and pack up her drinking for the afternoon. This done it was time to be on her way to work again, where she remains, without one minute's relaxation, till seven o'clock; she then comes home and throws herself into a chair exhausted. This is repeated six days in the week (save that on Saturdays she may get back a little earlier, say, an hour or two), can there be any wondering at their preferring to lie in bed till dinner-time, instead of going to church on the seventh?[17]

These conditions generated protests, expressed in strikes, trade unions, and the socialist movement, and gave rise to one of the major new conflicts of industrial societies.

Women, Factories, and the Home

New Views of the "Home." If industrialization transformed class structures, it also fundamentally altered family life and the roles of men, women, and children within it. In earlier agricultural societies, women combined productive labor on the farm or in the shop with their domestic and child-rearing duties because the family was the primary economic unit, and the home and the workplace were usually the same place. As industrialization moved the work site to factories and offices away from the home, that easy blending of women's productive and reproductive roles became more difficult. Middle-class women in particular largely withdrew from wage-earning labor. A new "ideology of domesticity" defined them as wives and mothers and charged them with making the home a "haven in a heartless world" of competitive industrial capitalism. Keeping women at home became a trademark of middle-class life that distinguished it from that of working-class families, fewer of whom could afford to do so. Thus, many working-class women joined the labor force as textile factory workers, as miners, and most often as domestic servants in middle-class households. But the new notion of women as homemakers and men as breadwinners penetrated the working class as well, and families in which married women worked outside the home were widely seen as failures. This novel division of labor between men and women proved to be a temporary adaptation to industrial life, as widening employment opportunities and the feminist movement brought many women of all classes back into the labor force in the twentieth century.

Children. More enduring perhaps were the changes in the lives of children. Early in the industrial era, many young children worked in the new factories and mines, an extension of long patterns of children contributing to the family economy. But this soon gave way to a concept of childhood defined in terms of school as compulsory education became common throughout nineteenth-century Europe. By the end of the century, a whole new stage of childhood had been invented—adolescence.

The teenage years had never before been defined as a unique stage of life, but as growing educational demands, required by an increasingly complex economy, kept young people out of the workforce for many years, that period of life acquired a distinct identity, especially in middle-class families, as a troublesome and traumatic passage from childhood to adulthood.

Politics and War

European political life also changed as a consequence of industrialization. Governments found themselves increasingly drawn into the economic life of their countries as they developed policies to enhance economic growth, to organize a growing educational system, to regulate industrial working conditions, and to moderate the disruptive social consequences of industrialization. Industrial development also played a growing role in the endlessly competitive relations of European states, especially as its military implications became apparent. By the end of the nineteenth century, a naval arms race between Germany and Great Britain fueled the instability of European international relations and helped to pave the way for World War I in 1914. That conflict disclosed the immense new destructiveness of industrialized warfare as barbed wire, machine guns, poison gas, tanks, and submarines took their place in the arsenals of the Great Powers and traumatized an entire generation as 10 million people perished in a few years. Further "progress" in the application of industrial and scientific techniques to military affairs in the twentieth century reached the point at which a global war with nuclear weapons raised the possibility of extinguishing human life—and perhaps all life—on the planet.

The Political Revolution

Accompanying Europe's industrialization was yet another revolutionary process, centered in the political arena and unfolding all around the Atlantic basin between the seventeenth and nineteenth centuries. Central to this upheaval was the French Revolution of 1789, but it was preceded by the English Civil War and the American Revolution of 1776 and followed by a massive uprising of slaves in Haiti in the 1790s and by Latin America struggles for independence in the early nineteenth century. Together, these revolutions gave the Western world of the nineteenth century a distinctive character and created societies unique in world history.

Kings and Commoners

At the core of the political revolution that swept Western societies in the eighteenth and nineteenth centuries was the replacement of monarchies by representative governments. In some cases, the monarch was removed and killed, as in the English Civil War of the 1640s and the French Revolution. In other cases, as in the establishment of the United States and most new Latin American republics, monarchy was denounced and ignored. But even when kings returned to more limited or "constitutional monarchies"—in England in 1689, in France briefly from 1814 to 1848, and in Brazil after 1822—the building of representative government continued.

The principles of this political revolution were enshrined in the declarations and political philosophies of the period. Initially calling for the "rights of subjects" and the need of monarchs to "consult" with parliament, as in the English Bill of Rights (1689), they broadened to protect "the rights of man and the citizen" in the French Declaration (1789) and to ensure the sovereignty of the people. All citizens were to be subject to the rule of law. Government and laws were to be created by representative assemblies of the people. The French Declaration and the U.S. Bill of Rights called for freedom of the press, freedom of expression, and freedom from arbitrary arrest. In practice, representative government meant political parties, elections, rules of procedure, and methods for determining the public, national, or majority will.

This political revolution was largely the act of the new middle class of merchants, producers, bankers, and capitalists with their wide range of supporters and allies—lawyers, doctors, writers, accountants, political leaders, and officials. The French called them the "bourgeoisie" and the German's "burgers" because they lived in the "burgs," the cities, both large and small. They were the urban money people—a "middle class" between the old landed aristocracy and the small rural peasants and farmers. In opposition to kings, aristocrats, and sometimes clergy, they claimed to represent all the people. But until the nineteenth century, they meant all the freeborn men with property. To secure life, liberty, happiness, and property, they pledged their lives and sacred honor but also their fortunes.

Revolutions are inherently destabilizing affairs. When one class of people demands power from another, the struggle can unleash the aspirations of those beneath both of them. In the English Civil War of the 1640s, the parliamentary party's demands of the king led to a civil war that not only resulted in the execution of King Charles I but also engaged landless laborers, calling themselves Levelers and Diggers, who were not satisfied by the replacement of the old rural propertied class by a new

urban propertied class. The political revolution of emerging capitalist society created not only the political conditions for a successful industrial revolution but the aspirations of a more socialist or communal world as well.

The American Revolution was also about property and principles. Opposition to the crown, while not universal, was as old as the colonies themselves. Some early settlers even returned to England to fight in the Civil War of the 1640s. But the more prosperous colonists of the eighteenth century were aggrieved by a British crown that seemed to them increasingly remote and unnecessary. The immediate cause was new taxation, made necessary, in British eyes, by the growing expenses of war and empire but bitterly resented in the North American colonies. The result was independence for the new United States of America, the first in a series of anticolonial struggles that would continue well into the twentieth century. Accompanying its independence was a self-conscious effort to create a "new order for the ages" based on a republican constitution and at least partially democratic principles.

The French Revolution of 1789, on the other hand, began as an internal affair, taking aim at a domestic monarchy and the ruling class of aristocrats who supported it. The French government was bankrupt, partly because of its support of the American Revolution and its many European wars. The French king, Louis XVI, and his queen, Marie Antoinette, were increasingly unpopular, and their court was widely viewed as basking in luxury and debauchery while ordinary people suffered terribly from various taxes, feudal payments, and a series of poor harvests, leaving many in hunger. Members of the emerging bourgeoisie resented the remaining privileges of the aristocracy, while many leading intellectuals had already lost confidence in the old regime. And the American example of republican revolution was contagious. In these volatile circumstances, the calling into session of an ancient assembly, the Estates General, for the purpose of raising taxes, served to trigger revolution.

In its most radical actions, that revolution executed the king and queen, abolished the ancient privileges of the nobility and the Catholic clergy, confiscated much of the Church's land, and unleashed a reign of terror against suspected enemies of the revolution, sending about 40,000 of them to the guillotine. In efforts to create a new society based on "liberty, equality, and fraternity," French revolutionaries such as Robespierre tried to replace Christianity with a secular "cult of reason" and, seeking to break decisively with the past, even promoted a new calendar for a new age. It was a far more revolutionary process than the Americans had undertaken.

The radical phase of the French Revolution came amidst a European wide war that required the revolutionary government to draft the first modern citizen army and establish the first modern procedures to confiscate and distribute food to the urban poor. Known as *sans-culottes* (those who wore long trousers rather than the knee-length breeches of the upper classes), they pushed the revolution into an increasingly radical and egalitarian direction and celebrated their differences from the dominant nobility and the propertied middle class. A pamphlet written in 1794 conveys something of their sense of themselves and of the class conflict that marked the French Revolution:

A Sans-Culotte[18] is a man who goes everywhere on his own two feet, who has none of the millions you're all after, no mansions, no lackeys to wait on him, and who lives quite simply with his wife and children, if he has any, on the fourth or fifth floor.[19] He is useful, because he knows how to plow a field, handle a forge,

Figure 9.3   Revolutionary market women marched to the king's residence at Versailles in 1789, forcing him to return with them to Paris. *Reunion des Musées Nationaux/Art Resource, NY. Musée de la Ville de Paris, Musée Carnavalet, Paris, France.*

a saw, or a file, how to cover a roof or how to make shoes and to shed his blood to the last drop to save the Republic. And since he is a working man, you will never find him in the Café de Chartres where they plot and gamble. . . . In the evening he is at his Section, not powdered and perfumed and all dolled up to catch the eyes of the *citoyennes* in the galleries, but to support sound resolutions with all his power and to pulverize the vile factions [of anti-revolutionaries]. For the rest, the Sans-Culotte always keeps his sword with a sharp edge, to clip the ears of the malevolent. Sometimes he carries his pike and at the first roll of the drums, off he goes to the Vendee,[20] to the Army of the Alps, or the Army of the North.[21]

Making New Societies

The "Enlightenment." Revolutionaries in both North America and France shared a novel idea derived from eighteenth-century European thinkers—that it was both possible and desirable for people to reconstruct their societies in a deliberate and self-conscious way. Such ideas grew out of an intellectual movement known as the "Enlightenment," in which scientific thinking spread to broader circles of the population and was applied to human affairs as well as nature. The Scottish professor Adam Smith, for example, found natural laws that explained the operation of the economy and argued that allowing them to operate freely would produce a good and prosperous society. Others addressed problems of politics and government. While they came to various conclusions, all believed that human reason, applied to human society, would generate unending progress. "The day will come," wrote the French thinker Condorcet, "when the sun will shine only on free men, born

knowing no other master but their reason; where tyrants and their slaves, priests and their ignorant hypocritical writings will exist only in the history books and theatres. . . . [T]he perfectibility of humanity is indefinite."[22]

Such criticism of European intolerance, superstition, and oppression flew in the face of conventional thinking in almost all of the world's large-scale agrarian civilizations. Human societies, it was widely held, were hierarchical, consisting of distinct, fixed, and unequal groups in which individuals would live and die. These societies and the kings or emperors who ruled them were ordained by God, an idea expressed in Europe as the "divine right of kings." Against this conception of society, American and especially French revolutionaries hurled their ideas of freedom from traditional beliefs and practices, the equality of all persons, and popular sovereignty, which meant that the right to rule derived from the consent of the people. The violent upheavals of the French Revolution were eventually tamed by military dictator Napoleon Bonaparte in the early nineteenth century, but his military campaigns and conquests throughout Europe spread the ideas of the revolution far beyond France. Those ideas came to define distinctively "Western" political and social values, often labeled "liberalism."

Liberalism. Rooted in the ideas of the Enlightenment, the core value of liberalism was the individual, and it sought to further individual liberation in every domain of life. Politically, liberals opposed arbitrary royal authority and the domination of society by privileged aristocracies. Intellectually, they sought liberation from ancient superstitions and religions, believing that human rationality was sufficient to understand the physical world and guide public affairs. Economically, liberals sought an end to restrictions on private property,

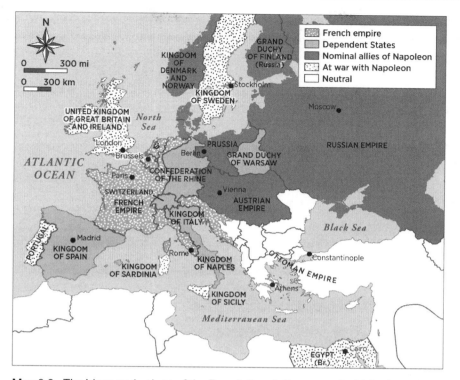

Map 9.2   The ideas and values of the French Revolution spread widely throughout Europe as Napoleon's conquests brought a huge area under French control.

believing that the public good would be best served by individuals pursuing their own economic interests. In the late eighteenth and early nineteenth centuries, these indeed were revolutionary ideas.

Who Benefited? Initially, these ideas and the legacy of the American and French revolutions benefited primarily white men of the professional and business classes, which capitalism and industrialization were simultaneously strengthening. In that sense, the political revolutions helped to create societies in which industrial capitalism could flourish. The beheading of the French king Louis XVI and his queen, Marie Antoinette, put more than a little dent in the divine right of kings, while the end of feudalism with its legal privileges for the aristocracy opened the way for wealthier

and more prominent members of the rising middle classes to share in political power and to acquire a greater measure of social prestige.

The expansion of the franchise or voting rights to men of property—and briefly during the French Revolution to all men—began a long process of political democratization but did not include women (except in a few places, like New Jersey during the American Revolution), people of color, or colonial subjects until the twentieth century. The idea of "careers open to talent" established the principle of merit rather than birth as the basis for social mobility, though those with education and property could more easily demonstrate their merit than those without. And the abolition of artisan guilds and internal trade barriers, together with development of commercial law and uniform weights and measures, facilitated the growth of industrial capitalism by allowing both workers and goods to move freely. More generally, the idea that human societies could be reshaped by human hands was an attractive and useful notion in a world where capitalism and industrialization were eroding the old system and creating the need for some new principles on which social order might be based.

The Revolution beyond America and France

Slave Rebellion and Independence Movements. In fairly short order, others found the ideas of the French and American revolutions useful in their own struggles as "liberalism" came to have a global impact. Slaves on the French island colony of Haiti in the Caribbean invoked the idea of human equality in a successful revolt in the 1790s. Unlike the revolt of the North American colonies, it was both a struggle for political independence from colonial rule and a violent social upheaval, shattering the illusion that slaves were a content and docile labor force and striking fear into slave owners throughout the Americas. Latin American revolutionaries in the early nineteenth century likewise found inspiration in the American and French experience as they pursued independence from Spain and Portugal. And Napoleon's occupation of those two countries during the wars that followed the French Revolution provided the occasion for launching independence struggles. But the violence of the French Revolution and the bloody slave uprising in Haiti made the elite leaders of these revolts very reluctant to encourage the participation of the masses and unwilling to extend the benefits of independence to them. Their societies were little altered when independence was achieved, though the ideas

of liberalism echoed frequently in the politics of independent Latin American states in the nineteenth century.

Challenging Old Oppressions. Aristocratic army officers in Russia, also influenced by the French example, attempted unsuccessfully to install a constitutional monarchy in 1825, thus challenging Europe's most autocratic state. "The Russian people is not the property of any one person or family. On the contrary, the government belongs to the people," declared one of their leading figures.[23] In places as far apart as Brazil, Japan, the Malay states, India, and the Ottoman Empire, nineteenth-century reformers who challenged old hierarchies of power and privilege found inspiration and support in the ideas of European liberalism. So too did reformers in Europe and the United States. Abolitionists seeking the end of slavery, democrats demanding an extension of the franchise, and women hoping to escape their age-old subordination to men were all acting on the basis of new ideas of freedom and equality. These ideas were revolutionary because they suggested that ancient inequalities and oppressions were neither natural nor inevitable; radical change was both possible and desirable.

Variations on a Theme

The British and French Paths. The industrial and French revolutions worked themselves out in different ways in different countries. England, of course, was the first center of industrial development, and those who followed sought to imitate the British example, borrowing or stealing its technology. Britain gradually extended democratic rights to ever-larger groups of men (but not to women) and after the Civil War did not experience the periodic violent upheavals that rocked France for almost a century after the revolution of 1789. Partly because of these political and social upheavals, French industrialization took place more slowly and gradually than in Britain. The absence of large coal fields also slowed industrial growth in France, as did the continued existence of small-scale peasant agriculture and relatively slow population growth.

The German Path. German industrialization, which took off after 1850, was far more rapid than the French, and it focused from the beginning on heavy industry—metals, chemicals, and electricity—rather than textiles, which had earlier led the way to industrialization in England. Germans organized their industries in very large companies or cartels rather than the smaller family-owned firms more common in England and France. By the end of the nineteenth century, Germany had taken the lead in the newer high-technology fields of chemicals and electricity. But this rapid economic progress took place in a society and a state that retained many of its earlier features—authoritarian government, militarism, and the continued prominence of aristocratic landlords. The democratic outcomes of the French Revolution had less impact in Germany than in France or Britain. Thus, Germany had fewer political outlets for the social strains of industrialization.

The Path of the United States. Like Germany, the United States industrialized rapidly in the second half of the nineteenth century and moved quickly toward large-scale business organizations. More so than elsewhere, these companies came to separate management from ownership, and without the pressure of family interests, managers were more free to innovate both production and marketing. A little later, Americans pioneered techniques of assembly-line mass production using interchangeable parts. They also applied industrial technology to agriculture more extensively than European countries and became a major exporter of agricultural goods. Furthermore, the United States depended quite heavily on Europe for capital investment. Because of its earlier involvement in the slave trade and massive immigration in the nineteenth century, the American labor force was far more diverse, racially and ethnically, than those of Europe. The divisions of race and ethnicity, in addition to the open frontier to the West, meant that workers' protests took a different form than in Europe. Socialist parties with their emphasis on class solidarity grew strong in Europe but found it far more difficult to take root in the United States. American labor protest was no less militant than in Europe, but it was less socialist.

The Russian Path. Russian industrialization was both later and less far reaching than in the rest of Europe. It got under way seriously in the 1880s and was concentrated in large industrial complexes in several major cities, such as Moscow and St. Petersburg. In the absence of a vigorous capitalist class, the state took the initiative with railroads and heavy industry leading the way. More than anywhere else, Russian industrialization took place in an otherwise backward country. Russian serfs won their freedom only in 1861, and the country remained overwhelming rural well into the twentieth century. The democratic ideas of the French Revolution had little impact in Russia, where the tsar retained absolute authority even after he reluctantly allowed a representative assembly to be elected in 1905. The strains of industrial development in an autocratic state exploded in revolution during World War I, leading to the world's first communist state. That state, the Soviet Union, then undertook a massive program of industrialization in the

1930s, but it completely rejected the capitalist framework within which all other processes of industrialization had developed.

New Identities, New Conflicts

Together, the industrial and political revolutions produced in the West were strikingly different from any in world history. They were enormously more productive and more commercialized. They engaged far more ordinary people in public life than in any of the older agrarian empires. Their military capacity surpassed anything known before. Social values highlighting competition among individuals as the route to a good society reversed traditional moralities that had emphasized community and cooperation. Finally, the worldview of the dominant elites was increasingly secular, seeking to explain the world in scientific rather than religious terms. In particular, Charles Darwin's theory of evolution challenged long-held notions about humankind as a distinct creation of God, while Sigmund Freud suggested that human beings were motivated largely by irrational drives, both sexual and aggressive.

Nowhere has the combined impact of the political and industrial revolutions been more apparent than in the growth of three movements—socialism, nationalism, and feminism—that appeared in nineteenth-century Europe and were appropriated in much of the rest of the world in the twentieth.

Socialism

Utopian Socialism. Socialism was a protest against the inequality of capitalist society. It had roots in biblical ideas of a peaceful future when "the lion would lie down with the lamb,"

in peasant yearnings for their own land, and in protests against the division of common grazing land into private property. Such early ideas and movements were later seen as nostalgic and naive. In one, Thomas More's *Utopia* (1516), the author imagined an ideal island in the Atlantic where a highly educated society had no private property, held everything in common, and needed neither money nor gold. In the English Civil War of the 1640s, poor peasants and revolutionaries called Levelers and Diggers briefly claimed the estates of lords for their own cultivation. During the French Revolution, in the 1790s, a firebrand named Gracchus Babeuf created a revolutionary group called "The Conspiracy of the Equals." During the first half of the nineteenth century, such ideas spread throughout Europe and North America. Some created utopian communities on the principle of "from each according to his abilities, to each according to his needs" or based on the idea that work should be an expression of personal passion rather than obligation to an employer. Some of these utopian colonies lasted into the twentieth century, especially in the rural United States.

Marxism. It was Karl Marx (1818–1883) who labeled these early efforts "utopian" in the sense of "unrealistic." For Marx, the utopian socialists were naive to imagine that they would change society by creating alternative models in the wilderness. They failed to understand that the capitalist class had created a new society, infinitely more productive than rural agricultural society but full of contradictions: between private gain and social well-being, its power to transform the world for the better, and its narrow selfishness. The goal of "scientific socialism," Marx believed, was to understand this process of historical change in order to exploit the contradictions of the capitalist system—to harness its enormous productivity to serve the common good.

Here was an economic system that could produce enough for everyone through the marvels of industrial technology but was absurdly unable to provide to its workers the fruits of their own labor. No wonder capitalism would be swept away in revolutionary upheaval featuring the urban industrial proletariat. Then its vast productive potential would be placed in service to the whole of society in a rationally planned, democratic, and egalitarian community. In such a socialist commonwealth, degrading poverty, conflicting classes, contending nations, and human alienation

generally would be but fading memories. From the ashes of capitalism, Marx wrote, there will emerge a socialist society in which "the free development of each [person] is the condition for the free development of all."[24]

Socialist Parties. In answer to the question of how this new world would come into being, the followers of Marx, not to mention other socialists, had diverse responses. Some believed that the downtrodden working classes would spontaneously rise up in a popular revolution. In 1848, the *Communist Manifesto*, by Marx and Friedrich Engels, fed such revolutionary energy with its call to struggle: "The Communists disdain to conceal

Figure 9.4 A socialist perspective on industrial capitalist society. The caption reads, "If only the chaps at the base, proletarians and peasants, should move . . . and the pyramid crumble." *The Granger Collection, New York.*

their views and aims. They openly declare that their ends can be attained only by the forcible overthrow of all existing social conditions. Let the ruling classes tremble at a communist revolution. The proletarians have nothing to lose but their chains. They have a world to win." But the middle-class revolution of 1848 did not turn into the working-class revolution that they urged. In Germany, where Marx and Engels were most hopeful, even the middle-class aspirations were brutally repressed. The first revolutionary socialist society was created by the people of Paris in 1871 after France was defeated by the new German Empire. They declared Paris to be an independent commune, governed by the workers and citizens. It lasted only a couple of months.

Nevertheless, by the time of Marx's death in 1883, there were socialist political parties throughout Europe. They agitated for the rights of workers, to vote, to organize in unions, and to gain political power. Socialist parties splintered and proliferated. Some remained revolutionary, in tune with the "Internationale," the anthem of the newly global movement:

> Arise you prisoners of starvation,
> Arise you wretched of the earth;
> For justice thunders condemnation,
> A better world's in birth.
> No more tradition's chains shall bind us,
> Arise, you slaves, no more in thrall,
> The earth shall rise on new foundations,
> We have been naught, we shall be all.

Western capitalists and governments countered the appeal of socialism in a number of ways. Capitalist governments recognized the need to integrate the worker classes into the political society. They initiated mass education and encouraged national rather than class

identity. In Germany, conservative governments lured away workers with an alternative state socialism of health, old-age, and unemployment insurance, creating the basis of what was to become the welfare state. By 1900, most socialist parties had dropped revolutionary ideology and adopted electoral politics. In France, a socialist party joined a conservative government. Accustomed to political power, the new socialists taught reform rather than violent struggle and evolutionary change rather than revolution. In the same period, Western corporations were able to raise the living standards of their domestic workers as they increased their exploitation of peoples in Latin America, Asia, and Africa. Western governments compensated for the depressed domestic markets of the late nineteenth century with a wave of "new imperialism" aimed at gaining cheaper raw materials and more global markets for European and North American corporations.

Nationalism

Western socialist movements were also undermined by the cultivation of appeals to the nation. The outbreak of World War I in August 1914 marked a capitulation by workers to this new identity. Some socialist leaders called on the workers to refuse participation in a conflict where they would be expected to kill fellow workers from other countries. But national loyalties proved stronger than class solidarity as European workers rallied to their respective flags and enthusiastically set out to slaughter fellow brothers of the Communist International rather than rising up against their capitalist overlords. Where had this compelling sense of national identity come from?

Nationalism as a Modern Idea. The national idea—that the world is divided into separate peoples each with its own distinct culture and deserving political independence—is some-times regarded as a natural and ancient orga-nization of human society. In fact, however, nationalism is a distinctly modern phenom-enon, dating back little more than two centuries in most places, and largely a European innova-tion. Before that most people regarded them-selves as members of small local communities such as clans, villages, or towns. Where they were bound to larger structures, it was as reli-gious believers, such as Christians or Muslims, or as subjects, not citizens, of dynastic states or empires, such as those that governed the Rus-sian, Chinese, or Ottoman empires.

The Origins of Nationalism. The emergence of what we now recognize as national identity occurred as Europe's modern transformation eroded older identities and loyalties. Science and rationalism weakened traditional religious loyalties. The emergence of separate states (Spain, Prussia, England, and France) under-mined dynastic imperial systems in which a sacred monarch ruled over a variety of cul-turally different peoples. The printing press standardized differing dialects and created a national language. By means of public educa-tion and popular media, print spelled out a national identity for a literate public.

Capitalism, industrialization, migration, and urbanization uprooted millions from long-established traditions and so created a need for new forms of community. The French Revolution and its democratic legacy encour-aged many people to feel that they had a right to participate in political life, for they were now citizens and no longer subjects. And lead-ers of that revolution called on these citizens to defend the French nation and its revolutionary achievements against attacks from conserva-tive forces in the rest of Europe.

Creating Nations. This was the brew from which nationalism emerged, first of all in France and England, where the modern trans-formation was most highly developed. In these countries, vernacular languages largely coin-cided with political boundaries, making the transition to a national consciousness easier. The political and economic success of these western European nations—especially through the conquests of Napoleon—soon gave the ideas of nationalism and the nation-state a great appeal in central and eastern Europe, where dynastic empires still held sway. There, during the nineteenth century, a distinctly national consciousness dawned for peoples who, unlike the French and the English, had no states of their own. Urban intellectuals—linguists, historians, writers, and students of folklore—took the lead in creating German, Italian, Hungarian, Czech, Bulgarian, Greek, Ukrainian, and many other nationalisms. Drawing on local folk cultures and selected aspects of their historical experience, these intellectuals shaped a conception of the nation that appealed to a widening circle of people. This process did not so much reawaken an-cient national feelings; rather, it "invented" or "constructed" new political loyalties—the "imagined communities" of the modern era.[25]

The Power of the National Idea. It soon proved to be a compelling identity. In Ger-many and Italy, scattered members of these "national communities" were gathered into new unified states, a process largely completed by the early 1870s. Governments increasingly based their authority on a claim to represent the "nation" rather than on divine right. They actively encouraged national loyalties in their schools, public rituals, newspapers, and mili-tary forces. Newly conscious "nations," such as Czechs and Hungarians, sought greater political independence from the ramshackle Austrian Empire; Greeks and Serbs revolted against Turkish rule in the Ottoman Empire;

and Poles and Ukrainians grew increasingly conscious of their subordination within the Russian Empire. As European imperialism intruded on Asia and Africa, stirrings of nationalism emerged in late nineteenth-century Egypt, India, China, and Vietnam. In the twentieth century, nationalism was thoroughly "internationalized" as it exploded across the globe, bursting apart any number of empires (Ottoman, British, French, Portuguese, and Soviet), triggering two world wars and the Holocaust, and serving to justify many regional conflicts and civil wars. New national identities may initially have been "imaginary," but modern political and economic changes forged them into powerful and competitive communities. Those national identities became a central element in the making of the modern world, a source of solidarity and immense sacrifice as well as a stimulus to bitter conflict.

Feminism

Although much smaller in size and impact than nationalism and socialism, the emergence of a feminist movement in nineteenth-century Europe and America represented something even more novel and unprecedented. Conflict between classes and countries was, after all, nothing new in world history. But the patriarchal double standard that allowed men to rule women had existed at least as long and had rarely been challenged. Now in the most advanced industrial societies of the West, such a challenge took shape and became a mass movement by the beginning of the twentieth century. How had it happened?

Roots of Feminism. Many elements of Europe's modern transformation paved the way for a feminist movement. Enlightenment thinkers challenged many of the received traditions of European society, including that of

women's intrinsic inferiority. The French and American revolutions raised the question of whether women were to be included in pronouncements of equality.

The growth of an industrial society with a much larger middle class, together with growing educational opportunities for girls, created a substantial group of educated women with the leisure to read, write, correspond with one another, and, eventually, organize. Both the slow progress of democracy and the challenge of socialism expressed ideas of equality with implications for women.

Feminist Beginnings. By the 1830s, small groups of educated middle-class women in Great Britain, France, Germany, and the United States, numbering in the hundreds or thousands, had come to a feminist awareness that completely rejected female subordination and inequality. "I came to the consciousness and to the knowledge that the position of women was absurd," wrote one German American feminist, "so I soon began to do as much as I could, in words and print, for the . . . betterment of women."[26] Many of them had prior experience in other reform movements, such as socialism, abolitionism, and religious freedom, and they took courage from a wave of short-lived revolutionary upheavals that broke out all over Europe in 1848.

These women established feminist newspapers and journals, founded schools and colleges, held numerous meetings and conventions of like-minded colleagues, and kept in touch with one another across national boundaries as they created the first international women's movement in world history. In the process, they questioned age-old traditions: some women wore pants, others declined to take their husband's name, and still others challenged patriarchal religious beliefs and practices. Women contested dominant male attitudes concerning sex, prostitution, rape, and divorce. They organized to gain equal employment opportunities, education, and political rights for women.

The American feminist Elizabeth Cady Stanton made the case in an eloquent address to a committee of the U.S. Congress in 1892:

> The strongest reason why we ask for woman a voice in the government under which she lives; in the religion she is asked to believe; equality in social life, where she is the chief factor; a place in the trades and professions, where she may earn her bread, is because of her birthright to self-sovereignty; because, as an individual, she must rely on herself. No matter how much women prefer to lean, to be protected and supported, nor how much men desire to have them do so, they must make the voyage of life alone, and for safety in an emergency they must know something of the laws of navigation. To guide our own craft, we must be captain, pilot, engineer; with chart and compass to stand at the wheel; to match the wind and waves and know when to take in the sail, and to read the signs in the firmament over all. It matters not whether the solitary voyager is man or woman.
>
> Nature having endowed them equally, leaves them to their own skill and judgment in the hour of danger, and, if not equal to the occasion, alike they perish.[27]

The Achievements of Feminism. The European feminist movement was temporarily silenced in the repression that followed the revolutionary upheavals in 1848. But it reemerged several decades later with a primary focus on the issue of suffrage and with a growing constituency. Now many ordinary middle-class housewives and working-class mothers joined their better-educated sisters

in the movement. By the outbreak of World War I in 1914, French feminist groups counted some 100,000 adherents, while the National American Women's Suffrage Association claimed 2 million members. Although most of these organizations pursued peaceful tactics of persuasion and protest, the British Women's Social and Political Union was deliberately more aggressive, engaging in civil disobedience and occasional acts of terrorism. One suffragette threw herself in front of the king's horse during a race in Britain in 1900 and died from her injuries. The violent hostility that such actions aroused revealed the depth of "sexual warfare," which an overt feminism provoked. In the most highly industrialized countries of the West, the women's movement had become a mass movement.

Greater access to university education, legal reforms giving women control over their property, and some liberalization of divorce laws owed much to the growing feminist movement, though widespread voting rights for women in national elections were not achieved until after World War I. Perhaps the most significant achievement of the movement, however, was to force the "woman question" onto the public agenda in the West far more extensively than it had ever been before. Novelists and dramatists challenged the institution of marriage. Henrik Ibsen's play *A Doll's House* (1879) riveted and sharply divided European audiences when the character of Nora abruptly left a confining marriage and her children to "find herself" in the larger world. An increasingly frank and public discussion of sexuality, including homosexuality and birth control, took place in literary, medical, political, and journalistic circles. Socialists debated whether a separate focus on women's issues might distract from the class solidarity that Marxism proclaimed. Feminists themselves

Figure 9.5 Women and men march in support of the vote for women in Britain in 1910. *Time Life Pictures/Getty Images.*

argued about the basis for women's rights. Did they arise from an emphasis on women as individuals with rights equal to those of men? Or was it rather women's unique role as mothers and their relationship to family life that provided the strongest case for reform?

Backlash. All of this, not surprisingly, provoked opposition. Some academic and medical experts proclaimed that women had smaller brains and that undue study would cause serious reproductive damage. Others defined feminists as selfish, pursuing their own interests at the expense of the family or even the nation. Public officials in France and elsewhere inveighed against feminism in general and birth control in particular on the grounds that it would depopulate the nation. Some saw

suffragists, like Jews and socialists, as "a foreign body in our national life." Women who worked outside the home were said to neglect their children and to overtax their reproductive capacities. Never before in any society had such a passionate and public debate about the position of women erupted. It was a novel feature of Europe's modern transformation.

Conclusion: Modernity as Revolution

By the beginning of the twenty-first century, modern life had become so familiar to people in the West that its unprecedented and revolutionary qualities were easily overlooked.

Historical study reminds us how new, how radical, and how relatively recent these transformations have been.

Like all great movements of historical change, the industrial and political revolutions both shattered old ways of life and gave rise to new ones. Technological change unleashed vast new productive forces. Aristocrats lost out to industrialists, who were themselves challenged by workers and socialists. Artisans and peasants declined in numbers as factory workers, salespeople, and typists took their place. Kings whose authority had long rested on "divine right" now had to accommodate elected assemblies based on notions of popular sovereignty and democracy. Children went to school rather than to work, and middle-class women increasingly stayed at home while their husbands went off to the factory or office. Class and especially national loyalties increasingly replaced those of local communities. Individualistic and secular values challenged traditional commitments to family, village, or religion. Military forces achieved immeasurably greater power. Never before in human history had so much changed so quickly.

These transformations certainly brought new freedoms and greater prosperity to many people as living standards slowly rose, education grew, and democratic practice was established. But they did not generate a lasting stability in European societies. Conflicts of class, nation, and gender continued to unsettle European life, and during the first half of the twentieth century, the "proud tower" of European modernity virtually collapsed in war, depression, and genocide. Furthermore, the modern transformation of European society inspired and enabled a new wave of European expansion that encompassed almost the entire planet and brought lasting changes to the rest of the world as well.

Suggested Readings

Anderson, Bonnie S. *Joyous Greetings: The First International Women's Movement, 1830–1860.* Oxford: Oxford University Press, 2000. A history of the beginnings of organized feminism in the West.

Eley, Geoff, and Ronald Grigor Suny. *Becoming National: A Reader.* New York: Oxford University Press, 1996. A collection of readings about the history of nationalism around the world.

Hobsbawm, Eric. *The Age of Revolution, 1749–1848.* New York: Vintage Books, 1996. A Marxist account of the French and industrial revolutions by a well-known and highly respected scholar.

Landes, David. *The Wealth and Poverty of Nations.* New York: Norton, 1998. A controversial but very readable book that seeks to explain why Europe grew wealthy while other areas of the world did not. Often criticized for being Eurocentric.

Marks, Robert. *The Origins of the Modern World.* Boston: Rowman & Littlefield, 2003. A short account of the beginnings of modernity that draws on much recent scholarship and places Europe in a global perspective.

Palmer, R. R. *The Age of Democratic Revolution.* Princeton, NJ: Princeton University Press, 1970. A classic account of the French Revolution that places it in a broader Atlantic context.

Stearns, Peter. *The Industrial Revolution in World History.* Boulder, CO: Westview Press, 1998. A global history of industrialization from its eighteenth-century origins through the end of the twentieth century.

Tilly, Louise, and Joan Scott. *Women, Work, and Family.* London: Routledge, 1987. Explores the changing roles of working-class women in France and England as they participated in the industrial revolution.

Notes

1. William H. McNeill, "*The Rise of the West* after Twenty-Five Years," *Journal of World History* 1, no. 1 (Spring 1990): 7.

2. E. L. Jones, *The European Miracle* (Cambridge: Cambridge University Press, 1981), 119.

3. David Landes, "Clocks: Revolution in Time," *History Today*, January 1984, 19–26.

4. Jack A. Goldstone, "Efflorescence and Economic Growth in World History," *Journal of World History* 13, no. 2 (Fall 2002): 323–89.

5. Kenneth Pomeranz, *The Great Divergence: Europe, China, and the Making of the Modern World Economy* (Princeton, NJ: Princeton University Press, 2000).

6. Colin Simmons, "Deindustrialization, Industrialization, and the Indian Economy, 1850–1947," *Modern Asian Studies* 19, no. 3 (1985): 600.

7. Kenneth Pomeranz and Steven Topik, *The World That Trade Created* (Armonk, NY: M. E. Sharpe, 1999), 7.

8. Arnold Pacey, *Technology in World Civilization* (Cambridge, MA: MIT Press, 1990), 117–20.

9. Janet Lippman Abu-Lughod, "The World System in the Thirteenth Century," in *Islamic and European Expansion*, ed. Michael Adas (Philadelphia: Temple University Press, 1993), 85–97.

10. Jones, *The European Miracle*, 82

11. Howard Spodek, *The World's History*, vol. 2 (Upper Saddle River, NJ: Prentice Hall, 2001), 519.

12. R. R. Palmer et al., *A History of the Modern World* (New York: McGraw-Hill, 2002), 556.

13. Clive Pointing, *A Green History of the World* (New York: St. Martin's Press, 1991), 355

14. Ramachandra Guha, *Environmentalism: A Global History* (New York: Longman, 2000), chaps. 1–4.

15. Spodek, *The World's History*, 531.

16. Roy Palmer ed., *Poverty Knock* (New York: Cambridge University Press, 1974), 24.

17. William Dodd, *The Factory System Illustrated* (London: John Murray, 1842), 108–10.

18. A class of workers and artisans defined by their clothes—long pants (literally without culottes, or breeches, which were worn by the upper classes).

19. French apartment buildings reflected French social structure. The wealthy lived in grand apartments on the first floor, while the lower classes had to climb the stairs to the upper floors.

20. Western France where the proroyalist antirevolutionary movement was strong.

21. Quoted in Mortimer Chambers et al., *The Western Experience* (Boston: McGraw-Hill, 2003), 730.

22. Marquis de Condorcet, *Sketch of the Progress of the Human Mind*. Translated from Marie Jean Antoine Nicolas Caritat, marquis de Condorcet, *Esquisse d'un tableau historique des progrès de l'esprit humain* (Paris: Librairie philosophique J. Vrin, 1970), p. 198.

23. Quoted in C. A. Bayly, *The Birth of the Modern World* (Oxford: Blackwell, 2004), 295.

24. Marx and Engels, *The Communist Manifesto* (New York: Signet Classics, Penguin Group, 1998), 46.

25. Benedict Anderson, *Imagined Communities: Reflections on the Origins and Spread of Nationalism* (London: Verso, 1983).

26. Bonnie S. Anderson, *Joyous Greetings: The First International Women's Movement, 1830–1860* (Oxford: Oxford University Press, 2000), 14. This paragraph is drawn from Anderson's book.

27. *Votes for Women: Selections from the National American Woman Suffrage Association Collection, 1848–1921*. Washington, DC: Library of Congress, American Memory: Historical Collections for the National Digital Library, December 3, 2001, http://www.wfu.edu/~zulick/340/solitude.html.

10

The Great Disturbance
by Global Empires
1750–1940

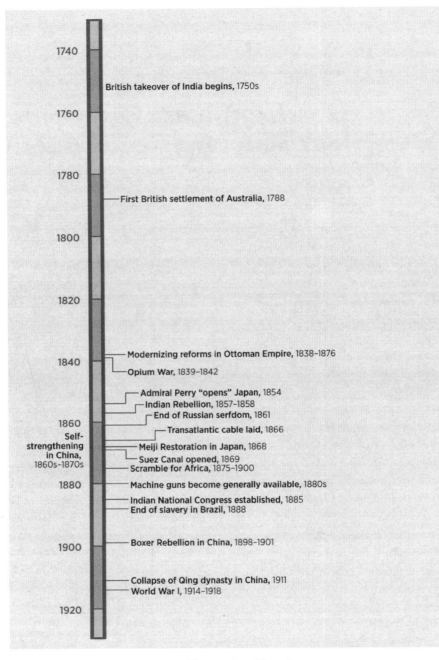

Figure 10.1 Time line.

T HE INDUSTRIAL revolution not only transformed the face of Europe, where it originated, but also set in motion dramatic changes—a great disturbance—throughout the entire world. While the world's various peoples outside the West retained their many differences after 1750, increasingly they had one thing in common—the need to confront the aggressive intrusion of Europeans into their affairs. Europeans of all kinds—soldiers and settlers, missionaries and explorers, businessmen and investors, and colonial administrators and technical specialists—now descended on Asian-Pacific and African societies. Most dramatic perhaps was Western military power, which brought many societies under European political control for the first time, some in formal colonies and others in semi-independent countries heavily influenced by their foreign intruders. With even longer-lasting consequences, European economic penetration confronted Afro-Asian peoples as Western industrializing societies sought raw materials for their factories, markets for their products, and investment opportunities for their profits. Afro-Asian societies also encountered and adapted some of the revolutionary ideas and techniques generated in Europe's modern transformation, such as socialism, nationalism, railroads, mechanized mining operations, and factory production. They were also exposed to the older features of European civilization, such as Christianity and European languages and literatures. These encounters generated new identities—racial, class, gender, ethnic, national, and religious—in Asian and African societies and provoked many of the world's peoples into transforming their own societies.

The dilemma that confronted many of the world's peoples is illustrated by the reaction of a well-educated Egyptian Muslim named Abd al-Rahman al-Jabarti as he witnessed Napoleon's conquest of his country in 1798. On the one hand, al-Jabarti was much impressed with French science and technology and was forced to the disturbing conclusion that a culture he regarded as inferior had superseded the technological and intellectual achievements of his own:

> The French installed . . . a large library with several librarians who looked after the books and brought them to the readers who needed them. . . . If a Moslem wished to come in to visit the place he was not in the least prevented from doing so. . . . The French especially enjoyed it when the Moslem visitor appeared to be interested in the sciences. They welcomed him immediately and showed him all sorts of printed books with maps representing various parts of the world and pictures of animals and plants. . . . One was positively astounded at the sight of all these beautiful things.
>
> . . . [T]hey [the French] were great scholars and loved the sciences, especially mathematics and philology. They applied themselves day and night to learning the Arabic language and conversation. . .
>
> An astronomer and his students had very precise astronomical instruments. One saw among them instruments

constructed in absolutely remarkable ways and which were obviously very expensive. . . . They also had telescopes which contracted and closed themselves in little boxes. They helped to observe the stars and determine their distances, volumes, conjunctions, and oppositions. They also had all sorts of time devices, including very valuable clocks which indicated the second very precisely, and many other instruments. . .

We also saw a machine in which a glass went around which gave off sparks and crackled whenever a foreign object was brought near it. . .

We had other experiences even more extraordinary then the first ones, and untutored intellects like ours could not conceive how they happened or give any explanations for them.[1]

But al-Jabarti reacted in a quite different fashion to another "face" of the West encountered during 1798—the arrival of the French occupying army in Egypt:

The French entered the city [Cairo] like a torrent rushing through the alleys and streets without anything to stop them, like demons of the Devil's army. They destroyed any barricades they encountered. . . . And the French trod in the Mosque of al-Azhar with their shoes, carrying swords and rifles. . . . They plundered whatever they found in the mosque. . . . They treated the books and Quranic volumes as trash. . . . Furthermore, they soiled the mosque, blowing their spit in it, pissing and defecating in it. They guzzled wine and smashed bottles in the central court.[2]

How to resist aggression, to accommodate superior power, and to appropriate what was useful from the invaders—here was the

dilemma faced by growing numbers of people and societies as a changing balance of global power allowed Europeans, for a brief time, to dominate virtually the entire earth.

Imperialism of the Industrial Age

The most visible though not the most lasting expression of Europe's global reach after 1750 lay in the wars of conquest by which Europeans extended their military and political power throughout the world. This process continued patterns of European imperialism that began in the fifteenth and sixteenth centuries, but this new phase of Western expansion differed in many ways from the earlier one. Now the primary focus lay in African, Middle Eastern, Asian, and Pacific societies rather than the Americas. And the cast of European players changed as well. The Spanish and Portuguese, so prominent in the early conquest of the New World, had only a marginal role in this new era of empire building. The British and French were the most significant European imperialists, while Germany, Italy, Belgium, the Netherlands, Russia, and the United States entered the fray on a more modest scale. Late in the nineteenth century, Japan joined the imperialist club as its only non-Western member and began to carve out an empire in East Asia.

Imperial Motives

Most of these countries had begun to industrialize, and that process shaped their imperial expansion even as it changed so much else as well. European motives now included the desire to export their surplus industrial production, to find more profitable investments for their capital, and to secure raw

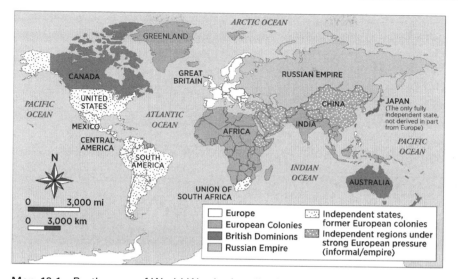

Map 10.1 By the eve of World War I, virtually the entire world was politically controlled by Europeans or people of European descent in one way or another.

materials needed for their factories. Some Europeans, particularly the wealthy, were aware of the social importance of foreign outlets for their goods and profits. Without them, many feared, prices would fall, unemployment increase, and socialism become more popular. "If you wish to avoid a civil war," wrote Cecil Rhodes, among the most ardent advocates of the British Empire, "then you must become an imperialist."[3] Older impulses toward imperialism growing out of European rivalries continued and even intensified in the late nineteenth century, as competing nationalisms now fueled Western expansion in Africa and Asia. Religion, however, declined among statesmen and diplomats as a motive for empire, though it remained strong among missionary societies and their supporters at home.

Underlying all this was a growing sense among Europeans that they were a superior form of humanity, as evidenced by their amazing technological progress. For some, this meant that "lesser breeds" or 'backward peoples" were destined to be displaced or

destroyed by superior races and that the war, bloodshed, and brutality associated with imperialism were the "natural" and even "progressive" mechanism by which the "survival of the fittest" unfolded. For others, this "social Darwinism," a harsh understanding of imperialism, was tempered with a genuine though condescending sense of responsibility to the "weaker races" that Europe was fated to dominate. Empire and trade, they felt, should bring the blessings of Western civilization to those less fortunate: Christianity, freedom, and material improvement. Rudyard Kipling's famous poem of 1899 gave this "paternalistic idealism" its classic expression:

Take up the White Man's Burden
Send forth the best ye breed
Go bind your sons to exile
To serve your captives' need;
To wait in heavy harness
On fluttered folk and wild
Your new caught, sullen peoples,
Half devil and half child.[4]

The Tools of Empire[5]

The industrial era provided new means as well as new motives for European expansion. Steam-driven ships facilitated the penetration of the Asian and African interiors along their river systems, and the discovery of quinine to prevent malaria reduced the risk of an extended stay in the tropics from quasi suicidal to merely dangerous. Breech-loading rifles, which became available about 1850 and machine guns a few decades later, provided the overwhelming firepower that decided many a colonial conflict. A much-quoted rhyme expressed the essential facts of the situation:

> Whatever happens, we have got
> The Maxim gun [machine gun], and they
>   have not.

Finally, the enhanced administrative capacities of an industrializing Europe as well as remarkable improvements in the technology of transportation and communication—larger and more efficient ships, the Suez and Panama canals, underwater telegraph cables, and the railroad—linked Europe and its new dependencies more tightly than ever before. All this—both motives and means—propelled Europeans' inland intrusion into Asian and African societies after 1750, following more than two centuries of being limited largely to fortified trading centers along the coasts.

Confronting Imperialism

The global encounter of European imperialism and various Afro-Asian peoples took shape in quite different ways. Much depended on the historical circumstances of particular cultures or civilizations as well as on the intentions of various groups of European intruders. It was clearly a two-way process although a highly unequal one in terms of power.

Some people and some groups in every society found advantage in the European presence and were inclined to cooperate, at least for a time. Rulers, caught in complex internal rivalries and external threats, might very well view the Europeans as useful allies. In Southeast Asia, for example, a number of highland minority groups, long oppressed by the dominant lowland Vietnamese, viewed the French invaders as liberators and assisted in their takeover of Vietnam. And once colonial rule was established, many traditional elite groups and other aspiring individuals eagerly served the new order as princes, chiefs, administrative officials, clerks, soldiers, and translators. Without them, colonial rule would have been impossible.

On the other hand, resistance was widespread, as witnessed by the endless and bloody wars of conquest that Europeans were required to fight in order to establish their control. Here is just one very small example drawn from the British conquest of Kenya in East Africa in the early twentieth century. It comes from the diary of a British soldier in 1902:

> I have performed a most unpleasant duty today. I made a night march to the village at the edge of the forest where the white settler had been so brutally murdered the day before yesterday. Though the war drums were sounding throughout the night, we reached the village without incident and surrounded it. . . . I gave orders that every living thing except children should be killed without mercy. I hated the work and was anxious to get through with it. So soon as we could see to shoot we closed in. Several of the men tried to break out but were immediately

Figure 10.2   The Suez Canal, opened in 1869, provided Europeans with a much quicker route to Asia and East Africa than ever before. *bpk, Berlin/Art Resource, NY.*

shot. I then assaulted the place before any defense could be prepared. Every soul was either shot or bayoneted, and I am happy to say that there were no children in the village. They, together with the younger women, had already been removed by the villagers to the forest. We burned all the huts and razed the banana plantations to the ground.[6]

Even after initial resistance had been crushed, hundreds of rebellions threatened the "colonial peace." And soon nationalist movements, led by Western-educated elites, took shape and eventually brought the age of global empire to an end in the second half of the twentieth century.

But the various peoples of Asia and Africa confronted quite different patterns of European intrusion, and their responses to it varied widely as well.

India

Mughal Decline. India was among the first to experience this new thrust of European imperial expansion. European traders, first the Portuguese and later the British and French, had been active along the coast of India for several centuries, but their trading companies had long operated under the control and with the permission of the powerful Mughal Empire. But in the eighteenth century, that empire began to disintegrate as the more aggressively Muslim emperor Aurangzeb (1658–1707) upset the delicate balance between the empire's Muslim rulers and its mostly Hindu subjects. As the central authority of the Mughal Empire weakened, regional rulers became more prominent, as did urban merchants and moneylenders. Many such people found an advantage in some connection with the French or British trading companies. European military technology and techniques for training troops were useful to aspiring regional authorities enmeshed in local rivalries. Some wealthy Indian traders and bankers, resenting the demands of Mughal authorities, helped finance the military forces of the British East India Company. Substantial numbers of Indian men joined European led armies, attracted by the security and opportunities for enrichment that they offered.

British Takeover. Without the authority of the Mughal Empire to provide law and order, the British East India Company, together with its French rival, found it useful and profitable to train and arm some of these Indian states and to involve themselves ever more deeply in the complex political affairs of India. Over the course of more than half a century after 1750, the British Company bested its French rivals, allied with some Indian rulers, opposed others, and found itself by the mid-nineteenth century ruling the Indian subcontinent. Although it involved the frequent use of British-led military forces, the British acquisition of India was not, precisely, a "conquest" of one state by another, and it occurred with the assistance of many Indian allies. Lest this seem unpatriotic, we need to remember that little sense of "India" as a nation had yet emerged. Local loyalties to caste, village, or region were far more important, and relationships with rulers at an all-India level fluctuated frequently on the basis of changing interests.

One witty observer quipped that Britain had acquired its Indian colony "in a fit of absence of mind." Certainly, the British government had no declared policy of conquering India, but it generally acquiesced to the actions of East India Company officials "on the spot" who often acted quite deliberately (and without consulting authorities in London) in carving out new territories to govern. Thus, the British takeover of India was carried out by a private commercial company, though the British government assumed official control of the country in 1858. The resources that made this remarkable acquisition possible did not initially involve industrial technology or superior firepower, for much of this process occurred before the industrial revolution kicked in. Rather, it was a matter of organizational technology in the form of disciplined military training and highly regimented tactics.

A broadly similar transition from a limited European commercial presence to outright political control also occurred in Indonesia as the Dutch East India Company took over that heavily populated archipelago. In both cases, the outcome was unexpected and was driven as much by events in Asia as by the intentions of European governments or commercial firms.

Rebellion. India was also the site of one of the largest rebellions in the colonial world. Known as the Indian, or Sepoy, Rebellion of 1857–1858, it began as a cultural clash in the military when Indian troops, known as sepoys, refused to use cartridges greased in animal fat. Hindus feared that the fat came from sacred cows, while Muslims feared it came from filthy and offensive pigs. The revolt attracted a variety of groups with grievances against the new British rulers: exploited peasants, landlords deprived of their estates, princes displaced by British rule, and religious leaders threatened by missionary activity. Nevertheless, divisions among the rebels and British military superiority crushed the revolt amid horrendous violence. In one display of extravagant revenge, British soldiers chained "disloyal" sepoys to the mouths of cannon and blew them apart.

Yet even failed rebels could become martyrs in later struggles for independence. One of these was the young Rani of Jhansi, a fierce fighting widow of an Indian raja who had been deprived by the British of her inheritance. The Rani led her own army of women as well as male troops against the British in 1858. Despite her death in the battle at the age of 23, her memory was honored in stories, films, monuments, and the naming of a women's regiment in the anti-British Indian National Army during World War II.

China

China and the West. China's confrontation with Western imperialism bore both similarities and differences to that of India. Like the Mughal Empire, China had controlled and contained European activity for some 300 years. Chinese authorities had admitted European missionaries to the court when they appeared respectful and useful and sharply restricted or prevented their activity when they became offensive. Western traders, like other "barbarians" seeking access to China's riches, were subject to strict monitoring and after 1759 were limited to trading in a single Chinese city, Guangzhou (Canton), and were compelled to conduct business only with authorized Chinese merchants. But by the early nineteenth century, the balance of power had begun to shift. China's Qing dynasty (1644–1911) weakened under the pressures of population growth, official corruption, and periodic peasant rebellion. Furthermore, the country faced a new problem, directly related to European activity—drug addiction.

Opium for Tea. British traders had long been frustrated by their inability to find Western products that the Chinese wanted to buy. By the eighteenth century, increased consumption of Chinese tea had to be paid for in silver, depleting British reserves. A solution was found in India, where opium had long been grown for medicinal purposes. Finally, a product with an unquenchable demand. The British East India Company increased production, and it and (after 1834) various American and other companies began to import huge quantities of this highly addictive drug into China, where it found a ready market. From the viewpoint of the Chinese government, here was a problem of major proportions. The opium trade, after all, was wholly illegal and contrary to Chinese law, thus creating a growing "law-and-order" issue. Furthermore, it corrupted Chinese officials who were bribed to turn their heads when boats laden with opium chests arrived. It was a terrible social problem as well, vastly increasing the number of addicts to perhaps 10 million by the mid-1830s. For the British, the trade was a huge success since it reversed the drain of silver, but now the Chinese suffered from a massive outflow of the precious metal in payment for an illegal addictive drug.

What followed was an intensive debate at the Chinese court in the mid-1830s between those who sought to control the opium trade by legalizing it and those who wanted to strictly enforce the laws against it. When the emperor finally decided on suppression, Chinese authorities acted decisively, seizing and destroying some 20,000 chests of opium in Canton and promising harsh punishment for Europeans who persisted in the trade. From the Chinese point of view, a crackdown on the sale and consumption of opium was a principled decision.

Figure 10.3   Chinese efforts to prevent their citizens from smoking opium, as in this opium den, led to humiliating military defeat and a century of semicolonial status. *The Stapleton Collection/ Art Resource, NY.*

The Opium Wars. But the British claimed a principle as well—free trade and the rights of private property. As the world's major commercial country, the British viewed free trade as an almost religious doctrine, and the seizure of British-owned opium had clearly violated the rights of private property. Emboldened by their new industrially based power, the British government in 1840 used novel steam-powered gunboats to coerce the Chinese state into more open trading relations. This was the Opium War (1839–1842), the first in a series of military conflicts in the nineteenth century in which various European powers (and later Japan) repeatedly inflicted humiliating defeats on the proud Chinese state. In one of these encounters in 1860, after the Second Opium War, the British vandalized and then burned to the ground the exquisite summer palace of the emperor.

Unlike European imperialism in India, the outcome was not a formal colonial takeover but rather a set of "unequal treaties" that sharply limited Chinese sovereignty while preserving its legal independence. Under these treaties, the Chinese were required to open up numerous ports to European merchants, to limit their tariffs on imported goods, to allow foreigners to be judged by their own courts, and to protect Christian missionaries. They also had to permit the continued trade in opium, which grew even larger. One of the treaties even forbade the Chinese to use the character for *barbarian* to refer to the British. It was a kind of semicolonial status that historians sometimes call "informal empire."

The Taiping Rebellion. Compounding China's external problems was a series of massive peasant rebellions that shook the country in the 1850s and 1860s. But unlike the Indian

Rebellion, which was directed against the British, China's largest upheaval, known as the Taiping Rebellion, took aim at the ruling Qing dynasty and the landlord class that supported it. The ideology of the Taiping rebels differed from earlier Chinese peasant movements in that it was based on a foreign set of ideas, a garbled version of Christianity picked up from missionary teachings. That ideology cast the rebellion's leader, Hong Xiuquan (1814–1864), as the younger brother of Jesus Christ, returned to Earth to expel the demons and to prepare the way for the "heavenly kingdom." Hong's message was genuinely revolutionary as it rejected Confucianism, Buddhism, and Daoism; proposed the elimination of private property; urged the equality of men and women; and sought to promote modern industrialization. While the Taiping Rebellion was crushed by the mid-1860s, the civil war that it occasioned devastated China economically, cost some 20 million to 30 million lives, and further weakened the Qing dynasty, which was already under growing pressure from foreign imperialists.

The Ottoman Empire

Something similar occurred in the Middle East, where the Ottoman Empire, which had long posed a threat to Europe, was suffering internal decline throughout the eighteenth and nineteenth centuries compounded by periodic military defeats and loss of territory at the hands of French, British, and Russian aggression. As the empire shrank in size as a result of European annexations, a lengthening set of "capitulations," similar to the "unequal treaties" later signed with China, gave foreign merchants immunity from Ottoman laws and legal procedures, exempted them from internal taxes, and limited import and export duties on their products. Foreign consuls could grant these privileges to Ottoman citizens, and hundreds of thousands of them, usually Jews, Greeks, and Armenians, received this privileged status, which effectively removed them from Ottoman control and greatly enhanced European control of the Ottoman economy. In 1838, the British and French forced Ottoman authorities to reduce their tariffs on imported goods, an action that made subsequent Ottoman efforts to industrialize even more difficult. Like China, the Ottoman Empire gradually slipped into the position of an "informal colony" of the European powers.

Africa

Patterns of Change in the Nineteenth Century. The nineteenth century in much of Africa was a period of dynamic, even revolutionary, change. In North Africa, some regions began to throw off the control of the Ottoman Empire. Egypt, for example, regained its independence, pursued an ambitious program of modernization, and carved out a large empire in the Nile River valley in what is now the modern country of Sudan. As the Atlantic slave trade diminished, a number of societies in West Africa reoriented their economies toward the export of other products—palm oil, peanuts, gum, coffee, and ivory. The interior of West Africa witnessed a series of religious wars intended to expand and purify the practice of Islam, a process that gave rise to a number of new Islamic states. In southern Africa, an enormous and bloody upheaval grew out of the conquests by the Zulu people, setting in motion a series of vast migrations and stimulating the formation of many new states and societies. Eastern Africa experienced a growing commercial integration of the interior and the coast, expressed tragically in a mounting slave trade that sought to supply laborers for Arab plantations on the coast and on the nearby islands of Zanzibar and Pemba.

From the Slave Trade to Colonial Rule. As Africa changed, so did European interest. The Atlantic slave trade gradually diminished in the nineteenth century. Europeans began to think about Africa in terms of "legitimate commerce," missionary activity, exploration of the continent's vast interior, and, in a few places, investment and settlement opportunities. Humanitarian and religious groups sought to end slavery and the slave trade after some four centuries of deep European involvement in it and to bring the alleged "blessings of Christianity and civilization" to what they saw as a dark and barbarous continent. But few European governments sought territory on the continent until the final quarter of the nineteenth century when they quite suddenly descended on Africa and divided it up among themselves.

As in India, African societies were incorporated into formal colonies, but conquest was extraordinarily violent and rapid, most of it occurring in the 1880s and 1890s, compared to a much more prolonged process in India. It was a final spasm of imperialist annexations, often called the "scramble for Africa," and pursued quite deliberately, even desperately, with little of the "absentmindedness" that shaped the takeover of India. Unlike the Dutch conquest of Indonesia or the British in India, the European conquest of Africa was highly competitive. British, French, German, Italian, Portuguese, and Belgian participants negotiated colonial boundaries among themselves and then bloodily subdued the African societies in their respective territories. The speed and ferocity of the scramble for Africa reflected the growing intensity of national rivalries in late nineteenth-century Europe and

the high point of Western military superiority over the rest of the world. These factors also brought much of Southeast Asia (Vietnam, Laos, and Cambodia) into the French Empire and Pacific Island societies under the control of various European powers and the United States.

Resistance and Cooperation. While Western conquest was relatively quick, it was not easy. Most African states and societies were not initially hostile to Europeans and often tried to work out some accommodation with them. But as they became aware of the unlimited aims of the intruders and their demand for political submission, resistance mounted. Any number of African states, both large and small, fought fiercely in defense of their sovereignty. Machembe, leader of the Yao people of modern Tanzania, defiantly told the Germans in 1890, "I have listened to your words but can find no reasons why I should obey you—I would rather die first. . . . If it should be war you desire, then I am ready . . . but to be your subject, that I cannot be."[7] In West Africa, Samori Toure, founder of a new empire based among the Mandinka people, sought initially to use the French as allies against his local rivals. But the persistent aggressiveness of the French provoked Samori into a 10-year military struggle against them. On the other hand, the Kingdom of Buganda in East Africa chose to ally itself with the British and in so doing greatly expanded its territory at the expense of its local rivals and vastly enriched a small class of chiefs who gained access to much of the best land in the kingdom.

By the early twentieth century, the initial resistance had been crushed, and all of Africa, except for Ethiopia and Liberia, had come under the control of Europeans. The overwhelming military advantage of the invaders was surely the most important factor, for by

Figure 10.4 European weapons and tactics overwhelmed African forces but not without a struggle. The battle of Omdurman on the Nile River in 1898 won British control of Sudan. *Eileen Tweedt. The Art Archive at Art Resource, NY.*

1900 the technological gap between Europeans and the rest of the world was at its widest. Also important were sharp divisions among African societies, as the absence of any common identity as "Africans" made lasting alliances difficult to achieve. And finally, the colonial invasion of Africa coincided with a 40-year period (1880s–1920s) of diminished rainfall, famine, and disease that greatly weakened African societies. Combined with the violence of conquest, this led to devastating loss of life in many parts of the continent. More than 20 years of on-and-off warfare between Italians and Libyans killed perhaps a third of the population. A similar mortality rate afflicted the peoples of German East Africa (modern Tanzania) in the repression and famine that followed a major rebellion in 1904–1905.[8]

Russian and American Expansion

Yet another pattern of Western expansion after 1750 involved Russia and the United States, both of which continued processes begun in the 1600s. These were overland rather than overseas empires, with Russian acquisitions in the nineteenth century focused largely in more densely populated Muslim areas of central Asia and the Caucasus and those of the United States in the vast sparsely populated regions of the American West. In these land-based empires, there was no sharp distinction between "mother country" and colony so characteristic of European empires in Asia and Africa. And in both cases, the "colonial power" had some experience with various forms of Western imperialism. The United States, of course, had originated as a set of British settler colonies, while Russia continued in the nineteenth century to suffer repeated military defeats and much foreign investment by stronger European countries. Both countries introduced substantial numbers of settlers into the newly conquered regions, though in the Russian territories indigenous peoples survived and their cultures endured rather more than was the case in the American West.

While Russian imperialism was limited largely to adjacent territories and peoples, its U.S. counterpart grew more expansive. By the late nineteenth century, American industrialization had made it an exporting nation. Now the products of America's farms and factories began to descend on Europe, Latin America, and even Asia. Foreign markets and the need to sustain them played an increased role in the thinking of American business leaders as the factories poured out more goods than their countrymen could afford to buy. By the 1890s, Americans were looking west toward Asia and south to Latin America for potential markets. Some argued for an expanded navy with which to protect American commerce abroad. This was accompanied by a revival of expansionist thinking reminiscent of the Manifest Destiny era. Senator Albert J. Beveridge of Indiana thrilled listeners with his oration "The March of the Flag," an updated version of Manifest Destiny, with more than a tinge of racism:

> God has not been preparing the English-speaking and Teutonic peoples for a thousand years for nothing but vague and idle self-contemplation and self-admiration. No! He has made us the master organizers of the world to establish system where chaos reigns. . . . He has made us adepts in government that we may administer government among savage and senile peoples. . . . We are the trustees

of the world's progress, guardians of its righteous peace.[9]

Beveridge later added, "The twentieth century will be American. American thought will dominate it. American progress will give it color and direction. American deeds will make it illustrious."[10]

The Spanish-American War of 1898 was the most visible result of this new interest in expansion. The United States wound up in possession of Guam, Puerto Rico, and the Philippine Islands. In separate actions, Hawaii was annexed in 1898 and the Panama Canal Zone in 1903. The United States entered the twentieth century as the newest of the overseas imperial powers. But it also practiced a form of noncolonial imperialism, or informal empire, in which nations nominally independent, largely in the Caribbean and Latin America, nonetheless were actually controlled by U.S. mining, agricultural, and commercial corporations, occasionally with the help of the Marine Corps.

Australia and New Zealand

A final pattern of European expansion, more closely resembling the earlier experience in the Americas, unfolded in Australia and New Zealand, both claimed by Great Britain. While no demographic catastrophe of American proportions had afflicted mainland Africa and Asia, a combination of imported firearms and disease decimated the previously isolated hunting and gathering Aboriginal people of Australia and the agricultural Maoris of New Zealand. While both peoples subsequently recovered demographically and have maintained a unique cultural identity into the present, their territories were overrun in the nineteenth century by European settlers who established fully Western societies in the South

Pacific. In New Zealand, for example, some 700,000 whites dominated the colony in 1896, while Maori numbers had been reduced to about 40,000, many of whom had converted to Christianity. This contrasts sharply with most Asian and African territories, which received few permanent European settlers and maintained demographic dominance in their own lands even as their cultures and economies changed considerably.

Global Imperial Economies

A Second Wave of Globalization

If Europe's expansion in the Atlantic basin during the sixteenth and seventeenth centuries initiated modern "globalization," its nineteenth-century empires deepened that process and extended its reach in Asia and Africa. Conquest and foreign rule, of course, were nothing new in world history. Earlier empires, whether dominated by Romans, Arabs, Mongols, or Turks, had also brought suffering to subject peoples. The uniqueness of Europe's global reach in the nineteenth and early twentieth centuries lay in the extent of change that it induced in the ordinary working lives of millions of people around the world. An industrializing Europe acted like a magnet, pulling raw materials and agricultural products from its formal colonies and informal empires alike in ever-growing quantities. Rice from Southeast Asia; indigo, tea, and opium from India; meat from Australia; rubber from Brazil and the Congo; palm oil and cocoa from West Africa; cloves from Zanzibar; sugar and coffee from Indonesia; cotton from Egypt; tin from the Malay Peninsula; and gold and diamonds from South Africa—all of this and much more was financed by Western capitalist enterprises

and produced by the low-wage labor of local people, which together generated an expanding stream of world trade moving generally to the west. In return Asian, African, and Latin American societies received a growing volume of Europe's manufactured products.

What made this economically integrated world possible was a host of communication and transportation innovations that emerged during the nineteenth century. The telegraph, underwater cables, steamships, railroads, and canals tightened the links among distant human communities. Messages that previously took months or years to arrive now could be transmitted in minutes. Falling transportation costs made it possible to carry bulk goods such as cotton, coal, grain, tea, tobacco, and opium over long distances. More and more people became dependent on these man-made linkages for their economic and sometimes their physical survival.

A Divided World

If the world was growing more connected, it was also increasingly unequal, as an international division of labor that had begun earlier in the Atlantic basin now took shape in the rest of the world. As late as 1750, India accounted for almost 25 percent of world manufacturing and China for another 33 percent, but by 1913, they produced only 1.4 and 3.6 percent, respectively.[11] To the massive inequalities between social classes, evident since the beginning of urban civilizations, was now added a new inequality among the nations or regions of the planet. Here were the roots of that "global rift,"[12] sometimes called the North–South divide, between the rich and poor regions of the earth that continues to bedevil the world in the twenty-first century. It was a novel division of global labor, casting the

Western world of Europe and North America as the center of manufacturing while the rest of humankind provided the raw materials and consumed the products of the industrialized West. Born of Europe's industrial revolution and its global empires, this emerging world economy departed sharply from the more regionally balanced world of earlier centuries.

India and Imperial Globalization

The consequences of this "imperial global-ization" became especially and tragically ap-parent in the last quarter of the nineteenth century as a worldwide wave of climate change and weather disruption, associated with what meteorologists now call the El Niño–Southern Oscillation, brought recurrent and widespread drought, famine, and death to many parts of the world, especially in the tropics. Mortality estimates for India, China, and Brazil range from a low of 32 million to a high of 61 million between 1876 and 1902. Many others perished in Africa. Much of this massive human suffer-ing was caused not by the weather alone but by the policies and practices of governments, both colonial and semi-independent, operat-ing within the emerging world of imperial globalization.

Famine and Free Markets. British-ruled India provides a case in point. When drought and famine struck India in 1876, the colonial state was unable—or unwilling—to respond effectively. Household and village grain re-serves, intended to provide a local safety net, had been transferred largely to central ware-houses using recently built railroads. Wheat exports to Great Britain almost doubled in 1877 despite widespread famine within the country. Food prices soared as private specu-lators took advantage of shortages to make a profit. Meanwhile, the colonial viceroy, Lord

Lytton, acting on the basis of laissez-faire free market economic principles, gave orders that "there is to be no interference of any kind on the part of the Government with the object of reducing the price of food." Nor did the gov-ernment make much effort to provide relief for those perishing from famine, believing that it was nature's correction to India's tendency to "overbreed." A Famine Commission argued the case against relief: "The doctrine that in time of famine the poor are entitled to demand relief . . . would probably lead to the doctrine that they are entitled to such relief at all times, and thus the foundation would be laid of a system of general poor relief which we cannot contemplate without serious apprehension." At the same time, extravagant expenditures on military campaigns in Afghanistan and on an elaborate ceremony proclaiming Queen Vic-toria as empress of India continued without pause, and the government refused to defer the collection of heavy land taxes. British rac-ism, no doubt, played a role in these decisions, as many senior officials were convinced that it was "a mistake to spend so much money to save a lot of black fellows."[13]

The outcome of these policies was disaster. In the 1876–1879 famine, hunger and disease claimed some 6 million to 10 million Indian lives. In some districts, this amounted to 25 percent or more of the population. Moth-ers sold their children for a meal, husbands drowned their wives to prevent them from dying of hunger, people sought imprisonment for the food it provided, and violence flared among groups and individuals struggling for survival. Between 1872 and 1921, the overall life expectancy of ordinary Indians fell by an amazing 20 percent.[14]

The Economics of Empire. Beyond the ca-tastrophes of the late nineteenth century, how did India fare economically under British rule?

Some Indians clearly benefited—merchants, producers of high-end textiles, upper-caste Indians closely associated with the British, larger landowners producing for export, and a few industrialists. But Indian entrepreneurs were slowly squeezed out of the ship-owning and shipbuilding business, prevented from entering the new railroad industries, and restricted in the profitable export trade—primarily because they lacked access to credit, insurance, technology, and information about the world market. These were monopolized largely by European interests in the British port cities of Calcutta, Bombay, and Madras.

But perhaps more important than what happened was what did not. In almost two centuries of British rule (1757–1947), while the "mother country" industrialized and raised its people's living standards sharply, India experienced no overall growth in its per capita income and only a very modest beginning of modern industrial production. This meant that India's handloom weavers, long the source of much of the world's textiles, had few alternatives when their traditional livelihood was destroyed by the massive importation of cheap mass-produced textiles from England. British weavers, similarly unemployed, could at least seek work in the burgeoning factories of industrial England.

Scholars have argued about the sources of India's modern poverty. Many have focused on internal factors, such as a weak internal market, the continuation of rural mentalities among workers, and inadequate Indian entrepreneurs. Critics of British imperialism have pointed to the almost religious belief in free trade and the political influence of English manufacturing interests, which produced a virtual refusal to provide tariff protection for India's infant industries. Certainly, the unwillingness of the British government of India to actively foster industrial growth (as the governments of Germany, Japan, and Russia were doing in the late nineteenth century) played an important role in its retarded industrialization.

Yet another inhibition of British colonial rule on India's economic growth lay in the substantial wealth the British carried home from India, draining the country of investment capital needed for development. Some of this drain came in the form of profits made by British banks and corporations, some as pensions sent to retired soldiers and officials, and some as various expenses that the British government charged off to the Indian treasury. Indian taxpayers had to foot the bill, for example, for the Indian army, which was used in places as far away as China and Ethiopia to further British imperial interests. While the size of this drain is in dispute, its existence is not. In short, 200 years of colonial rule by the world's first industrial power did not make a substantial dent in India's traditional poverty and in fact created new forms of modern poverty.

Africa and Imperial Globalization

Colonial rule likewise brought African societies more fully into a new world economy as growing numbers of people were drawn into producing goods for distant markets. Their experience illustrates the various ways in which this process took shape and the kinds of changes it brought to this most recently colonized continent.

Forced Labor. Even after the end of the slave trade, European imperialists of the late nineteenth century subjected Africans to very crude and direct forms of exploitation. In one form or another, forced labor was practiced in almost all the colonies and was used for building roads, railroads, and government buildings as well as providing workers for private enterprises. The worst abuses occurred in the Congo Free State, personally controlled by Leopold II, king of Belgium. Here, private companies were granted huge concessions of forestland rich in rubber, which was much in demand for bicycle and automobile tires in the early twentieth century. With political and administrative authority over their concessions, these companies compelled local Africans to collect the rubber and enforced their demands through hostage taking, torture, and murder. A reign of mass terror lasted a decade until the Belgian government, acting under the pressure of massive public protest, took direct control of the colony in 1908.

Cash Crops. In many places, particularly West Africa, colonial governments came to rely on African farmers to produce the export products that would generate a taxable trade. Somewhat to their surprise, they found many African peoples both willing and able to respond to new market opportunities. Peanuts in Senegal and Gambia, cocoa in the Gold Coast, cotton in Uganda, and coffee in Tanganyika were among the cash crops African farmers began to produce for the world market and in considerable quantities. Many African farmers gained substantial cash incomes with which they could pay their taxes and school fees and buy a variety of imported goods. But in linking their economic lives so heavily to a world market over which they had little control, Africans also came to experience the fluctuations of the capitalist world economy, as many discovered painfully during the Great Depression of the 1930s. The uncertain rhythms of the international marketplace were now added to those of the seasons and weather.

In addition, most colonies came to specialize very heavily in a very limited range of products and had the bulk of their trade with the country governing them. This very narrow

base for economic development proved a serious obstacle to balanced growth after independence. Furthermore, some African colonies devoted so much land and labor to producing luxury crops for export that they had to rely on imported food to feed their own people. This happened first in Senegal and Gambia, where peanut production was so intensive that rice had to be imported from Asia. By the 1970s, such deficiencies had become common throughout the continent, caused in part by an overemphasis on export agriculture and a corresponding neglect of domestic food production. Here was one source of the terrible vulnerability to famine that afflicted so much of Africa in the 1970s and 1980s.

The Loss of Land. Elsewhere, in colonies with a large and permanent European population, production for export was undertaken primarily by resident white settlers. Colonial governments intervened decisively on behalf of European settlers, took large areas of African land, and reserved it for exclusive white ownership. In Kenya's "white highlands," some 4,000 European farmers owned 7.3 million acres of the colony's richest land. Even more extreme was the situation in South Africa, where the Land Act of 1913 legally reserved 88 percent of the land for whites, who constituted less than 20 percent of the population.

Settler colonies created vastly overcrowded and impoverished "native reserves," as areas limited to Africans were known in British territories. Especially in South Africa, these "reserves," or "homelands," of the country's African population often became "rural slums," undeveloped, overgrazed, and seriously eroded. Nor was this accidental, for limiting the size of African reserves was one means of forcing Africans to work on European-owned farms and plantations. The experience of rural wage labor for white settlers became a familiar one for hundreds of thousands of Africans who lived in or near settler territories. By the early 1950s, about 30 percent of the African male population of South Africa worked and usually lived on European-owned farms.

Mining and Migration. Many others came to work in the copper-, gold-, and diamond-mining industries of central and southern Africa. Such enterprises created a vast pattern of labor migration all over southern Africa, as men by the hundreds of thousands left their homes in the rural areas for work in the mines. To prevent the growth of a stable and permanent black urban population, the South African government enforced a pattern of circulating labor migration. Without their wives and children, men would come to the mines on contract for a fixed term and then be required to return to the overcrowded reserves,

only to repeat the whole process sometime later. Such a pattern, involving by the early 1950s more than 2 million men, undermined rural society, for it meant the absence of large numbers of men and prevented the development of a normal urban society because settled family life was forbidden. African laborers were caught in the middle.

Global Migration

The new world economy of the nineteenth and early twentieth centuries put people into motion not only in Africa but around the world as well. Between 1800 and 1914, some 50 million Europeans, many from impoverished regions of southern and eastern Europe, migrated to the United States, Canada, Argentina, Brazil, Australia, New Zealand, and South Africa in search of land and jobs. In doing so, they created "neo-Europes," or Western-style

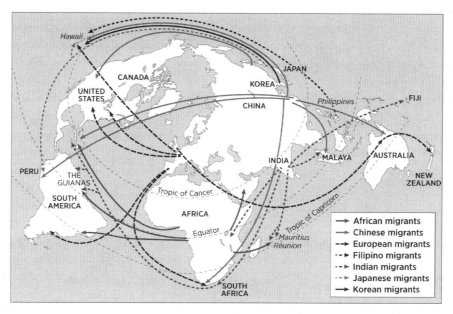

Map 10.2 The worldwide movement of people tightened the links among the world's various regions and cultures in the nineteenth century and gave rise to much cultural conflict as well.

societies, in these temperate regions. Another migratory stream brought indentured laborers from India to the plantations of the West Indies, South and East Africa, Southeast Asia, and the Pacific Islands, generating sizable Indian minorities in these areas. The so-called coolie trade pulled large numbers of impoverished Chinese workers to Malaya, Peru, California, and elsewhere, while other Chinese settlers followed earlier migrants to colonial Southeast Asia, where they often became a prosperous mercantile minority. A recent estimate suggests that some 38 million Asians (19 million from India and 19 million from China) migrated to Southeast Asia between 1850 and 1940, a vast movement of people comparable to the better-known European migrations to the Americas.[15]

Global Imperial Society and Culture

Nineteenth-century European imperialism also created global societies and cultures. Sometimes these new social and cultural developments were intentional creations of the Europeans, sometimes they were the indirect product of European economic dominance, and sometimes they were the product of Asian and African initiatives.

Population Patterns

Among the most significant consequences was the quickening of population growth in several places as modern public health measures and improved food supplies took hold. Rates of growth were most rapid in the Americas, where a massive influx of European immigrants contributed to the process. Japan and India also grew rapidly and China's already

huge population somewhat less so. On a global level, the 1800s witnessed an 80 percent increase in human numbers, compared to 30 percent in the 1700s and no more than 10 percent for previous centuries. More isolated peoples, however, suffered greatly, and their populations declined sharply as they came into contact with the diseases and the firepower of European intruders. These included the native peoples of the American West, Australia, New Zealand, the Pacific Islands, the Arctic, central Africa, and the Amazon River basin. The original population of Tasmania, an island south of Australia, disappeared entirely as the last native person died in 1876. Her name, for the record, was Trucanini.[16]

Slavery and Race

An End to Slavery. A further social change induced by the impact of an industrializing Europe involved slavery, for centuries an integral part of colonial economies in the Americas. In some places, such as the southern United States, Cuba, and Brazil, the initial impact of Europe's industrial revolution was to intensify the use of slaves as the demand for slave-produced products such as coffee, cotton, and sugar increased. African producers of palm oil in West Africa and Arab producers of cloves in East Africa also made extensive use of slave labor in the nineteenth century.

In the long run, however, slavery came to be considered incompatible with both Christian morality and a capitalist economic system dependent on free labor. Furthermore, periodic slave revolts raised the cost of slavery. Abolitionist reformers in both Europe and the Americas put pressure on their governments to take legal action against it throughout the nineteenth century. The British outlawed the slave trade in 1807 and slavery itself in 1833;

other countries followed suit. With the ending of Brazilian slavery in 1888, four centuries of Atlantic slavery came to an end. A parallel process brought the abolition of serfdom in central and eastern Europe, most notably in Russia in 1861. While pockets of slavery remained until recently, capitalism and Christianity made the practice both inefficient and immoral for most people in the nineteenth century. For many people, however, legal slavery or serfdom was replaced by new forms of oppression and exploitation, including forced and indentured labor and permanent indebtedness. Typically, former slaves became landless laborers or tenant farmers, while immigrants were imported to replace them. Cuban sugar planters imported Chinese contract laborers to work with and replace African slaves, and Brazilian coffee growers near São Paulo recruited migrants from Italy rather than take newly freed Africans from its own northeast.

The Growth of "Scientific Racism." While slavery gradually declined, the racial distinctions so often associated with it assumed even greater significance. Earlier, in the eighteenth and early nineteenth centuries, Europeans living in Asia and Africa had attempted to adapt to local cultures. Dutch gentlemen in Java often wore the long skirtlike garb of Javanese aristocrats and lived with and frequently married local women. Until the 1850s, the British governed India ostensibly as agents of the Mughal emperor, making use of Indian political rituals and ceremonies, patronizing Hindu temples, and sharply restricting Christian missionary activity for a time. Eighteenth-century European intellectuals praised China for its long political unity and its remarkable system of civil service examinations. It was, declared the French writer Voltaire, "a model, even for Christians."

But increasingly in the nineteenth century, this more fluid and tolerant pattern of race relations sharply declined as Europeans living in the colonies withdrew into their own restricted communities. Steamships and the opening of the Suez Canal after 1869 brought wives and families to the little Englands in the hill stations of British India and Malaya. There, British magistrates and family men began to worry about sexual relations across racial lines and to deal with "natives" only as servants or subjugated people. One English missionary in early twentieth-century East Africa objected to teaching English to "natives" on the grounds that it would endanger white women if African men could speak their language.

The new intensity of colonial racism reflected an emerging ideology of race in Europe and the United States. With their marvelous technological inventions and their immense economic and political power, many westerners came to believe in their innate biological superiority. To many people, "social Darwinism," based on the "survival of the fittest," seemed a sufficient explanation for Western dominance in the world. Invoking the prestige and apparatus of science, "phrenologists" used allegedly scientific methods to classify the size and shape of human skulls and concluded, not surprisingly, that those of whites were larger and therefore more advanced. "Race is everything," declared British anatomist Robert Knox in 1850; "civilization depends on it."[17]

Race and Colonial Life. Race thus became the central division of all colonial societies, affecting job opportunities, political participation, educational provisions, wages, and daily social interactions. The earliest colonial settler societies in the Americas experienced this new postslavery racism earliest. The Civil War in the United States brought an end to slavery but not racism. In fact, after 1875, the United States initiated racial segregation of public facilities; pioneered pseudoscientific racist studies meant to prove the inferiority of blacks, Jews, immigrants, and poor rural Americans; and tolerated racial violence against blacks by white mobs, police, and government officials.

Among later settler colonies, South Africa was the most extreme case. There, a long history of racial conflict culminated in twentieth-century apartheid, which established race as a legal, not just a customary, feature of South African society and provided for separate "homelands," educational systems, residential areas, public facilities, and much more. South African whites sought to maintain an advanced industrial country by incorporating Africans into the economy as cheap labor while attempting to limit their social and political integration into South African society in every conceivable fashion.

Similar efforts to maintain racial barriers, though less formal and rigid than in South Africa, occurred all across the colonial world. Where these barriers were threatened, European reaction was vociferous. Outraged British residents of India in 1883 protested massively and bitterly against a proposal to allow Indian judges and magistrates to hear cases involving Europeans, "the conquering race." A debate about domestic servants in colonial Southern Rhodesia illustrates the complex sexual politics of race. There white men favored using African females as household servants, fearing that African men had uncontrollable designs on their women. But European women preferred African male servants, fearing the temptations that female help presented to their husbands.

Western-Educated Elites. Those most directly affected by colonial racism were members of the "educated elite," Asians and Africans trained in mission or government schools and employed in the modern sector of the economy or the colonial bureaucracy. Their familiarity with Western ways set them apart from others and introduced a new cultural division into their societies. Many among them enthusiastically embraced Western culture. The first generation of Western-educated Bengalis in northeastern India of the early nineteenth century came to believe that much of old Indian culture was obsolete and needed an infusion of European civilization. They demonstrated their modern "enlightenment" by speaking and writing in English, wearing European clothing, and eating European foods, often to the distress of their elders. Subsequent generations of educated Indians sought to reform certain features of Indian society, such as child marriages or harsh caste restrictions, while vigorously defending Indian culture and especially its unique spirituality in the face of racially based and highly negative European views of India.

Colonial racism impelled some among the educated elite to political action as well. Among the earliest was the Indian National Congress, established in 1885 by a group of educators, lawyers, and journalists. Inspired by Western political ideals, this organization later led the drive for India's independence and became a model for anticolonial movements in Asia and Africa. More than military conquest or economic exploitation, racial discrimination was responsible for the bitterness of educated Asians and Africans, who otherwise saw much to admire in modern Western culture. What they found so offensive was Western hypocrisy—the contradiction between the "civilizing" and "modernizing" rhetoric and the reality of racial exclusiveness—together with a frequent disparagement of their cultures for being backward, primitive, or savage. Thus, in a strange irony of colonial history, those most deeply involved in Western culture became the chief critics of Western domination and in the twentieth century the leaders of mass movements that brought colonial rule to an end. In this explosive combination of Western education and colonial racism lay yet another process of change generated by the global extension of European power.

New Identities

Beyond Western education, other patterns of change in the colonial world also generated new ways of thinking and new conceptions of community. Millions of Asians and Africans found their way to cities, mines, plantations, and mission stations far from home where they mixed and mingled with people quite culturally different from themselves while competing for jobs, school places, and living space. In the process, new identities took shape as earlier fluid and flexible cultural loyalties became more rigid and sharply defined. Some Africans began to see themselves as "black" in response to "white" racism and even to forge connections with black people in the Americas in the beginnings of a pan-African identity. Others identified with various "tribes," many of which had been invented by European colonial officials to administer complex African societies more easily. In the Belgian Congo, colonial authorities applied the "tribal" label of "Bangala" to men from a number of small and quite separate communities along the Congo River who worked in colonial enterprises. The Belgians adopted one of the river dialects as their means of communicating with these Africa workers, and thus it became Lingala, or the language of the Bangala. Prior to the coming of the Belgians, the notion of a Bangala identity had simply not existed; it was the creation of the colonial state, appropriated by various Africans as its usefulness in

the colonial situation became apparent. Then, typically, colonial authorities like the British in East Africa would informally sponsor the publication of "tribal" histories in order to blunt the force of more inclusive African nationalisms.

"India" likewise took on a new national meaning for some elite South Asians confronting British rule. At the same time, the old distinction between Muslim and Hindu communities in India became sharper and more competitive as the British defined separate law codes for the two groups and organized political representation along religious lines. Growing numbers of African and Indian peoples found these new racial, national, ethnic, or religious identities useful as they sought a measure of security and solidarity in a rapidly changing colonial environment.

Colonized Women

European Reforms. Colonized women were also put to the European global standard. Horrified European officials, aided by some Indian reformers, attempted to abolish sati, the practice in which a devoted Indian widow, usually from an upper caste, followed her husband in death by burning herself alive on his funeral pyre. In Africa, missionaries and some colonial officials attacked polygamy and female circumcision, or the cutting of the clitoris, while in Polynesia, nudity and sexual permissiveness deeply offended European sensibilities. While none of these efforts were wholly successful, they introduced new ideas about the roles of women and stimulated local reformers. In 1819, for example, the king of Hawaii declared an end to the traditional taboo on men and women eating together.

Coping with Colonial Economies. More significant, however, were the indirect consequences of economic transformations. As India was flooded with machine-produced textiles from British factories, large numbers of Indian women lost their livelihood as handicraft producers of cotton textiles. And these women had little chance to find alternative work in the few modernized industries that did emerge in India during the colonial era. Thus, the economic gap between men and women grew, and opportunities for male domination increased. Furthermore, as Asian and African men focused more of their attention on producing cash crops or were pushed into working in distant plantations, mines, or cities, women found themselves saddled with increasing workloads at home, where they assumed greater and sometimes sole responsibility for domestic food production and child rearing.

Education and Opportunity. But new opportunities as well as new burdens beckoned in the colonial order, at least for a few. Western education offered modern employment possibilities to a handful and stimulated some to raise questions about the role of women. Huda Shaarawi, daughter of a prominent Egyptian family, was among the first of her generation to appear in public without a veil and went on in 1923 to establish the Egyptian Feminist Union, which pushed for the rights of Muslim women. Many more found opportunities in the burgeoning cities of colonial Africa and Asia, where they might escape the oppression of patriarchal families or the heavy labor demands of the colonial era. A growing exodus of women to the towns of colonial Zimbabwe in southern Africa in the early twentieth century prompted a joint and not very successful effort by colonial officials and senior African men—chiefs, elders, and household heads—to restrict the mobility and sexual activity of women and to confine them to the rural areas.[18] The control of women was one area in

which European officials and African or Asian patriarchs had something in common.

Missionaries and Conversion

A final notable change, born of the European disturbance in world affairs, involved the activities of Christian missionaries who fanned out over much of the Afro-Asian-Pacific world in the nineteenth and twentieth centuries. Their schools provided basic literacy to many and more advanced education for a few, their clinics and hospitals introduced modern medicine to Asian and African societies, and their teachings challenged traditional conceptions of social and family life, sexual morality, and, of course, religious ideas as well. While Indian, Chinese, and especially Islamic societies proved resistant to the religious message of the missionaries, the peoples of New Zealand, the Pacific Islands, and especially non-Muslim Africa were highly receptive and Christianity spread rapidly. This was a remarkable cultural change, due in part to opportunities for education, employment, and status available to people identified as Christians. However, many Africans also saw in Christian rituals, symbols, and practice a powerful religious resource for dealing with the problems of everyday life: illness, infertility, the need for rainfall, protection from witchcraft, and the many upheavals and disruptions of the colonial era. These had been among the concerns of traditional African religions, so it was not surprising that Africans would think that people so obviously as powerful as Europeans should have access to supernatural power that might be applied to such problems. In addition, some historians have suggested that Christianity, a world religion focused primarily on an all-powerful creator, was becoming more relevant than local divinities and ancestral spirits in explaining and controlling the new and wider world of the twentieth century. To people who interpreted the world in religious terms, a universal religion might well seem more appropriate than a local one in the new circumstances of the colonial era. Christianity, in short, could provide both secular opportunities and religious resources for dealing with societies in the process of rapid change.

But while Christianity spread widely in Africa, it was also widely Africanized, particularly in thousands of independent church movements that broke away from their European missionary mentors. In the Belgian Congo, for example, a young educated Baptist convert named Simon Kimbangu had a series of visions and, in 1921, began a ministry of healing and preaching in very Christian terms. In just a few months, he had attracted an amazing following and so frightened the Belgian government that he was imprisoned for the rest of his life. But the movement spread, largely underground, and Kimbangu came to be regarded as an African prophet with a status equivalent to that of Moses, Jesus, Muhammad, or Buddha.

Changing Defensively

In many places, the transformations of the great disturbance arose less from direct European intervention than from local efforts to defend themselves against it. Some societies did so by drawing on their own cultural resources. In a number of American Indian societies of the later nineteenth century, hard pressed by settler expansion and the disappearance of their precious buffalo, prophets arose who declared that performing a particular "ghost dance" would bring back the vanishing buffalo, restore the dead to life again, and cause Europeans to vanish or at least to live peacefully with their Indian neighbors. Likewise, the Xhosa of South Africa, beset by diseases that decimated their cattle herds, followed the teachings of a young woman prophet to kill their remaining cattle and destroy their grain crops in the belief that this sacrifice would bring the ancestors back to lead an Xhosa revival. The cattle would return, grain would grow again, and Europeans would be driven into the sea.

Trying to Catch Up

Elsewhere and with more lasting impact, societies threatened by Western power but not fully colonized sought to borrow elements of European technology, culture, or practice to protect themselves against the external threat. Known as "defensive modernization," this course of action brought substantial changes to a number of societies.

Perhaps the most common pattern of borrowing involved military technology. This was at the heart of Peter the Great's reforms in eighteenth-century Russia, as he imported western European officers to train his armed forces, adopted modern muskets and artillery, and introduced administrative and educational practices drawn from Europe. The desire to buy or reproduce European weapons was in fact practically universal. Such borrowing was obviously useful in defending against European aggression, but it also permitted local states to carve out their own empires. Late nineteenth-century Ethiopia, for example, used its access to modern military technology to defeat the Italians, becoming the only African state to retain its independence throughout the scramble. But it also considerably expanded its own territory and thus participated in the partition of the continent.

Ottoman Modernization

Efforts at defensive modernization often provoked serious internal conflict as they challenged existing power relations and cultural values. Did borrowing from the West offer protection from European aggression, or did it undermine traditional cultures and erode the privileges of established elites? It was a question that the Ottoman Empire confronted when, beset by European pressures, that Muslim state finally began to reform its military and taxation practices along European lines in the early nineteenth century. These actions appeared threatening to elements of the older military units—the janissaries—who feared being replaced by more modern military forces. Some Muslim religious leaders—the ulema—saw a danger to Islam itself in borrowing from the Christian infidels. Their combined opposition forced the reforming sultan from power in 1807. When the reform process resumed in the late 1830s, it deepened to include Western-style legal codes and schools; telegraphs, steamships, and railroads; and the concept of equality for all citizens regardless of religion. By then, advocates of still further westernization pushed for political change. A constitution limiting the power of the sultan was adopted in 1876 but lasted only briefly as yet another conservative backlash took shape. Similar conflicts about what to borrow from the West and how quickly to implement reform accompanied defensive modernization in many places.

Comparing China and Japan

Chinese Self-Strengthening. The various ways that defensive modernization actually worked out are perhaps best illustrated by the contrasting cases of China and Japan. In nineteenth-century China, repeated military defeats and massive internal peasant rebellions finally persuaded the conservative Qing dynasty to undertake reforms in the 1860s and 1870s. Known as "self-strengthening," these reforms combined a reassertion of Confucian education and principles of government with modest borrowings from the West, including the creation of modern arsenals and shipyards, translation services, and even a few industrial enterprises manufacturing iron, steel, and textiles. A Chinese general Li Hongzhang made the case for adopting elements of Western technology:

> I have been aboard the warships of the British and French admirals and I saw that their cannons are ingenious and uniform, their ammunition is fine and cleverly made, their weapons are bright, and their troops have a martial appearance and are orderly. These things are actually superior to those of China. . . . I feel deeply ashamed that Chinese weapons are far inferior to those of foreign countries. Every day I warn and instruct my officers to be humble-minded, to bear the humiliation, to learn one or two secrets from the Westerners in the hope that we may increase our knowledge.[19]

But it was all a rather superficial and reluctant effort, in large part because members of the Chinese gentry class, with their wealth and privileges rooted in the rural areas, feared that thorough urban and industrial development would erode those privileges. Many felt that even limited borrowing from the West would undermine a Chinese regime based on Confucian principles. Court officials likewise inhibited a thoroughgoing reform program, severely criticizing as greedy and unduly ambitious those who were involved in foreign commerce and making no overall plans for improving banking, communications, or industry.

The results of such an approach soon became apparent. Further humiliating military defeats at the hands of Europeans and Japanese between 1884 and 1901 revealed the failure of China's efforts at defensive modernization. The imperial system itself, some 2,000 years in the making, collapsed in 1911, and not until the communist seizure of power in 1949 was the country able to achieve a measure of stability, independence, and modern development.

Japan's "Revolution from Above." Japan began its encounter with Europeans in a broadly similar fashion to that of its giant neighbor. Like China, Japan had held the Europeans at arm's length and strictly limited and controlled interaction with them for several centuries. And also like China, Japan was forcibly opened to Western penetration in the form of an American naval expedition led by Commodore Matthew Perry in 1854 and subjected to a series of "unequal treaties." But there the similarity ceased, for Japan responded to the new Western threat far differently than China.

The humiliation of the "unequal treaties" prompted a political upheaval in Japan known as the Meiji Restoration, which brought to power in 1868 a remarkable group of samurai

Figure 10.5
Nineteenth-century empire building was a highly competitive process. This French cartoon shows Britain, Germany, Russia, France, and Japan carving up the "cake" of China. *The Granger Collection, New York.*

reformers, governing ostensibly in the name of the emperor. This new regime undertook a dramatic—even revolutionary—process of modernization, far more extensive than anything the Chinese state had even contemplated. It drew heavily on European experience while maintaining Japanese control and much of Japanese culture intact. The feudal domains of Tokugawa Japan were abolished, and a new centralized bureaucratic structure took its place. A new national army based on universal conscription was established in 1873, and the samurai lost their identity as a privileged military caste. A program of state-directed industrialization initiated the first industrial revolution outside the West, while Western-style legal codes, based on individual ownership of property, were adopted. The government imported hundreds of Western experts and sent students and study missions abroad. And they even adopted the forms of a Western political system with a constitution, an elected parliament, and political parties, though real power continued to reside with the

reforming oligarchy and the emperor. For a time, many Japanese enthusiastically imitated even the superficial aspects of Western culture, such as ballroom dancing, shaking hands, and European-style haircuts.

The outcomes of this process sharply distinguished Japan from China. Based on an intensifying industrialization and legal reform, Japan persuaded the Western powers to revise the "unequal treaties" and to acknowledge Japan as an equal power. Its military defeat of China in 1895 and Russia in 1905 launched Japan on an empire-building path of its own, gaining colonial control of Taiwan and Korea. Thus, while China continued to languish under the umbrella of European "informal empire," Japan had joined the imperialist club of nations and emerged as one of the industrial "great powers" of the early twentieth century. The rise of Japan echoed loudly throughout the colonial and semicolonial world, suggesting that European dominance need not be permanent.

In 1907, one of Meiji Japan's leading political figures, Shigenobu Okuma, looked back

Figure 10.6   Japan's modernizing efforts involved selective borrowing from the West, including at least the outward forms of a parliamentary government. © *Bettmann/Corbis/AP Images.*

with great satisfaction on the preceding half century while seeking to explain his country's remarkable transformation:

By comparing the Japan of fifty years ago with the Japan of today, it will be seen that she has gained considerably in the extent of her territory, as well as in her population, which now numbers nearly fifty million. Her government has become constitutional not only in name, but in fact, and her national education has attained to a high degree of excellence. In commerce and industry, the emblems of peace, she has also made rapid strides. . . . Her general progress, during the short space of half a century, has been so sudden and swift that it presents a rare spectacle in the history of the world. This leap forward is the result of the stimulus which the country received on coming into contact with the civilization of Europe and America. . . . Foreign intercourse it was that animated the national consciousness of our people, who under the feudal system lived localized and disunited, and foreign intercourse it is that has enabled Japan to stand up as a world power. We possess today a powerful army and navy, but it was after Western models that we laid their foundations. . . . We have reorganized the systems of central and local administration, and effected reforms in the educational system of the empire. All this is nothing but the result of adopting the superior features of Western institutions. . . .

For twenty centuries the nation has drunk freely of the civilizations of Korea, China, and India, being always open to the different influences impressed on her in succession. Yet we remain politically unaltered under one Imperial House and sovereign, that has descended in an unbroken line for a length of time absolutely unexampled in the world.

We have welcomed Occidental civilization while preserving [our] old Oriental civilization.[20]

Perspectives on the Nineteenth Century

The nineteenth century witnessed dramatic and unprecedented changes in the older patterns of world history. With the industrial, American, and French revolutions, western Europeans and their North American cousins created new and modern societies unique in their wealth and power. These societies then came to dominate—or at least to seriously influence—much of the rest of the world while creating a global web or network of communication and exchange that encompassed and transformed the entire planet. These changes have been so profound and far reaching that it is hardly surprising that they have been assessed in many different ways. Both scholars and participants in these processes have sought to define the significance of this grand upheaval in world affairs and to give it some larger meaning.

Progress or Exploitation?

Celebrating Western Achievement. For some, especially those who benefited most, the nineteenth century represented a dramatic and recent example of progress and the human capacity for self-improvement. Vast increases in material well-being, a doubling or more of the human life span in industrialized countries, and enormous new knowledge about the world—is this not compelling evidence for an essentially positive view of these great changes? Certainly, these benefits were experienced most fully in the more developed societies of Europe, North America, and Japan, but even in the colonial or semicolonial regions of the world, the extension of European political and economic power laid the foundations for modern development. Railroads, ports, telegraphs, roads, schools, medical facilities, technological innovations, and the very idea of progress itself—all this accompanied European imperialism. Certainly, there was violence, exploitation, and brutality, but over the long run, the West, through the vehicle of empire, transmitted its modernizing impulses to the more stagnant societies of Asia and Africa, jump-starting their own processes of modern development. This has been the core argument of those who have celebrated the Western achievement and sought to justify the West's global reach.

Alternative European Voices. Critics obviously saw things differently. Within Europe, socialists applauded industrialization for its potential to liberate humanity from the ancient scourge of scarcity while denouncing the inequalities and exploitation inherent in the capitalist system of private ownership and rampant competition. Conservative critics bemoaned the destruction of traditional communities, which they idealized as ordered, hierarchical, and organic with a place for everyone, and foresaw a future of crass materialism, individual self-seeking, and the loss of religious faith. The first half of the twentieth century, with its devastating global wars, its murderous fascist and communist regimes, and its economic disasters, seemed to confirm the critics' view that Europe's modern transformation bore self-destructive tendencies. And the environmental protests of the later twentieth century suggested that unchecked technological development was eroding the very ecological foundations of sustainable modern societies.

Critics from the Colonies. Asian and African intellectuals have articulated a somewhat different critique, with a focus, obviously, on empire. It was not so much that European pressures had undermined traditional societies, for that was perhaps inevitable, but that so little had been done to construct viable modern societies. In Europe and America, industrialization had been at the very heart of the modernizing process, but in colonial and semicolonial societies, very little progress had been made toward developing modern manufacturing industries, even where it might have been profitable to do so. The profits from foreign investment were mostly remitted abroad rather than invested locally, and few local capitalists had sufficient wealth to make a real difference. Furthermore, little change in techniques of food production occurred in the colonies as Europeans focused their attention on the development of export crops. Thus, rapid population growth occurred without an agricultural revolution to provide adequate local food supplies, and massive urbanization took place in the absence of an industrial revolution to meet basic material needs or to provide employment opportunities. The result was social crisis or distorted development rather than the transmission of a balanced modernity.

Other voices within the Afro-Asian world called into question the very desirability of imitating the European model of society. The West African intellectual Edward Blyden in the early twentieth century compared European and African civilization and found the West wanting. Africa's uniqueness, Blyden wrote, lay in its communal, cooperative, and egalitarian societies, which contrasted sharply with Europe's highly individualistic, competitive, and class-ridden societies; in its harmonious relationship to nature as opposed to

Europe's efforts to dominate and exploit the natural order; and particularly in its profound religious sensibility, which Europeans had lost in centuries of materialism. To Blyden, Africa had a distinct global mission:

> Africa may yet prove to be the spiritual conservatory of the world. . . . When the civilized nations, in consequence of their wonderful material development, shall have had their spiritual sensibilities darkened and their spiritual susceptibilities blunted through the agency of a captivating and absorbing materialism, it may be, that they may have to resort to Africa to recover some of the simple elements of faith; for the promise of that land is that she shall stretch forth her hands unto God.[21]

Many Indian intellectuals likewise contrasted a spiritual East with a materialistic West. The great Indian nationalist leader Mahatma Gandhi largely rejected industrialization as a future direction for his country. Rather, he envisioned an India of harmonious self-sufficient villages that would make their own cloth, practice agriculture in cooperative ways, eliminate discrimination against women and the lowest castes, and keep in touch with the ancient traditions of Indian civilization.

Actors and Re-actors

Beyond the debates about modernity and empire lies the issue of agency: who shaped the changes associated with the great disturbance? Until fairly recently, historians generally pictured Europeans as the primary actors in the drama of modernity, casting Asians and Africans in the role of victims or beneficiaries but in either case largely passive in the process. But many elements of the modern

transformation—urbanization, commercialization, technological change, and participation in the world economy—had deep roots in African and Asian societies and were well under way long before Western dominance was established. Furthermore, European modernity itself can hardly be understood without including Islamic scientific traditions, China's economic achievements in the eighteenth century, the stimulus of India's textile industry, the labor of countless African slaves, the wealth of the Americas, and the markets of the world.

In many cases, including Russia, China, Japan, and the Ottoman Empire, reformist and modernizing programs were established, with varying degrees of success, by existing state authorities, albeit under pressure from encroaching Europeans. Even in formal colonies, the apparatus of colonial rule was largely in the hands of the colonized. In French West Africa, an area eight times the size of France itself with a population of some 15 million in the late 1930s, the colonial state consisted of 385 French administrators and more than 50,000 African chiefs. And Asian and African intellectuals were culturally active in creating new identities of race, nation, and ethnicity; in reforming and reviving older religious traditions; and in adapting European ideas to the local environment. The spread of Christianity in Africa and the Pacific Islands was largely the work of indigenous catechists, priests, and teachers rather than the direct result of European missionaries. While large numbers of people "converted" to Christianity, they also converted that Christianity to their own cultures. For many Africans, the new religion was more akin to a traditional healing cult rather than a vehicle for salvation from personal sin and eternal damnation as the missionaries had taught. Whether for good or for ill, the great disturbance was never a wholly European enterprise but also the outcome of a collaborative though unequal venture.

Nor was it a one-way street. It brought change not only from the West to the rest but also in the other direction. The development of jazz in the United States was derived in large part from African musical traditions. Asian religions, especially Buddhism, have long attracted attention from westerners disaffected from the Christian faith and seeking an alternative spiritual path. Patterns of migration that brought South Asians and West Indians to Britain, Algerians to France, and Latin Americans and Asians to the United States have given rise to both social tensions and opportunities for cultural synthesis.

Change and Persistence

A final question of perspective involves that enduring issue of historical analysis—change and continuity. Most historians have described the nineteenth century as a period of profound change in human affairs. And surely it was. But are we in danger of overlooking the continuities of the historical process or the more subtle relationships between the old and the new?

Religious Revival and Consolidation. The nineteenth century is often viewed as a time of modernization that undermined or pushed aside religious belief as material progress and the secular ideas of science, liberalism, nationalism, and socialism took center stage. Yet that century was also a time of great religious vitality, expansion, and consolidation all across the world.[22] The renewed energy of Christianity was most evident in the massive missionary movement that scattered representatives of the faith around the globe with perhaps 100,000 of them in Africa alone by 1900, all supported by the prayers and contributions of churches

and congregations back home. Revivalist Islam took shape all across the Muslim world as ardent believers sought to purify and extend the faith. Religious revolutions in West Africa, for example, created a series of new Islamic states during the nineteenth century. Other Muslim intellectuals, such as the Egyptian Muhammad Abduh and the Indian Sayyid Ahmad Khan, laid the foundation for Islamic modernism as they argued for a synthesis between Islamic and Western traditions. And Islam continued its centuries-long expansion in Africa even while the continent was under the control of Christian European powers.

The nineteenth century also witnessed the emergence of a more distinctly "Hindu" religious tradition from what had been a vast array of sects, practices, rituals, and beliefs on the South Asian peninsula. Modern reformers and some Indian nationalists presented a revitalized "Hinduism" as India's national religion, spiritually equivalent and in some ways superior to Christianity. Efforts to reconvert those who had turned to Islam or Christianity made Hinduism for the first time something of a missionary religion. In 1893, Swami Vivekananda, a leading figure in the revival of Hinduism, made a deep impression at the World Parliament of Religions in Chicago. There, he articulated a more or less unified Hinduism as a major world religion, casting India as a repository of a deep spirituality in contrast to the shallow materialism of the West.

The forces of "modernity" have in various ways strengthened rather than eroded long-established religious traditions. The European intrusion with its denigration of Afro-Asian belief systems and its efforts at Christian conversion stimulated a desire to revive and redefine these religions as a means of cultural defense. Railroads and later airplanes have enabled many to make a pilgrimage to Christian,

Hindu, Buddhist, or Muslim holy places, while the printing press, radio, and television allowed a wider dissemination of their sacred literatures and enabled much wider audiences to read or hear popular and simplified versions of ancient and complex texts.

Powers and Privileges. If older cultural and religious traditions persisted throughout the nineteenth century, so too did older patterns of society despite the pressures of revolution, capitalism, industrialization, and modernity. Global slavery, for example, died a slow death and was often replaced by other forms of coerced labor, such as indentured servitude, coolie labor, and colonial forced labor, where conditions of life were not far removed from that of slavery. Even in the United States, perhaps the most self-consciously modern nation and committed to the "rights of man," the end of slavery was bitterly resisted in the Civil War and was followed by a system of sharecropping and pervasive racial discrimination. For many, it was a "new slavery."

Landlords, aristocracies, and royal families likewise showed a surprising resilience in the face of liberal and democratic thinking. Landowning aristocrats dominated the highest levels of the British and German governments even at the end of the nineteenth century and often presented themselves as bearing the authentic national traditions of their countries while protecting the poor from exploitation at the hands of moneygrubbing capitalists. The Chinese imperial system and its scholar-gentry class also survived the many upheavals of the nineteenth century and made plans for more substantial reforms as the new century dawned. Japan's emperor emerged as a more central figure in the Meiji regime, and members of the elite samurai class found positions of power and wealth in a modernizing country even as they lost their legal privileges.

Colonial rulers in Asia and Africa frequently allied with the most conservative and established elite groups—Indian princes and high-caste elites, Muslim emirs, and African chiefs and kings—freezing their privileges and protecting them from further change. In the colonies, European authorities were highly suspicious of both modern education and urban life, fearing that these influences would "detribalize" their colonial subjects, making them less easily controlled. Thus, they often acted to reinforce or even create what they regarded as "traditional" identities of tribe, caste, or religion. The colonial experience was deeply ambiguous, simultaneously driving and retarding the modernizing process.

Nor did the nineteenth century fundamentally transform that most ancient of social hierarchies: the unequal relationship between men and women. Life certainly changed, especially for elite women in the West, but voting privileges came more slowly—first in New Zealand in 1893 and some European states and settler dependencies soon after but not until World War I for most women of the West. Colonial law codes in Asia and Africa usually entrenched male privileges, while capitalist enterprises such as mining and settler farms removed large numbers of men from rural villages, throwing an added burden on women. "Most historians of the family," writes a leading scholar, "see few major changes in the structure of the family across the world in the course of the nineteenth century."[23]

Conclusion: Toward the Twentieth Century

Thus, the full impact of the "great disturbance" occurred only in the wars and revolutions of the twentieth century. Industrialization, restricted to a few places in the 1800s, became then a global process. It brought with it a range of familiar problems—changing class structures, urbanization, and new roles for women, for example. But it also generated qualitatively new features in the new century, including massive population growth, environmental disruption on an unprecedented scale, and the challenge of communist revolutions. The new century also began with Europe's global empires intact and apparently secure, but by the 1970s, those empires had disintegrated, dozens of new nations emerged from their ruin, and a very different balance of power prevailed. Both global connections and global divisions, forged in the nineteenth century and before, became deeper and more pronounced in the twentieth.

Suggested Readings

Adu Boahen, A. *African Perspectives on Colonialism*. Baltimore: Johns Hopkins University Press, 1987. The colonial experience through the eyes of a prominent African intellectual and historian.

Bayly, C. A. *The Birth of the Modern World, 1780–1914*. Oxford: Blackwell, 2004. An examination of the "long nineteenth century" on a global basis, emphasizing the role of the "non-West" in the emergence of modernity.

Conklin, Alice L., and Ian Christopher Fletcher, eds. *European Imperialism, 1830–1930*. Boston: Houghton Mifflin, 1999. A collection of classical and contemporary scholarship on Europe's nineteenth-century empires.

Davis, Mike. *Late Victorian Holocausts*. London: Verso, 2001. Examines El Niño–induced famines in the colonial world and the failure of governments to deal effectively with them.

Orwell, George. *Burmese Days*. New York: Harvest Books, 1974. An insightful novel about the British colonial experience in Burma.

Said, Edward W. *Orientalism*. New York: Random House, 1978. A now classic account of how empire shaped and distorted European perceptions of the Islamic world.

Smith, Bonnie G. *Imperialism: A History in Documents*. Oxford: Oxford University Press, 2000. A combination of pictures, primary sources, and commentary by a prominent American historian.

Waley, Arthur. *The Opium War through Chinese Eyes*. Palo Alto, CA: Stanford University Press, 1979. Various Chinese perspectives on European aggression in the nineteenth century.

Notes

1. Quoted in James Kritzeck, *Modern Islamic Literature* (New York: New American Library, 1970), 18–22.

2. Quoted in Magali Morsy, *North Africa: 1800–1900* (London: Longman, 1984), 79.

3. Quoted in Heinz Gollwitzer, *Europe in the Age of Imperialism* (London: Thames and Hudson, 1969), 136.

4. Rudyard Kipling "The White Man's Burden," in *Rudyard Kipling's Verse* (Garden City, NY: Doubleday, 1940), 321.

5. See Daniel Headrick, *The Tools of Empire: Technology and European Imperialism in the Nineteenth Century* (New York: Oxford University Press, 1981).

6. R. Meinertzhagen, *Kenya Diary* (London: Oliver and Boyd, 1957), 51–52.

7. Quoted by Basil Davidson, *The African Past* (London: Longman, 1964), 357–58.

8. John Iliffe, *Africa: The History of a Continent* (Cambridge: Cambridge University Press, 1995), 208–11.

9. Quoted in Claude Bowers, *Beveridge and the Progressive Era* (New York: Houghton Mifflin, 1932), 121–22.

10. Quoted in John Dos Passos, *U.S.A.: The 42nd Parallel* (New York: Modern Library, 1937), 5.

11. Colin Simmons, "Deindustrialization, Industrialization, and the Indian Economy, 1850–1947," *Modern Asian Studies* 19, no. 3 (1985): 600.

12. L. S. Stavrianos, *Global Rift* (New York: William Morrow, 1981).

13. This section is drawn from Mike Davis, *Late Victorian Holocausts* (London: Verso, 2001). The quotes are on pp. 31, 33, and 37, respectively.

14. Davis, *Late Victorian Holocausts*, 312.

15. Adam McKeown, personal email, August 1, 2010, regarding previous posting on H-World, February 23, 2001. See also Adam McKeown, "Global Migrations, 1846–1940," *Journal of World History* 15, no. 2 (2004): 155.

16. J. R. McNeill and William H. McNeill, *The Human Web* (New York: Norton, 2003), 215–16.

17. Robert Knox, *Races of Man* (Philadelphia: Lea and Blanchard, 1850), v.

18. Elizabeth Schmidt, *Peasants, Traders, and Wives: Shona Women in the History of Zimbabwe, 1870–1939* (Portsmouth, NH: Heinemann, 1992), chap. 4.

19. Teng Ssu-yu and John K. Fairbank, eds. and trans., *China's Response to the West: A Documentary Survey, 1839–1923* (New York: Atheneum, 1963), 69.

20. Shigenobu Okuma, *Fifty Years of New Japan* (Kaikoku Gojunen Shi), 2nd ed. (London: Smith, Elder, 1910).

21. Edward Blyden, *Christianity, Islam, and the Negro Race* (Edinburgh: Edinburgh University Press, 1967), 124.

22. C. A. Bayly, *The Birth of the Modern World* (Oxford: Blackwell, 2004), chap. 9.

23. Bayly, *The Birth of the Modern World*, 399.

11

The Modern World and Global Realignments

THE PAST CENTURY

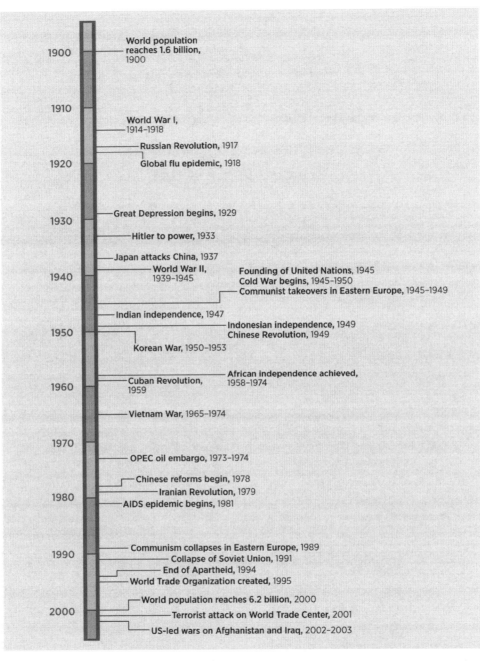

Figure 11.1   Twentieth-century time line.

A HUNDRED years ago, Europeans dominated the world. The past century, however, witnessed a series of challenges, shocks, or realignments that substantially altered that pattern. This chapter highlights these global realignments: six "political earthquakes" that in rapid succession transformed older patterns of world history and reshaped the lives of billions all across the planet. Chapter 12 continues this exploration of the past 100 years by examining a set of global processes that, perhaps less visibly and more slowly, have changed our lives.

The European Crisis, 1914–1945

As the twentieth century dawned, world power was pretty much in European hands. Europeans directly governed colonies encompassing Africa, South and Southeast Asia, and elsewhere; they indirectly dominated China and much of the Middle East through periodic military intervention and economic penetration; and people of European descent ruled in the Americas, Australia, New Zealand, and much of the Pacific. The industrial economies of Europe and the United States generated unprecedented wealth and power while commanding the natural resources and the markets of the world. Militarily, European states

were vulnerable only to one another. Their schools and universities produced the best-educated citizens and the most advanced scholars and technicians. And their scientists had unlocked many of the secrets of the universe. No wonder most Europeans felt self-assured, even arrogant and superior, when comparing themselves to the world's other peoples.

But the first half of the twentieth century brought down this "proud tower"[1] of European civilization, and much of the destruction was self-inflicted. In just over three decades (1914–1945), Europe seemed to self-destruct in an orgy of violence known as the world wars. Their vaunted capitalist economic system unraveled in the Great Depression of the 1930s. Their claims to moral superiority lay in tatters as the rise of fascism—a highly emotional, nationalistic, authoritarian, and revolutionary movement—mocked Western rationalism, democracy, and humanitarian values. In Germany and eastern Europe, it led to the grotesque horrors of the Holocaust and the slaughter of millions of citizens. What had happened?

World War I

The Roots of War. This "European crisis" was the product of Europe's own deeply rooted internal flaws, cracks in the foundation of the "proud tower." Perhaps the most serious of those flaws was the endemic rivalry of European states, which both generated and glorified war. For nearly a century (1815–1914), a precarious balance of power had kept European states generally at peace. But by the early twentieth century, those rivalries were upset by the emergence of a recently unified Germany as a new and ambitious "Great Power," aspiring to its "place in the sun." The growth of popular nationalism, an accelerating arms

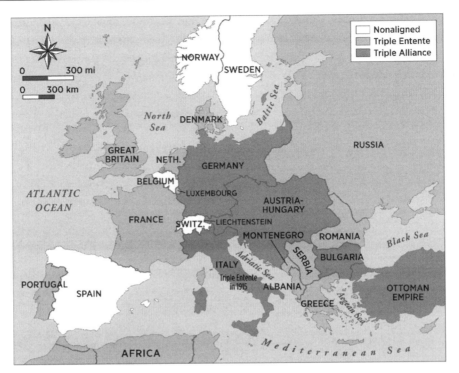

Map 11.1 Despite its remarkable achievements, Europe in the early twentieth century was precariously divided between two rival alliances, each armed to the teeth with modern weapons. World War I demonstrated the fragility of the European peace.

race in highly destructive weaponry, and a system of rigid alliances that divided Europe into two armed camps by 1914 compounded the tensions, raised the stakes, and created a crisis waiting to happen. Then a single spark, the assassination of an Austrian archduke by a Bosnian-Serb nationalist, ignited a war that set Great Britain, France, and Russia (and later the United States) to war against Germany, the Austrian Empire, the Ottoman Empire, and briefly Italy, which switched sides in 1915. It was a war that no country had actually intended but also one that no statesmen, despite much last-minute diplomacy, were able to prevent. The Great War was an accident, but Europe's system of competitive nation-states made it accident prone. The conflict ground

on for four long years, much of it bogged down in "trench warfare," before the British and French, joined now by the Americans, staggered to victory over Germany and its allies.

The Costs of War. It was a war of unprecedented and appalling casualties, caused in part by the introduction of various new weapons, such as poison gas, tanks, machine guns, submarines, and airplanes. Single battles produced deaths numbering in the hundreds of thousands, while a total of some 10 million lives were lost during the four years of the conflict (1914–1918) with perhaps twice that many wounded or maimed for life. On the home front, it was a "total war" in which governments took control of their economies,

Figure 11.2 Although India was half a world away from Europe, its people, as colonial subjects of Great Britain, participated in World War I. *FPG/ Getty Images.*

set women to work in factories producing munitions, and in wartime propaganda depicted the enemy in the most brutal and inhumane terms. A conflict of entire societies, not simply their military forces, took shape during World War I.

A Global Conflict. Although focused primarily within Europe, the war was global in several ways. Parts of it were fought in the colonies, as British and French forces seized German territories in Africa. Millions of colonized people from Africa, India, and elsewhere were drafted into the service of European powers. Japan took over German possessions in China and made heavy demands on China itself. Australia and New Zealand entered the world stage, suffering devastating losses in an attack on the Ottoman Empire near Istanbul at Gallipoli. Finally, the United States joined the war in 1917, marking its emergence as a global military power. With fresh American help providing a key boost to the Allies, Germany surrendered in November 1918.

Reverberations. The legacy of World War I was evident throughout the twentieth century.

That conflict destroyed the Russian, Ottoman, and Austro-Hungarian empires, which had long been prominent features of Europe's political order. In Russia in 1917, it prompted a massive revolutionary upheaval that toppled the tsar, brought communists to power, and initiated a century-long struggle with the capitalist countries of the West. Amid the rubble of the Ottoman Empire, the war redrew the map of the Middle East, creating the countries of Turkey, Syria, Iraq, Jordan, Palestine, and Lebanon. All except Turkey were placed under the control of the British or the French. Conflicting British promises to both Arabs and Jews regarding Palestine set the stage for an enduring struggle over that ancient and holy land. Europe's political map also changed as a bevy of new independent states appeared—Poland, Czechoslovakia, Hungary, Yugoslavia, Lithuania, Estonia, Latvia, and others. The principle of national "self-determination," articulated by the victors, echoed loudly throughout the twentieth century as subject peoples all across the world used it to further their own drives for greater freedom or independence from imperial rule. Within Europe, the war generated despair and disillusionment among educated people as they contemplated the immense and senseless horrors of that conflict. For many intellectuals, the very idea of progress, so prominent in nineteenth-century European thinking, was among the casualties of the war.

Capitalism in Crisis

The Great Depression of the 1930s disclosed another crack in the foundation of European civilization—the instability of its capitalist economy. To be sure, that economy in its industrial phase had given Europeans wealth and power unknown in human history. But it had also generated intense class conflict and inequality, and it had shown a tendency toward instability as the imbalances between capital and labor left many unemployed. In the 1930s, stock prices dropped sharply, banks failed, factories closed, unemployment skyrocketed in the major industrial countries, breadlines and soup kitchens sprouted in many cities, and, more than ever, the poor despised the rich and the rich feared losing what they had. It seemed almost that the predictions of Karl Marx about the inevitable collapse of capitalism were coming true. Instead, the governments of Western countries learned how to manage—or at least to moderate—these instabilities through government spending and controlling the supply of money. Nevertheless, the vicious downturn in the economy wrought terrible damage, leaving millions impoverished. It also created conditions in which the Nazis came to power in Germany. A fringe racist and highly nationalist party with minimal popular support before the Depression, the Nazis, under the leadership of the charismatic Adolf Hitler,

rode that disaster to power as they blamed Germany's problems on Jews and communists and claimed to have answers to all the country's economic and political woes.

Racism and the Holocaust

With its anti-Jewish, anticommunist, and intensely nationalist message, the Nazis gained growing support in Germany during the early 1930s and came to power constitutionally in 1933. They then proceeded to dismantle Germany's young and fragile democracy, arrested hundreds of thousands of opponents, and established a single-party dictatorship. They also began to put their racist ideas into practice. At the heart of this effort lay tightening restrictions on the country's Jewish population and then during World War II a systematic program to kill them all. The Nazi phenomenon and the ghastly Holocaust that followed from it grew out of a further flaw in European civilization—racism. That racism had found expression earlier in the African and Asian colonies of the major European powers, but in Europe itself it now joined an ancient anti-Semitism and a modern narrow nationalism to provide the conditions in which the Holocaust occurred. In the deliberate murder of 6 million Jews—and as many communists, Gypsies, Poles and other Slavs, and people with disabilities—a modern administrative and technological apparatus for death served Europe's oldest and most traditional hatreds. The Holocaust and the terrible war during which it took place greatly undermined those European claims to progress, virtue, benevolence, and civilization that had justified its global empires. Western pretensions to superiority rang hollow in the aftermath of two world wars and barbarities beyond imagination.

Another World War

World War II. The roots of World War II lay in the peace settlement of the first one. The Treaty of Versailles (1919) put the entire blame for World War I on the Germans and imposed very harsh terms on them. Much of Hitler's popularity derived from his vociferous opposition to this treaty and his determination to end its restrictions on Germany. Once in power, Hitler rebuilt German military forces and set about a program of territorial expansion by which Germany absorbed Austria and Czechoslovakia (1938–1939) and then attacked Poland (1939), France (1940), and the Soviet Union (1941). These efforts to carve out for Germany a larger empire, a "living space" brutally cleansed of Jews, led to war in Europe beginning in 1939. The major theater

of that war was the "Eastern Front," in which the Soviet Union first absorbed invading German forces and then slowly pushed them out, suffering 25 million or more deaths in the process.

Japan was the Germany of Asia. In fact, as early as 1931, a militarized Japan carved out an empire that consisted of parts of China, Dutch possessions in Indonesia, British Malaya and Burma, and French colonies in Southeast Asia. It was a continuation of Japan's remarkable rise to world power that had begun with its unique industrialization in the late nineteenth century. While Japan presented itself as leading an effort to oust Western imperialists from Asia, its brutality toward other Asians, particularly Chinese, marked it as yet another empire designed only to further its own economic and territorial interests. When the Japanese

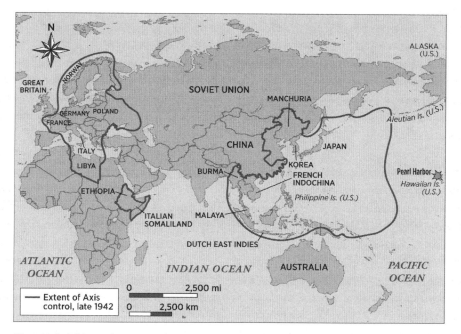

Map 11.2 This map shows the extent of German and Italian conquests in Europe and Africa and Japanese conquests in Asia before the tide of war turned against them.

attacked the American base at Pearl Harbor in Hawaii in December 1941, the Asian and European conflicts were joined as Germany backed Japan and the United States declared war on both of them.

Thus, World War II took its final shape as Nazi Germany, fascist Italy, and a militarized Japan (the "Axis") faced off against Britain, the Soviet Union, China, and the United States (the "Allies"). Fought in Europe, North Africa, Asia, and the Pacific, it was even more of a "total war" since it not only militarized the home front but also targeted civilians in massive numbers. The war claimed perhaps 60 million fatalities, about 3 percent of the world's population. Heavy bombing of entire cities from the air proved far more devastating to the civilian populations than during World War I, a trend that culminated in 1945 in the destruction of the Japanese cities of Hiroshima and Nagasaki by the United States with newly created atomic bombs. A centrally directed Soviet economy and American techniques of mass production combined to vastly outproduce the Germans and Japanese and laid the foundations for military victory in 1945.

A World Reshaped

World War II pressed "reset" to global politics. Western Europe, which had largely dominated the globe for the previous 150 years, had been physically devastated, morally tarnished, and politically weakened. Recovering economically from these conflicts with substantial American assistance in the form of the Marshall Plan aid, Europe put aside some of its historical rivalries and moved toward greater cooperation. But Europe's dominant position in global affairs was gone, replaced by that of the Soviet Union and the United States. The Soviet Union, battered by more than 25

million deaths, had nonetheless performed heroically, and its communist regime gained credibility. It also gained a major ally, as the Chinese Communist Party took power in that enormous country in 1949. The United States, with some 300,000 deaths, far fewer than other key combatants, and no invasion of its own territory, emerged as the single most powerful country in the world and the clear leader of the advanced capitalist nations. The wartime alliance between the Soviet Union and the United States soon gave way to a bitter and intense rivalry known as the Cold War. This new conflict largely structured international relations until the collapse of the Soviet Union in 1991.

Revolution and Communism

War and revolution go together like, well, revolution and war. One often causes the other. It is hard to envision the French Revolution without the European and Napoleonic war or the American Revolution without the War for Independence. Similarly, it is hard to imagine the Russian Revolution of 1917 without World War I or, for that matter, the Chinese Communist Revolution without World War II. In fact World War I produced not one but two revolutions in Russia in 1917—a sort of middle-class parliamentary revolution against the tsar and then, later in the year as the war dragged on, the revolution in which V. I. Lenin and the communists seized power. It is that second revolution that changed Russia and shook the world.

The Russian and Chinese communist revolutions inspired potential revolutionaries throughout the world. In addition to transforming the largest and the most populous countries on the planet, they offered an alternative to Western capitalism that appealed to many. Through the use of state power, they would mobilize their people and their resources to construct in record time thoroughly modern industrial societies. And by substituting a rationally planned economy for private property and the market, they would do so without the painful consequences of the capitalist path—repeated recessions and depressions, the gross exploitation of workers, endemic conflicts between rich and poor, and economic rivalries that led to war and imperial aggression. That was the promise of communist revolutions.

The Birth of Communism

Russia. Revolutionary and democratic socialist parties flourished in Europe and even parts of the Americas during the decades before World War I, but they were blindsided by a revolution carried out in the name of Marx in distant Russia. Communism was born in a place far removed from the advanced capitalist industrialized countries that Karl Marx saw as the seedbed of socialism. V. I. Lenin knew that Marx and the Western socialists held a historical interpretation that envisioned socialism emerging from advanced capitalist society, when the contradictions of capitalism—abundance and inequality—could no longer be held together by markets and capitalists. But Lenin thought that Russia could be made to jump-start a socialist revolution even though capitalism had barely begun. It would just have to be dictatorial rather than democratic, organized by a tight cadre rather than an open parliament.

Russia was awash with revolutionaries. The war only magnified ancient inequalities, conflicts, and divisions in Russian society—the great gulf between a small landowning nobility and a vast peasant class, the dominance of Russians over the empire's many other peoples, and the absolute authority of the tsar over all other groups in society. But the revolution also grew out of the country's nineteenth-century efforts to modernize and industrialize as a means of maintaining its Great Power status. These efforts created or enlarged both an educated professional class of people and a heavily exploited urban working class, neither of which could find an outlet for their grievances in the autocratic tsarist system.

Revolution broke out as women demonstrated for lack of bread, soldiers mutinied and deserted, peasants seized land from the nobility, workers took over factories, and non-Russian nationalities asserted their independence. Within a year, the centuries-old tsarist monarchy was gone, and the Bolsheviks, more in tune with the revolutionary mood than rival parties, catapulted into power.

Few people expected this fragile toehold to last, but the Bolsheviks consolidated their power after a bitter civil war, renaming themselves the Communist Party. They even renamed their country the Union of Soviet Socialist Republics (the Soviet Union) after the "soviets" or grassroots workers' councils that had sprung up in 1917 to assume local power as the tsar's authority collapsed.

Eastern Europe. For 30 years, the Soviet Union remained the sole world outpost of an alternative to capitalism. But then in the late 1940s, communism began to spread as communist parties took power in eastern Europe after the end of World War II. Unlike the Soviet Union, where the Bolsheviks initially had considerable popular support, eastern European communist governments were created largely by occupying Soviet troops, determined to impose "friendly" communist states in an area through which Russia had been repeatedly invaded from the West.

China. Even more significant was the triumph of communism in China in 1949 in a revolutionary process quite different from that of Russia. Socialist parties had existed in Russia for decades before the collapse of the tsarist system, and the Bolsheviks came to power less than a year after the tsar abdicated. But few Chinese had even heard of Karl Marx or socialism when the Qing dynasty collapsed in 1912. The Chinese Communist Party was founded only in 1921 and then had to struggle for 28 years before coming to power. Furthermore, it was a struggle occurring largely in the countryside with communists finding their chief supporters among impoverished peasants, while Russia's communists were based in the cities among industrial workers. Finally, Russian communists gained support by taking their country out of a much-despised World War I, while China's Communist Party, led by Mao Zedong, gained credibility by leading China's heroic resistance to Japanese aggression in World War II.

When Mao triumphantly proclaimed the People's Republic of China in 1949, communism became a global movement with an enormous foothold in Asia. And over the next several decades, communism also took hold in North Korea, Cuba, Vietnam, Cambodia, and Laos. At its high point in the 1970s, communist rule encompassed perhaps a third of the world's population. And even where they did not seize power, communist parties attracted considerable support, for example, in France, Italy, Greece, the Philippines, Indonesia, and South Africa. While democratic socialist parties remained active in these and other countries, the political success of communist parties often gave them the upper hand. Democratic socialists argued that the authoritarian regimes of Russia, China, and eastern Europe lacked all the ingredients of

socialist revolutions since they did not emerge from advanced capitalist societies, but power seduced many who were eager to find an alternative to capitalism. On the other side of the political spectrum, capitalist media found the communists to be an easy stand-in to discredit all socialist parties and critics. Russian commissars and American capitalists could agree that there was only one kind of socialism, and that was practiced in the Soviet Union and China.

Making Communist Societies

Even though the Russian and Chinese revolutions were distortions of the Marxist vision of superseding advanced capitalism, they changed Russian and Chinese societies in ways that others found worth emulating. In their language at least, they echoed Marx and European socialists. The social promise of these revolutions was equality—the end of a humiliating domination by landowners and capitalists and the birth of new opportunities for peasants and workers in a socialist society. In eliminating these old elites of landlords and capitalists, the communist regimes went some distance toward fulfilling those promises. For example, in the course of the Chinese Communist Party's long revolutionary struggle, party officials encouraged ordinary peasants to confront landlords, to "speak the bitterness" of their personal experience with oppression, and to "settle accounts" with their class enemies. In the process, men and women who had long been passive or inarticulate in the face of landlord oppression became politically conscious and active, while large numbers of landlords, perhaps a million or more, were killed. In the rural areas of both China and the Soviet Union, peasants got access to land that they had previously worked as serfs or tenants.

Rural Communism. The end of landlord domination soon brought a kind of communalism to the countryside in both societies as Communist Party organizers established large collective farms as the centerpiece of the new agriculture. Large-scale farming was thought to be more modern and efficient, while collective or state ownership and the end of most private property in land made it more equal. Heavily resisted in the Soviet Union, collectivization occurred more peacefully in China, where the Communist Party had a much longer and more deeply rooted rural presence than in Russia.

In the Soviet Union, young urban activists sent to the countryside to assist in collectivization were enthusiastic about its potential. One young woman wrote to a friend,

> I am off in villages with a group of other brigadiers organizing *kolhozy* [collective farms]. It is a tremendous job, but we are making amazing progress. . . . [O]ur *muzhik* [peasant] is yielding to persuasion. He is joining the *kolhozy* and I am confident that in time not a peasant will remain on his own land. We shall yet smash the last vestiges of capitalism and forever rid ourselves of exploitation. . . . The very air here is afire with a new spirit and a new energy.[2]

To many peasants, it was a very different story, and collective farms were widely viewed as a "second serfdom." Furthermore, collectivization in the Soviet Union was accompanied by an assault on the churches that had long nurtured peasant life and by the deportation of a million or more kulaks, or rich peasants. A huge famine in the early 1930s, caused by the state's relentless efforts to force more grain out of the countryside to support its industrialization drive, cost millions of lives. Active resistance soon gave way to lingering resentment at the second-class status to which collectivized farmers were subjected. Through very low prices paid for their compulsory deliveries of food products, they were exploited for decades on behalf of the country's industrialization effort. Until the 1970s, they were denied the internal passports that permitted legal movement within the country. The results of this resentment were described by an outside observer in 1971:

> The collective farm "serf" discharges his labor obligation to the "master" carelessly, grudgingly. He refuses to concern himself with the fertility of the "collective" land. It is not his. He does not see the public weeds, nor the rust on the collective machinery, nor the private cow that grazes just inside the collective cornfield. He steals from the collective or habitually turns a blind eye when his fellows do so.[3]

Broadly similar patterns, including an even greater famine in the late 1950s, occurred in China. Peasant discontent there was dramatically evident when reforms in the late 1970s permitted private farming, and millions of Chinese immediately abandoned collectivized agriculture in favor of their own family farms.

Communist Industrialization. In the cities, rapid industrialization was the goal, and state planning, nationalization of industry, and priority to heavy industry were the means. "We are fifty to a hundred years behind the advanced countries," declared the Soviet leader Joseph Stalin in 1931. "We must make good this distance in ten years. Either we do it or we shall perish." In many ways, they did it. In both the Soviet Union in the 1930s and China in the 1950s, industrial growth rates were astonishing. Iron, steel, and coal production leaped ahead. New cities and industries boomed, and the urban workforce expanded rapidly. The contrast between a rapidly growing Soviet economy and the Great Depression in the capitalist countries was particularly striking. By the end of the 1930s, the Soviet Union was clearly one of the world's modern industrial states, an achievement that went a long way to explaining its victory over Nazi Germany in World War II. Centralized planning by an authoritarian state seemed to work, and many people—some intellectuals in the West and some political leaders in European colonies—saw communism as the wave of the future and capitalism as exhausted.

In the cities of communist societies, a rapidly growing urban working class gained much in terms of educational opportunities and social mobility. In the Soviet Union, Stalin's desire to create a technically competent and thoroughly communist elite, drawn from the working class, provided great opportunity for hundreds of thousands of these young people—manual laborers and low-level white-collar workers—who streamed into the new technical schools that opened after 1928. Those who graduated (mostly in engineering of some kind) in the early 1930s experienced rapid promotion in the party, state, or industrial bureaucracies and considerable upward social mobility. Here was the basis for some of the support and even enthusiasm that Soviet communism was able temporarily to generate. "I am a Tatar," wrote one grateful Soviet citizen:

> In old tsarist Russia we weren't even considered people. We couldn't even dream about education, or getting a job in a state enterprise. And now I'm a citizen of the USSR. Like all citizens, I have the right to a job, to education, to leisure. . . . From a common laborer I

have turned into a skilled worker. I was elected a member of the city soviets. . . . I live in a country where one feels like living and learning. . . . I will sacrifice my life in order to . . . save my country.[4]

But some people clearly benefited more than others from communism. A "new class" of party leaders, industrial managers, technical experts, and bureaucrats emerged in all the communist countries, eroding socialist commitments to equality. This new class was privileged in many ways: its members gained access to special stores, hospitals, schools, and apartments; luxurious vacations and country homes; higher salaries; servants and chauffeurs; and high social status. But these privileges derived from their positions in the hierarchy as communist officials, not from their ownership of property as in capitalist societies. And those positions were highly insecure, dependent on the approval of party authorities, as millions discovered in wave after wave of party purges.

Confronting Privilege and Inequality in China. The Chinese Communist Party faced the same problem as a new elite took shape, but unlike the Soviet Union, which largely accepted this reality, the Chinese leadership under Mao Zedong tried to combat it. They sent high-ranking officials out to the farms to renew their relationship with the "masses" and purged from the party those who resisted this effort to continue the revolutionary tradition. By the mid-1960s, Mao became convinced that many within the Communist Party itself, including top officials, had become complacent, were focusing on their own careers, and had lost touch with the ordinary people of the country. He launched a so-called Cultural Revolution in which millions of young people, organized as Red Guards, were encouraged to "make revolution" against such people, including often their own teachers, party leaders, and even their parents. The chaos that this movement generated finally came to an end only after Mao died and a new communist leadership decisively repudiated the Cultural Revolution.

Any modern industrial society, whether capitalist or communist, seems to require some kind of elite—managers, technicians, administrators, and experts. This reality flew in the face of more radical socialist visions of equality. In one early Soviet experiment, Russian orchestras tried to perform without a conductor. Mao Zedong famously dismissed the need for professionals with the dictum "Better red than expert." But the Soviet revolution was based not on the Marxist vision of the withering away of the state; it relied on Lenin's conviction that revolution in an undemocratic society could be accomplished only by a "dictatorship of the proletariat" and a secret and centralized party. In addition, the Soviet effort to industrialize the economy and modernize the society required a wide range of experts and administrators.

Totalitarianism and Terror. In both Russia and China, the Communist Party was everywhere. Education, the arts, the media, and social life—all of this, in addition to the economy and politics, was monopolized by the party and enforced by repeated purges, imprisonment, and executions in an effort to achieve almost total control of society. Membership in the party provided the chief means to status and privilege. But divisions within both communist parties triggered an escalating search for "enemies," those who rejected or even questioned the policies of the leadership. In the Soviet Union, it was known as "the Great Terror" of 1936–1939, in which millions were arrested and hundreds of thousands executed,

many of them high-ranking communist officials accused of horrendous and altogether unlikely crimes. A self-perpetuating wave of fear engulfed much of the country, particularly in elite circles, as citizens denounced one another for fear of being denounced themselves. Something similar took place during China's Cultural Revolution in the late 1960s as party leader Mao Zedong mobilized millions of young people, the Red Guards, and sent them streaming across the country to confront any who might be "taking the capitalist road." Something close to civil war ensued before Mao called a halt to the upheaval. These brutal state-controlled regimes were a far cry from the humane and democratic socialism of Marx and most European socialist parties of the period.

The Communist World and the "Free World"

On the global stage, the rise of communism split the world through the late 1980s. Known as the Cold War, that intense conflict found expression as a bitter ideological rivalry pitting Western market economies, democratic politics, and ideals of personal freedom against communist state-managed economies, single-party politics, and ideals of social equality. On both sides, the stakes seemed total, as entire ways of life, systems of value, and alternative visions of the future were at issue. More concretely, the Cold War gave rise to military and political rivalries throughout the world. Europe, Germany, and the city of Berlin were sharply divided with their eastern halves in the Soviet bloc and their western halves allied with the United States, now the clear leader of the so-called free world. Beyond Europe, the former colonies, now becoming independent nations, became yet another arena of Soviet–American

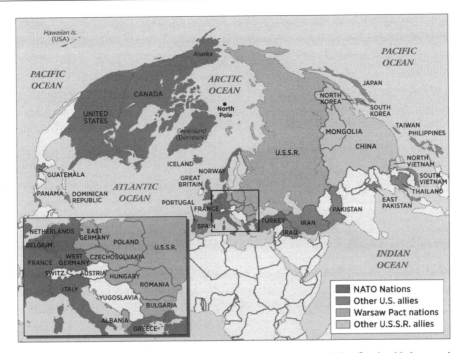

Map 11.3   The bitter rivalry between the United States and the Soviet Union and their respective allies divided the world sharply and dangerously in the second half of the twentieth century

rivalry with each side attempting to recruit allies with economic enticements, military aid, and diplomatic pressure. The early economic success of the Soviet Union and China and their apparent commitment to social equality attracted favorable attention in many of the new nations. The flashpoints of these Cold War rivalries spanned the globe—Korea, Cuba, Vietnam, Cambodia, the Middle East, Afghanistan, Ethiopia and Somalia, Angola, and elsewhere—sometimes erupting into war and other times merely threatening it.

What made these conflicts so dangerous was an escalating arms race, especially in nuclear weapons. Serious scientists and political leaders on both sides were aware of the wholly unique potential of these weapons such that their use in any widespread way meant mutual destruction at the least and possibly

the extinction of life on Earth. In a nuclear war, Soviet leader Khrushchev once opined, "the living will envy the dead." This awareness explained in large measure the surprising absence of any direct military encounter between Soviet and American forces despite the bitterness of their rivalries. In that respect, the Cold War never became hot. But the world lived on the precipice of disaster for several decades. Perhaps the most chilling confrontation occurred in 1962 when the Soviet Union attempted to install missiles with nuclear weapons in Cuba. A U.S. naval blockade of Cuba ultimately persuaded the Soviet Union to withdraw the weapons, but for a period of several weeks in October 1962, the world held its breath as nuclear war seemed imminent.

Communism, in short, was an enormous shock to the capitalist world system of the twentieth century. For those living in communist countries, it transformed conditions of life, bringing rapid economic growth, vast social upheaval, and great oppression. It threw the West on the defensive; challenged its political, economic, and religious values; and set in motion a historic confrontation between rival ideologies and social systems.

The United States as a Global Power

If world wars, depression, and communist revolution were not enough to shake Europe's confidence, the emergence of the United States as global superpower made up the difference. But the emergence of the United States on the global stage also suggests that European or, more broadly, Western dominance had not so much ended as acquired a new center across the Atlantic. After all, the United States was dominated by people of European origin, however much Americans might seek to distinguish themselves from the "Old World." And Americans certainly bore the legacy of European history in their commitment to Christianity, capitalism, democracy, and industrial development. Whether the rise of the United States challenged or extended European dominance, the second half of the twentieth century witnessed the emergence of the United States as the world's most powerful state. It was yet another of the major realignments that transformed the world of the twentieth century.

An American Century?

In 1941, the publisher Henry Luce, whose *Time*, *Life*, and *Fortune* magazines had become mainstays of American popular culture, wrote that the twentieth century would be "the American Century." "Our Bill of Rights, our Declaration of Independence, our Constitution, our magnificent industrial products, our technological skills" would be shared by all peoples, he declared. The United States must become the "training center for the skilled servants of mankind."[5] An audacious boast in the wake of the Great Depression became reality by the end of World War II. The United States emerged in 1945 alone among the combatants stronger than it had been. The American flag flew over defeated Germany and Japan. Even American allies—England, France, the Soviet Union, and China—were decimated by the war. The United States led the formation of the United Nations, writing the rules and ensuring the votes; created the International Monetary Fund and the World Bank; and provided extensive aid packages for the rebuilding of allies and former enemies. Producing over half the world's manufactured goods and controlling two-thirds of the world's gold supply, the American economy dominated the world as had no other in history. As Britain, France, and other European countries abandoned their empires, the United States stepped in to exert its will and support its manufacturers.

Between 1945 and 1975, the American empire provided factory workers with middle-class homes, secure retirements, and inexpensive college educations for their children. While American workers produced for the world, the U.S. government wrote constitutions for governments (beginning with Japan in 1945), toppled and selected governments (especially in Latin America), and sent military expeditions throughout the world.

Containing Communism

The most visible international role of the United States was its leadership in the effort to contain what it saw as the expansive forces of global communism. Already in 1945, President Harry S. Truman's decision to drop the atomic bomb on Japan was motivated partly by the fear of Soviet expansion in Asia. In 1947, the Truman Doctrine pledged support for virtually any government threatened by communist subversion or aggression. The North Atlantic Treaty Organization (NATO) soon followed, designed to counter any Soviet military threat to western Europe. Further alliances, such as the Southeast Asian Treaty Organization and the Central Treaty Organization, ringed the Soviet Union. By 1970, according to one historian, "the United States had more than 1,000,000 soldiers in 30 countries, was a member of four regional defense alliances and an active participant in a fifth, had mutual defense treaties with 42 nations,

was a member of 53 international organizations, and was furnishing military or economic aid to nearly 100 nations across the face of the globe."[6]

Containment also led to prolonged wars in Korea (1950–1953) and Vietnam (1955–1975). These bitter, bloody, and costly conflicts were based on a new official American understanding of the world.[7] Communism in this view was a global movement, coordinated from the Soviet Union and China, an infinite peril to free societies and personal liberties everywhere as well as to American economic interests around the world. A significant communist success could well trigger an escalating domino effect of further communist victories throughout Asia and beyond. Communist insurgencies in Burma, Indonesia, Malaya, and the Philippines represented the dominoes

Figure 11.3 The unsuccessful American war in Vietnam resulted in scenes such as this, in which a U.S. soldier throws a rice basket into flames after a peasant woman retrieved it from the burning house in background. *AP Photo/Dang Van Phuoc.*

waiting to fall. Only unwavering American commitment held the promise of containing that threat. "The aim [of the communists] in Viet-Nam is not simply the conquest of the South, tragic as that would be," argued President Lyndon Johnson in 1965. "It is to show that the American commitment is worthless. Once that is done, the gates are down, and the road is open to expansion and endless conquest."[8] For American leaders, the failure to oppose an expansionist Hitler in the 1930s had led to World War II; it was a lesson that had to be applied to containing communist expansion in the 1960s.

Beyond these major wars, a multitude of briefer interventions in Cuba, the Dominican Republic, Iran, Chile, Guatemala, Haiti, Panama, and elsewhere were intended to prevent or remove leftist governments and to provide support for many anticommunist regimes, even though they might be corrupt, undemocratic, and brutal. The shah of Iran, the famously corrupt dictator Sese Seko Mobutu of the Congo (then Zaire), Ferdinand Marcos in the Philippines, and any number of military governments in Latin America were among U.S. client states. They were surely "bastards," commented one official, but they were "our bastards." A further American ally was the apartheid state of South Africa, where fear of instability and communist penetration was among the factors that inhibited American willingness to strongly confront that country's racist policies.

Aid, both military and economic, was a further weapon in the Cold War. Beginning with the program to assist Greece and Turkey in combating communism in 1947, the United States funneled substantial sums of money and equipment to almost 100 countries in far larger amounts than the Soviet Union could afford. Its Peace Corps program, begun in the early 1960s, scattered tens of thousands of young Americans all across the Third World to assist in education and development projects and to win friends for the United States. Furthermore, private corporations and banks fostered trade and investment in many Third World countries, strengthening their ties to the West. All this was useful, many leading Americans believed, in enabling Third World countries to make the difficult and often destabilizing transition to modernity without succumbing to the "disease" of communism. Aid, trade, and investment in this view represented a kind of inoculation against that disease.

When the Soviet Union collapsed in 1991, the United States was the world's only military superpower. Its wars in the Persian Gulf (1991), Afghanistan (2002), and Iraq (2003) confirmed the military and political dominance of the United States.

An Empire of Culture

In the wake of American political, economic, and military power came heavy doses of American culture as well. American movies attracted and influenced millions. The works of American authors were translated into dozens of languages. American music, particularly jazz and, much more extensively, rock and roll, became a major form of entertainment the world over. And the brand names of American products like Ford, Spam, Kleenex, McDonald's, and Coca-Cola became part of the consumer culture of many countries. An ideology of consumerism, pioneered in the United States and driven by mass advertising, penetrated much of the world.

Resisting the American Empire

American dominance has not gone unchallenged. From the communist point of view, the Cold War was largely an effort to resist American global domination and to bring the blessings of socialism to those oppressed by capitalism. Mexico nationalized foreign-owned railroads and oil companies in the late 1930s, while Cuba escaped American domination and nationalized U.S. corporations during its revolution beginning in 1959.

Nor was the United States able to completely dominate its supposed Third World allies in the Cold War. Many sought actively to remain "nonaligned" in the global rivalries of the Cold War or to play off the global superpowers against one another. India routinely took aid from both sides and criticized both while resolutely maintaining its neutrality. Egypt turned decisively against the West in the mid-1950s, developing a close relationship with the Soviet Union, but in 1972 it expelled 21,000 Soviet advisers and aligned more clearly with the United States. Ethiopia, long a close ally of the United States with a large American communications base in its country, underwent a major change of government in the 1970s, becoming for a time a Marxist state and a Soviet ally. Neither side in the Cold War found it easy to impose its will in the Third World.

Culturally, Americans continued to be very influential in the world, but a vocal minority of intellectuals, writers, and political leaders in Europe and in developing countries strenuously objected to the new "cultural imperialism" or the "Americanization" of their countries. Both the assertion of political Islam and the rise of China as a major world power represented challenges to U.S. hegemony. The economic revival of Japan and western Europe, together with the industrial development in East Asia, eroded American economic dominance and created a massive trade deficit. And the war against Iraq in the early twenty-first century witnessed a global outcry of opposition to this unilateral exercise of American power.

The emergence of the United States as a global power marked both the end of western European dominance in world affairs and the continuation of Western political power, cultural values, and economic interests on a global level. It contributed to the epic conflict of the Cold War and provoked opposition from some allies in the Western alliance as well as from developing countries intent on preserving their hard-won independence.

Achieving Independence

The End of Empire

The past century was also the end of the age of empires. In 1914, many of the world's peoples lived not in independent national states but in multinational empires. Today, virtually all of the world's territorial empires have disintegrated. They have been replaced by dozens of newly independent nation-states. World War I witnessed the disintegration of the Habsburg, Ottoman, and Russian empires. During World War II, Germany's and Japan's empires dissolved in military defeat. The postwar decades saw the collapse of the overseas empires of France, Great Britain, Belgium, Holland, Portugal, and the United States. And in the years between 1989 and 1991, the Soviet empire likewise came apart as both its eastern European dependencies and the various non-Russia nationalities within the Soviet Union asserted their political independence.

This was a momentous change. It cultivated and authorized an array of new national identities. It mobilized millions of people to enter the political arena in search of independence for their countries and a better life for themselves and their families. It generated enormous conflict and bloodshed as struggles for independence unfolded around the world. And it set the stage for even more conflicts to follow as newly independent states quarreled with one another and sought to maintain a fragile internal unity.

Two factors underlay this remarkable and rapid transformation of the world's political architecture. The first was war, either hot or cold. Both world wars and the Cold War that followed smashed or weakened imperial powers and allowed subject peoples an easier exit from colonial dependency than might have been otherwise possible. The second was nationalism, a political ideology nurtured in nineteenth-century Europe and appropriated now on a universal basis by colonized people everywhere. The nationalist idea—a belief that one's own people share a common and distinct culture and deserve therefore a separate and independent political status—proved to be a powerful solvent of empire.

Afro-Asian Struggles

The Foundations of Anticolonialism. European colonies in Africa and Asia were most swept up by the call of national independence. Millions of colonized people had participated in World Wars I and II. They had gained military skills and political exposure, listened to wartime propaganda about freedom and self-determination, and had watched Europeans butcher each other in record numbers.

Western racism also weighed heavily on the colonized. Europeans had promised to accord their Western-educated colonial subjects a degree of equality and privilege. But European racial exclusiveness undermined these promises and alienated the educated elite in the process. Everywhere in the colonial world, these elites took the lead in struggles

for independence, seeking to create their own modern societies after being excluded from those of their European rulers. Particularly in Africa, racial consciousness became an important ingredient of nationalist movements and generated a sense of pan-African kinship between Africans and black people in the Americas. Gandhi's philosophy of nonviolence, the U.S. civil rights movement, and African struggles for independence reinforced one another and created a sense of global solidarity among people of color oppressed by whites.

Much else stoked the fires of anticolonial nationalism. The very example of European nationalisms had a corrosive effect on empire. In 1913, for example, the Dutch colonial regime in what is now Indonesia organized celebrations to mark the independence of the Netherlands from France 100 years earlier. It did not take long for Indonesian intellectuals to draw the logical conclusion: if the Dutch nation had liberated itself from France, why should not Indonesians do the same from the Netherlands? Furthermore, both the Soviet Union and the United States opposed formal colonial European empires, and the newly established United Nations provided a global forum for the expression of anticolonial demands. Like slavery in the nineteenth century, "imperialism" in the twentieth century lost its international legitimacy and became by the 1950s a term of opprobrium, widely used to insult one's opponents. The idea of the "nation" as a new, modern, and independent community appealed to peoples uprooted from their traditional societies and often impoverished by colonial economies. In these ways, the logic of nationalism itself undermined the foundations of colonial empires.

Independence Achieved. As the colonial powers of Europe rebuilt after the wars—Britain, France, the Netherlands, Portugal, and Belgium in particular—they had neither the

Figure 11.4   Gandhi (on the right) and Nehru came to symbolize the struggle for independence not only within their own country of India but also throughout the colonial world. © Bettman/Corbis/AP Images.

will nor the means to contest these movements indefinitely. Furthermore, world opinion, reflected in the newly formed United Nations, had turned decisively against imperialism. The moral legitimacy of empire now came under ferocious assault. In these circumstances, political leaders all across Asia and Africa created political parties and mobilized support from landless or exploited peasants, from impoverished or unemployed urban workers, and from enthusiastic young people eager for change. In rallies, marches, strikes, demonstrations, and sometimes guerrilla warfare operations, they made the colonies increasingly ungovernable. And so colony after colony—some 90 of them—emerged into what seemed then like the bright and optimistic light of freedom and political independence. India led the way in 1947, followed by Indonesia in 1949 and much of Africa from the late 1950s. By the 1970s, only scattered remnants of Europe's global empires remained. From the ashes of these empires emerged one of the novel features of twentieth-century political life: dozens of "new nations," each eager to assert its sovereignty in a world of equal states, to develop its economy

in a modern and industrial direction, and to secure the position of its dominant elite. The world of European empires was over.

Variations on a Theme

Anticolonial revolts took various forms. Some African states achieved independence peacefully, as did India eventually. The independence struggles of Vietnam and of Africans in Portuguese colonies were particularly violent. Algerians fought bitterly for some eight years before achieving independence from France in 1962. Some countries achieved independence almost overnight, as in the case of the Belgian Congo, where the struggle began only in 1956 with independence coming in 1960. The longer struggles, like that of India, may have provided a more experienced political leadership for the newly independent states. Some anticolonial struggles were associated with revolutionary social movements, such as those in Vietnam and China, while most African nationalist movements were rather more conservative in their social goals, seeking political independence but not socialism. Some, especially in the Islamic world, defined themselves in terms of religion, while most others maintained a secular focus. Where the people of a colony shared a common language or culture that was different from that of the colonial power, such as in the non-Russian republics of the Soviet Union and in Vietnam, China, Egypt, and elsewhere, new nations had a more solid cultural foundation and identity. But in much of Asia and Africa—India, Indonesia, Nigeria, and Congo, for example—no common language or culture existed. In some of these cases, India most notably, the language of the colonial power, English, was the language that most educated Indians knew, complicating the struggle for independence. But even where colonial powers had trained a colonial elite in European universities, the experience often served to create a common hostility to colonialism and helped forge a new national identity.

Whatever their distinctive features, the outcome of these anti-imperial nationalisms was the proliferation of dozens of new independent nation-states. Each of them, no matter how small, claimed sovereignty and legal equality with all the others and a rightful place in various international organizations, such as the United Nations. Their leaders and elites were committed to modernizing and catching up with the more advanced countries of the world. Collectively, they represented the triumph of the national ideal over discredited imperial ideologies. By the middle of the twentieth century and certainly by its end, traditional notions of empire had lost credibility in global discourse, while that of the nation reigned supreme.

New Nations on the Global Stage

Between 1900 and 2000, the number of independent countries in the world almost quadrupled, from 57 to 192. Many of these new states were former colonies that achieved political independence without economic development. Along with previously independent states like China and most of Latin America, these countries became known as the Third World, developing countries, or the global South. They made up the vast majority of humankind, some 75 percent of world population, and accounted for almost all the enormous increase in human numbers that the world experienced in that century. They also represented the locus of massive and pervasive poverty, punctuated by pockets of prosperity.

These countries adopted various strategies to generate economic development, ranging from total state control to free market capitalism. Politically, they tried single-party states, military regimes, communist governments, and variations on parliamentary democracy. For these and other reasons, many became pawns in the Cold War. In Korea, Vietnam, Cuba, the Middle East, Angola, Ethiopia, Afghanistan, and elsewhere, the superpowers took sides in local conflicts and projected them onto a global stage.

The experience of developing countries also raised questions about the meaning and significance of political independence. Although direct imperial control was a thing of the past, the optimistic expectation that independence would mean prosperity was often deeply disappointed. Continuing or even deepening poverty in many former colonies suggested that the unequal ties of the world economy—reflected in massive indebtedness, frequently declining terms of trade, intrusive foreign investment, export of raw materials, and dependence on foreign manufactured goods—survived intact even after independence. Nor did old-style colonialism disappear completely. France intervened militarily on many occasions in its former African colonies. The United States did the same in the independent states of the Caribbean and Central America. These realities gave rise to the notion of "neocolonialism," which suggested that only the political trappings, not the real substance, of Western dominance had really changed. The sharp division between the rich and poor countries in the contemporary world was a reminder that the global inequalities associated with the rise of the West still persisted into the twenty-first century.

But developing countries were actors on the global stage as well as spectators and victims of the new world order. Beyond their own internal processes—sorting out political conflicts, establishing economic policies, and managing the tensions of cultural diversity—they also shaped the world they inherited.

The Rise of the Third World

The "Third World" as an Idea. The *idea* of the Third World was as powerful as the fact. Articulated by intellectuals, journalists, scholars, and politicians in the developing countries, it cast as heroes men such as the Latin American revolutionary Che Guevara; the Algerian intellectual Franz Fanon; Jawaharlal Nehru, India's first prime minister; and Egypt's charismatic Gamal Abdel Nasser, who defeated British and French attempts to seize the Suez Canal in 1956. The idea of a Third World was an assertion of the historical significance of *their* movements and *their* countries in a world focused largely on the conflicts of the capitalist West and the communist East. It sought to distill a common and larger meaning from the variety of struggles that had recently won independence. Spokesmen for the Third World idea decisively rejected the notion of

industrialized countries bestowing civilization and development on less fortunate regions, they viewed colonial rule as the cause of their backwardness and poverty, and they saw the world instead as a struggle between an imperialistic, exploitative West, intent on maintaining its unjust privileges, and a progressive, revolutionary South. Their countries would be laboratories for land reform, state building, industrialization, and grassroots democracy. The Third World would chart the way to a rejuvenated future for themselves and for all humankind. This kind of "talking back" to the West also appealed to many idealistic young people in Europe and America who were disillusioned by the complacency, conservatism, and consumerism of their own societies.[9]

Nonalignment. The political expression of Third World thinking lay in efforts to chart an independent course in world affairs, maintaining a degree of neutrality in the face of competing demands of rival superpowers. Led by Nasser of Egypt, Nehru of India, and Sukarno of Indonesia, a conference in Bandung, Indonesia, in 1955 brought together 29 African and Asian heads of state, claiming to represent some 1.3 billion people. It was a symbolic assertion that global leadership no longer resided solely in London, Paris, or Washington. At this and subsequent meetings, Third World leaders pressed for more rapid decolonization and urged the United Nations to focus on issues other than the Cold War. The growing numbers of newly independent states transformed the United Nations from a group of 50 countries, mostly European and Latin American, to an organization numerically, if not politically, dominated by Afro-Asian states. While real power still rested with the Security Council of major capitalist countries and the Soviet Union, Third World countries pushed the United Nations to pay attention to issues of social and economic development and turned this international body into a "court of world opinion" on critical issues of the time.

Nonalignment (to the United States or Soviet Union) still left many options. India maintained a Western-style parliamentary democracy while tilting toward the Soviet Union in its foreign policy. Indonesia, having received large amounts of Soviet and eastern European aid, destroyed the Indonesian Communist Party in 1965, butchering half a million suspected communists in the process. Many Arab countries gratefully received Soviet support in their struggles against Israel while routinely jailing their own communists. And perhaps most famously, communist China broke decisively with its Soviet ally, creating a de facto alliance with the United States in the late 1970s.

A New International Economic Order? For most Third World countries, the core issues of international life were economic. By the 1960s, many of their leaders had come to believe that an unfair world economy, created and maintained by Western imperialism, made their own economic progress extremely difficult. If the poorer countries were to develop, they argued, the international economic system would have to change substantially. These demands continued the struggle against European political dominance that had occupied so much of the world's history earlier in the century. It was an effort to use a newly won independence to gain greater economic advantage on a global level, much as the lower classes in Europe and America had used political pressure and the vote to demand economic improvements within particular countries. The creation of the United Nations and other international bodies provided a forum in which these demands could be expressed and

negotiated. In 1964, at a UN Conference on Trade and Development, a number of Third World states joined together in the Group of 77 to demand concessions from the wealthy countries. This was the real beginning of organized class struggle at the international level.

But more than anything else, the success of the Organization of Petroleum Exporting Countries (OPEC) in quadrupling the world price of oil in 1973 stimulated the movement for international economic reform. Here was a dramatic breakthrough in the struggle of the poor against the rich, for OPEC, led by oil-rich Arab states, presided over the most rapid transfer of wealth the world had ever seen. In 1972, a barrel of oil could be exchanged for a single bushel of wheat; eight years later, Americans and Europeans had to pay the equivalent of six bushels of wheat for that same barrel of oil. Many people in developing countries saw it as a kind of historical justice after centuries of Western imperialism. Capitalizing on this remarkable success, virtually every country in the Third World coalesced around the demands for a New International Economic Order (NIEO) at the Sixth Special Session of the UN General Assembly in 1974. What they sought was a revolutionary overhaul of the existing international economic system, including higher and more stable prices for their exports, easier access to world markets in the rich countries, more foreign aid, and greater power in international economic agencies.

Resistance by the Rich. It is hardly surprising that the Western industrialized countries, led by the United States, were decidedly unenthusiastic about most of these proposals. Despite frequent conferences and much negotiation, little real headway was made in substantially reforming the international economic system in favor of the poor countries. The wealthier countries rejected the implication that Third

World poverty was the result of a capitalist world economy rather than the mismanagement, corruption, and inefficiency of Third World governments themselves. In addition, many Third World spokesmen argued that the West owed them some compensation for centuries of imperialist exploitation. This view hardly appealed to Western leaders or to their voting publics. Furthermore, the NIEO demands sought to interfere with the free working of the market economy, which many in the West held sacred.

The Debt Problem. In the 1980s and 1990s, international economic confrontations focused on the question of Third World debt, which had risen from about $100 billion in 1970 to $1.6 trillion in 1990. Making payments on those debts meant cutting other essential spending. In Ethiopia during the 1990s, for example, where perhaps 100,000 children died every year from preventable diseases, the country was spending four times as much on debt repayment as on public health.[10] Such conditions generated various proposals for canceling or restructuring the debt burden of poor countries. By the mid-1990s, the International Monetary Fund and the World Bank, controlled largely by the wealthy countries, conceded that some of this debt might have to be canceled in order to safeguard the world economy generally. And beyond debt, the issue of reparations, raised again at the turn of the twenty-first century, posed an even more disturbing question: did the currently rich countries owe some repayment to the developing world for centuries of slavery, colonial exploitation, and oppression?

The Assertion of Islam

The Revival of the Middle East. Among the various regions of the Third World, none made a more dramatic entry on the global stage than that of the Middle East or, more broadly, the Islamic world. The larger background to this vigorous assertion of Islam in the twentieth century lay in 1,000 years of Islamic expansion (622–1600) followed by three centuries of increasingly humiliating subservience to European imperialism. Then during the twentieth-century, a Middle Eastern revival took shape as Islamic civilization reasserted itself. It began, like that of other colonized regions, with powerful nationalist movements that broke Europe's political hold and gave rise to strong states, such as Turkey, Egypt, Algeria, and Iraq, committed to the modernization and economic development of their societies. Turkey in particular pioneered a unique Islamic path to modernity by pushing thoroughgoing westernization, a secular educational system, and centralized planning on the Soviet model while relegating Islam to the realm of private life.

By the 1960s, a number of these states, such as Egypt and Algeria, had governments proclaiming allegiance to an even more radical transformation of society under the banner of "Arab socialism." And in the 1970s, the oil-producing states in the Middle East took dramatic advantage of their political independence and sharply raised the price of this precious commodity, thus gaining a measure of revenge on the West for centuries of economic exploitation. Meanwhile, the competing claims of Palestinian and Israeli nationalisms made the Middle East a focal point of the Cold War, providing Arabs in particular and Muslims generally a focus for united action and feeling, a means of overcoming, at least occasionally, their many divisions.

The Roots of Islamic Renewal. But for growing numbers of Muslims, disappointments abounded. Despite numerous experiments, little overall economic improvement occurred; poverty and inequality deepened in many countries, especially in rapidly grow-ing cities; economic dependence on the West remained; and the Islamic world showed few signs of "catching up" in the race to moder-nity. Despite the successes of Arab national-ism, Arab armies had been repeatedly defeated by Israel, heavily supported by the United States. Imperialism, it seemed, had not been fully vanquished, and Israel was its Middle Eastern outpost. Furthermore, Western cul-ture continued to make inroads within the Islamic world. Secular courts and educational systems proliferated; unaccompanied women, immodestly dressed, appeared on city streets; Western-style movie theaters sprang up; oil wealth generated materialism; and political leaders paid only lip service to Islam. All this and more made many people sympathize with the cry of the early twentieth-century Indian Muslim writer Muhammad Iqbal:

> Turk, Persian, Arab
> Intoxicated with Europe
> And in the throat of each
> the fish-hook of Europe.[11]

In response to these disappointments, move-ments all across the Islamic world strongly asserted distinctly Muslim values in the face of modern materialism, secularism, and permis-siveness. They represented a sharp criticism of the West generally for its political, economic, and cultural imperialism; of communism for its atheism and materialism; and of women's "liberation" for its subversion of the proper relationship between the sexes. Known vari-ously as Islamic revival, renewal, renaissance, or awakening, these movements saw the deep-ening problems of the Islamic world as a direct consequence of departing from the original principles of the faith and from the practices es-tablished by Muhammad in the seventh century

CE. The solution therefore lay in returning to those principles and putting them into practice throughout society and in political life as well as in personal behavior. Islam, after all, embraced all of life with no distinction between sacred and secular, between the mosque and the state.

Such movements of renewal had occurred periodically throughout Islamic history. But for most of the twentieth century, revivalist Islam was a minor theme in an Islamic world dominated by the more secular concerns of nationalism, socialism, and economic devel-opment. But since the 1970s, it became a pow-erful current in Middle Eastern political and cultural life. Governments committed to the Islamization of public life came to power in Libya, Iran, Sudan, northern Nigeria, and Af-ghanistan. Elsewhere, growing movements of Islamic awakening challenged existing govern-ments in Egypt, Pakistan, Indonesia, and even Turkey. In 1992 in Algeria, a revivalist party called the Islamic Salvation Front seemed poised to assume power through democratic elections, a threat that provoked the military to cancel the elections and assume power it-self. Islamic groups responded with an armed insurrection that killed thousands.

Islamic Renewal in Practice: The Case of Iran. The Iranian Revolution of 1979 gave Islamic revivalism its first major international exposure. Its leader, the Ayatollah Khomeini, articulated clearly the values and outlook of Islamic revival:

> Islam is the religion of those who struggle for truth and justice, of those who clamor for liberty and independence. It is the school of those who fight against colo-nialism . . .
>
> The homeland of Islam, one and indi-visible, was broken up by the doings of the imperialists and despotic and ambi-tious leaders. . . . And when the Ottoman

Empire struggled to achieve Islamic unity, it was opposed by a united front of Russian, English, Austrian and other imperialist powers which split it up among themselves.

Moslems have no alternative, if they wish to correct the political balance of society, and force those in power to conform to the laws and principles of Islam, to an armed holy war against profane governments . . .

What do you understand of the harmony between social life and religious principles? And more important, just what is the social life we are talking about? Is it those hotbeds of immorality called theatres, cinemas, dancing, and music? Is it the promiscuous presence in the streets of lusting young men and women with arms, chests, and thighs bared? Is it the ludicrous wearing of a hat like the Europeans or the imitation of their habit of wine drinking?. . . Let these shameful practices come to an end, so that the dawn of a new life may break!

Islam has precepts for everything that concerns man and society. . . . There is no subject upon which Islam has not expressed its judgment.[12]

After overthrowing the secularizing, corrupt, and American-supported regime of the shah of Iran, Khomeini established the Islamic Republic of Iran. The government has been called a mixture of theocratic, authoritarian, and democratic elements. The ayatollah was supreme leader over a body of religious leaders called the Council of Guardians. This council was directed to oversee the elected parliament and president. In practice, religious leaders replaced secular bureaucrats, and the goals of Islamic fundamentalists directed policy. The 97 percent of the population who were Muslim were to abide by a reading of Islamic law that required women to be veiled, the sexes separated in schools and mosques, and a ban on alcohol consumption. Members of minority religions—Jews, Christians, and Zoroastrians—were to be administered by their own religious communities. Since 2009, the president has weathered opposition and protests with the aid of an elite military unit called the Islamic Revolutionary Guard Corps, which has become the nation's most powerful political, social, and economic institution.

Islamic Assertion on a Global Stage. Most Islamic activists attempted to further their cause peacefully through political means, religious education, providing social services for the poor, and changing their personal behavior. But some Islamic activists turned to violence in the form of assassinations, suicide bombings, and rebellions. The primary target of this violence has been the secularizing leadership of Islamic states. The leader of the group that assassinated President Anwar Sadat of Egypt in 1981 explained,

> Fighting the near enemy is more important than fighting the distant enemy. . . . There can be no doubt that the first battlefield of jihad is the extirpation of these infidel leaders and their replacement by a perfect Islamic order. From this will come release.[13]

Of course, Western interests were attacked as well. The Iranian Revolution held dozens of Americans hostage for a year following their seizure of power. Well-organized Muslim militants brought the struggle to the citadel of Western power in the destruction of the World Trade Center in New York City in September 2001, an action that prompted American wars against Afghanistan in 2001–2002 and Iraq in 2003. By the beginning of the twenty-first century, for growing numbers of people in the

West, the threat of militant Islam had replaced that of communism.

The possibility of a more secular and liberal turn appeared in the "Arab spring" of 2011 when young, middle-class, and religious protesters joined in the streets and public squares of Tunisia and Egypt, successfully bringing down autocratic regimes. The demand for popular government, jobs, and an end to corruption spread throughout the Middle East, with mixed success but a vision of a very different future.

Successes, Failures, and Fissures

Other regions of the Third World likewise asserted themselves on the global stage in various ways. China in particular and East Asia in general experienced remarkable economic growth in the final quarter of the twentieth century and became major players in the international marketplace. Africa, on the other hand, entered the global arena largely as a consequence of its deepening problems and failures: economic disasters, famine, the AIDS epidemic, genocide in Rwanda in 1994, and many cases of political instability and disintegration. Latin America was the site of the Western Hemisphere's only communist regime (Cuba), and its alliance with the Soviet Union gave rise to the Cold War's most threatening moment during the missile crisis of 1962. Massive indebtedness to Western banks in many Latin American countries triggered a major international financial crisis in the early 1980s. Large-scale migration from the Third World to the West occasioned considerable cultural conflict as Algerians went to France, West Indians to Britain, Yugoslavs to Germany, and Mexicans to the United States—all in search of a better life.

But too many differences separated Third World countries for them to act as a single

force. Did a huge and economically booming China have much in common with a small, impoverished, and conflicted Sierra Leone? What did an oil-rich conservative Islamic monarchy such as Saudi Arabia share with a war-torn communist Vietnam? Beyond these obvious differences lay often intractable and bloody conflicts between Third World countries. India and Pakistan, both armed with nuclear weapons, fought several wars since their independence from Great Britain in 1947 and faced off over the disputed territory of Kashmir. Iran and Iraq, neighboring Muslim states, fought a terrible war in the 1980s, costing perhaps a million lives. Nor did a common commitment to communism prevent war between China and Vietnam or between Vietnam and Cambodia. The genocidal suppression of the Tutsi people of Rwanda in 1994 set in motion bitter conflicts among the many states of central Africa. Any unity to which the Third World once aspired proved enormously difficult to achieve in practice.

The Collapse of Communism

A final realignment of the last turbulent century lay in the collapse of communism, a remarkable event in itself made even more so by the unexpectedness, rapidity, and peacefulness with which it occurred. Within a few years, a major source of inspiration, horror, and global conflict in the world of the twentieth century had largely vanished.

Three Routes to the End of Communism

The Soviet Union. The chief event in this process—but not the first—was the disintegration of the Soviet Union as a country along with its state-run economy, its Communist

Party, and its ideology, as Mikhail Gorbachev's efforts to reform the Soviet system badly backfired and led to its collapse in 1991. That event marked the disappearance of the world's largest state, one that had been central to Eurasian political life, and it generated new instabilities in many places along the borderlands of the former Soviet Union. It also signaled the end of the great global rift of the Cold War that had shaped so much of the twentieth century. And because communism had become so identified with socialism in the popular imagination of so many, the fall of the Soviet Union seemed to bring at least a temporary closure to a 150-year ideological debate about capitalism and socialism as distinct and rival systems.

Eastern Europe. In 1989, two years before the Soviet Union disintegrated, the communist regimes of eastern Europe were swept away by popular upheavals and by the unwillingness of their Soviet sponsors to rescue them. These revolutions marked the demise of the Soviet empire in eastern Europe and the end of the division of Europe between East and West. Germany was subsequently reunified, and a number of the eastern European states actually joined the Western military alliance of NATO.

China. A further component of the collapse of communism occurred in China, beginning in the late 1970s. While communism disintegrated from within in the Soviet Union and was overturned by popular rebellion in eastern Europe, in China it was largely abandoned as an economic practice in favor of private farming, attractive terms for foreign investment, and a much-expanded role for the market, even while maintaining Communist Party control of political life. In the process, China emerged as an economic giant and a major political force in East Asia and beyond.

Taken together, these three routes to the end of communism represent a remarkable conclusion to one of the twentieth century's most ambitious experiments and deepest conflicts. How should we explain it?

Explaining the Soviet Collapse

In the case of the Soviet Union, the core failure was economic. The country's rigid centralized economy, despite impressive earlier successes, could not keep pace with more dynamic Western economies, especially as the information age required flexibility and innovation rather than simply replicating existing technologies. Soviet citizens able to travel abroad were often stunned at the availability of consumer goods in the West compared to the paltry choices in their own state-run stores. The burden of very heavy military spending, intended to catch up and keep up with American power during the Cold War, further sapped the Soviet economy. A sharp decline in Soviet economic growth in the 1970s and 1980s shocked and embarrassed Soviet leaders and finally stimulated a serious effort at reform, reducing the role of the state and introducing elements of the free market. But those reforms, under the leadership of Mikhail Gorbachev in the late 1980s, made a bad situation worse as state planning mechanisms were dismantled before a functioning market system had emerged. As the Soviet economy contracted, millions experienced new hardships in the form of widespread shortages, mounting inflation, and the threat of unemployment.

Furthermore, Gorbachev's reform program also featured semidemocratic elections for a new parliament and a range of new freedoms for newspapers, magazines, and intellectuals generally. The result was an avalanche of political organizing, historical revelations, exposures of corruption and privilege, and new novels, plays, poems, and films, all of this

Figure 11.5 This sign in the Moscow airport in 1988 reflected the growing economic integration of the world, including its communist countries. It was a process that many Soviet democrats welcomed and many supporters of communism despised. *Photo courtesy of Robert Strayer.*

devoured by a public long starved of such opportunities. These new freedoms unleashed a torrent of public discussion that both revealed the long alienation of many people from the communist regime and deepened the gulf between them. The shock of "therapy by truth" comes through in this excerpt from an essay by Soviet writer Alexander Tsipko:

> No people in the history of mankind was ever enslaved by myths as our people was in the 20th century. We had thought that we had tied our lives to a great truth, only to realize that we entrusted ourselves to an intellectual fantasy which could never be realized. We thought we were pioneers leading the rest of mankind to . . . freedom and spiritual blessing, but realized that our way is the road to nowhere. We thought that building communism in the USSR was the greatest deed of our people, but we were purposefully engaging in self-destruction. We thought that capitalism was a sick old man sentenced to death, but it turned out that capitalism was healthy, powerful. . . . We thought that we were surrounded by people with the same ideals, grateful to us for saving them from capitalist slavery . . . but it

turned out that our friends and neighbors were only waiting for a chance to return to their old lives. We thought that our national industry, organized like one big factory . . . was the ultimate achievement of human wisdom, but it all turned out to be an economic absurdity which enslaved the economic and spiritual energies of . . . Russia.[14]

The new freedoms also opened the door to large-scale public protest—by workers stunned by new economic insecurities, by champions of democracy who despised the corrupt and authoritarian Soviet system, and by non-Russian nationalities who saw an opportunity to escape from their long domination by Russians. Furthermore, many among the Soviet elite readily abandoned communism as widespread opportunities for personal enrichment became available in the rapid and largely corrupt privatization of state enterprises. These combined pressures led to the dramatic collapse of the entire Soviet system in 1991, following a failed attempt by conservative forces to roll back Gorbachev's reforms. While the Soviet collapse had deep roots, there was little sign of it in 1985 when Gorbachev came to power. In that sense, it was less the product of the country's many diseases than of the treatment that the doctor prescribed.

The Chinese Difference

As in the Soviet Union, economic problems, plus the immense disruptions of the Cultural Revolution, brought communist reformers to power in China after the death of Mao Zedong in 1976. Led by Deng Xiaoping, the reform process unfolded quite differently than in the Soviet Union. The most dramatic Chinese reforms took place in the rural areas where collectivized agriculture rapidly gave way to individual family farms and a great increase in agricultural production that raised rural living standards substantially. Nothing of the kind occurred in the Soviet Union. But in dealing with state-owned industrial enterprises in the cities, Deng moved much more gradually than Gorbachev, maintaining overall state control while slowly introducing market prices. China also opened itself to the world economy far more successfully than the Soviet Union, welcoming foreign investment in "special enterprise zones" along the coast. Rural industry likewise flourished in a unique form called "township and village enterprises," owned and managed jointly by local governments, private entrepreneurs, and various collective groups.

These reforms, which increased in the decades after 1979, amounted to an abandonment of communist economic policies and the introduction of a largely capitalist or market economy, all of this, amazingly, under the direction of the Chinese Communist Party. Furthermore, and in sharp contrast to the economic disaster of the Soviet Union, these reforms were remarkably successful, generating the world's most rapid economic growth

and raising the living standards of millions of Chinese people.

China's reform process also differed from that of the Soviet Union in its refusal to accompany its economic changes with Soviet-style political and cultural freedoms. When demands for such freedoms erupted in demonstrations in central Beijing's Tiananmen Square in 1989, they were harshly and decisively suppressed. Reflecting memories of the chaotic Cultural Revolution, Deng Xiaoping declared,

> Talk about democracy in the abstract will inevitably lead to the unchecked spread of ultra-democracy and anarchism, to the complete disruption of political stability, and to the total failure of our modernization program. . . . China will once again be plunged into chaos, division, retrogression, and darkness.[15]

Such policies enabled China's Communist Party to maintain its monopoly on power even while presiding over what was rapidly becoming a market economy. And despite the presence of many minorities, the overwhelming numerical dominance of ethnic Chinese meant that China did not face the kind of intense nationalist demands that led to the unraveling of the Soviet Union.

The triumph of communism in China in 1949, the country's impressive military performance in the Korean War (1950–1953), its dramatic break with the Soviet Union in the 1960s, and its growing appeal in parts of the Third World had already given China an important international presence. Now in recent decades, its remarkable economic success made it a major player in the markets of the world and a great power to reckon with in East Asia and beyond. The rise of China to great-power status both reshaped the lives of the fifth of the world within its borders and reconfigured the contours of global power.

The End of the Cold War

The collapse of communism in eastern Europe and the Soviet Union and the abandonment of long-established communist economic policies in China brought an end to the Cold War. Russia and China actively sought foreign investment and entry into international capitalist bodies such as the World Trade Organization. Reductions in nuclear and other weapons followed. Although tensions remained between Russia, China, and the West, they now lacked the bitter ideological dimension and sense of immediate military threat that had characterized the Cold War. Throughout the world, communism had been discredited, and state management yielded to the market as the primary mechanism for generating the holy grail of economic growth. Having surmounted communist challenge, the supporters of capitalist democracies had reason to feel triumphant as the twenty-first century dawned.

But the communist challenge had long affected the development of capitalist societies. In the United States, for example, the Cold War drove an enormous expansion of the role of government as defense spending ballooned, it fostered increased funding for higher education as a means of keeping up in the arms race, and it contributed much to the growth of executive power in what was termed an "imperial presidency." It also made many Americans deeply suspicious of those with socialist sympathies or left-wing views and gave rise in the early 1950s to a wave of anticommunist purges.

The communist threat also stimulated Western reforms of capitalism, aimed at overcoming some of the insecurities, inequalities, and instabilities that unfettered market economies seemed to generate. During the twentieth century, state authorities in capitalist societies learned how to use their taxing and spending policies and adjustments in the supply of money to moderate the ups and downs of their economies. They proved increasingly willing to regulate banks, stock markets, and factories to protect their citizens from earlier abuses. And they constructed various kinds of welfare measures—unemployment insurance, national health care programs, minimum-wage laws, and tax breaks for the poor—to provide a measure of social and economic security in the face of unpredictable market forces. The collapse of communism coincided with—and perhaps caused—a retreat from these state welfare policies in many countries, but the triumphant capitalism of the twentieth century's end was quite different from that of its beginning.

Conclusion: Something New; Something Old

From the perspective of 1900, who would have predicted that established European states would exhaust themselves in two bitter wars within 50 years, that Europe's empires would come apart by the 1960s, that the Islamic world would reassert its values so dramatically, or that the United States would emerge as the leading power of the twentieth century's second half? Who could have foreseen the revolutions that brought down ancient regimes in Russia and China or the global division of the Cold War? Who could have realistically anticipated trips to the moon, artificial satellites circling the earth, or the instantaneous communications of the late twentieth century?

And yet, at least in hindsight, these changes had roots in earlier patterns and periods of world history. The world wars reflected the centuries-long inability of European states to re-create the kind of unity that had characterized the Roman Empire long ago. Twentieth-century communism represented an effort, even if misunderstood, to apply the ideas of Karl Marx and European socialists of the preceding century. Islamic revivalism drew on vivid memories of Islamic centrality in the Afro-Eurasian world for 1,000 years and on equally vivid memories of 300 years of Western imperialism in the Middle East. The struggles for independence and the emergence of new nations in Africa and Asia paralleled an earlier process in the Americas.

Recognizing the new in the context of the persistent is the challenge not only of historians but also, more important, of citizens, whether they are comfortable with what is or are searching for what might be.

Suggested Readings

Betts, Raymond. *Decolonization*. London: Routledge, 1998. A short account of the struggles for independence in Asia and Africa and the end of European empires.

Chatterjee, Choi, et al. *The 20th Century: A Retrospective*. Boulder, CO: Westview Press, 2002. A thematic rather than a region-by-region examination of recent world history.

Esposito, John. *The Islamic Threat: Myth or Reality*. New York: Oxford University Press, 1992. A concise account of Islam in the twentieth century, with a focus on its revivalist wing.

Kershaw, Ian. *The Nazi Dictatorship*. New York: Oxford University Press, 2000. A survey and assessment of conflicting interpretations of the Nazi phenomenon.

LaFeber, Walter. *America, Russia, and the Cold War, 1945–2000*. New York: Longman, 2002. A global account of the Cold War, emphasizing its impact on American life.

Read, Christopher. *The Making and Breaking of the Soviet System*. New York: Palgrave, 2001. An up-to-date examination of the rise and fall of the Soviet Union.

Spence, Jonathan. *Mao Zedong*. New York: Penguin, 1999. A brief biography of China's revolutionary leader.

Tuchman, Barbara. *The Guns of August*. New York: Macmillan, 1962. A popular and riveting account of the origins of World War I.

Notes

1. The term comes from Barbara Tuchman, *The Proud Tower* (New York: Ballantine Books, 1996).

2. Maurice Hindus, *Red Bread* (Bloomington: Indiana University Press, 1988), 1.

3. Quoted in Sheila Fitzpatrick, *Stalin's Peasants* (New York: Oxford University Press, 1994), 316.

4. Quoted in Stephen Kotkin, *Magnetic Mountain: Stalinism as a Civilization* (Berkeley: University of California Press, 1995), 221–22.

5. *Life*, February 17, 1941.

6. Ronald Steel, *Pax Americana* (New York: Viking Press, 1970), 254.

7. See Robert McNamara, *In Retrospect* (New York: Random House, 1995).

8. Quoted in Ralph B. Levering, *The Cold War, 1945–1987* (Arlington Heights, IL: Harlan Davidson, 1988), 105.

9. Robert Malley, "The Third Worldist Moment," *Current History*, November 1999, 359–69.

10. David Ranson, "The Dictatorship of Debt," *New Internationalist*, May 1999, 1–4.

11. Quoted in Francis Robinson, *Atlas of the Islamic World since 1500* (New York: Facts on File, 1982), 163.

12. *Sayings of Ayatollah Khomeini* (New York: Bantam Books, 1980), 3–29.

13. Quoted in Bernard Lewis, *What Went Wrong? Western Impact and Middle Eastern Response* (Oxford: Oxford University Press, 2002), 107–8.

14. From *Novy Mir*, 4 (1990): 173–204. Cited in Alexander Dallin and Gail Lapidus, eds., *The Soviet System from Crisis to Collapse* (Boulder, CO: Westview Press, 1995), 283–84.

15. Deng Xiaoping, "The Necessity of Upholding the Four Cardinal Principles in the Drive for the Four Modernizations," in *Major Documents of the People's Republic of China* (Beijing: Foreign Language Press, 1991), 54.

12

Beneath the Surface of
Globalization and Modernity
The Past Century

Communism and Women
Western Feminism
Women's Movements in the
    Third World
Feminism on a Global Scale
Conclusion: Coming Together and
    Growing Apart

BENEATH THE great public events of the past century—wars, revolutions, the end of empires, the collapse of communism, and changes in the balance of power—lay a set of related global processes that influenced those events and affected the lives of virtually everyone on the planet. Population growth, industrial development, environmental deterioration, globalization, and the worldwide spread of modern science, the English language, feminism, democracy, and nationalism—all of these less visible or more slowly developing processes shaped the world of the past century just as much as the more dramatic surface events of public life and with perhaps more lasting impact.

More of Us: Population Growth in the Past Century

For starters, world population quadrupled from 1.6 billion in 1900 to 6.2 billion in 2000. This rate of increase was unprecedented, peaking in the late 1960s at 2.1 percent per year. Since then, global population has increased as a slower rate (about 1.2 percent yearly since 1990). At this rate, UN specialists expect global population to reach 10 billion but then slow down further to replacement level and stabilize in the next 200 years. Why was there such a rapid increase? And why is it now abating?

A Demographic Transition

A graph of human population would show a line meandering at a steady low level from the urban revolution until the seventeenth century, at which point the graph would climb at almost a 90-degree angle up the page. Only very recently has that spike begun to slow down. The reason for that spike around 1700 was the beginning of a radical decline in death rates (the percentage of people who died in any one year). The cause of declining deaths was due to the improved nutrition of newly imported American crops like corn and potatoes and scientific and technological breakthroughs in sanitation, medicine, and immunization. These changes were initially felt in the richer industrializing countries but gradually extended to European colonies and developing countries in the nineteenth and twentieth centuries.

In India, for example, an annual mortality rate of about 50 per 1,000 people in 1900 dropped to 15.3 in 1970. Public health measures, pushed by colonial governments, independent states, and international agencies, contributed much. Vaccinations, draining swamps, the use of pesticides, wider availability of sulfa drugs and penicillin, and health education promoting the germ theory of disease—all of this brought down death rates throughout the world. One of the most successful efforts occurred in communist China. Life expectancy was perhaps 30 years when the revolution triumphed in 1949, but it had grown to over 70 years by 2000 through the use of "barefoot doctors" to bring basic health care to the masses and massive nationwide campaigns to promote cleanliness and better hygiene.

The crucial impact of lower death rates was not so much that old folks lived longer. There were always some who lived into their nineties. Life expectancy rose dramatically because more women survived child birth and more infants grew to be adults. In traditional societies, high birthrates compensated for high death rates. Children were old-age insurance policies as well as necessary helpers and breadwinners. With high death rates, a mother might have 10 children to ensure that a few would survive. Suddenly, in family after family, from 1700 to 1900, more children survived long enough to have their own families. New crops, expanded farmlands, and advanced technologies helped the process continue.

The custom of having lots of children lasted beyond the period it was necessary to balance high death rates. Eventually, as families grew in size, parents realized that they did not need so many children. Governments also felt population pressure as a disruptive force. In cities and in societies that sent children to schools, the young ones became extra mouths to feed. In societies that offered social security, they became less essential.

By the end of the twentieth century, global population growth began to moderate as birthrates also dropped. This transition had occurred earlier in the more urbanized industrial countries, where birth control measures were widely available, educated women were pursuing careers, and large families were economically burdensome. As the world urbanized, such logic began to take hold in developing countries as well, assisted by vigorous family planning programs in many places.

Consequences

Variations and Redistributions. The population explosion of the twentieth century was highly uneven. Its most intense effects were felt in developing countries after 1950. For the preceding century and a half, the most rapid growth had occurred in the rich countries; now the poorer regions of the world took the lead. Asia, Africa, and Latin America gained at the expense of Europe and Russia. Thus, behind the struggles for national independence, the Chinese Revolution, and Islamic renewal movements lay the surging populations of Third World regions.

Enough to Eat? While population growth put great pressure on rural areas of the world, it did not lead to global food shortages and famines of the kind predicted by some observers in the 1950s. Food production on a world level more than kept up with population growth, in part because of "green revolution" technologies, such as high-yielding seeds and chemical fertilizers. But famines there were, such as those in China and Russia following collectivization and in Africa in the 1970s and 1980s. These were the result of poverty or government policies that emphasized food exports instead of local food production.

To the Cities. Population growth contributed to rural misery in many places. Popular upheavals of the twentieth century—the Mexican Revolution, the Chinese Revolution, and rebellions in Peru, Kenya, Zimbabwe, and Chiapas—testified to that misery. So too did the massive urbanization in developing countries everywhere as rural people flocked to what they believed to be better opportunities in the cities. By the end of the century, close to half of the world's population were urban residents, another startling reversal of older patterns, and many of the largest and most rapidly growing cities were in the global South: Mexico City, Bombay (Mumbai), São Paulo, Shanghai, Lagos, Calcutta, and Buenos Aires. The population history of Egypt provides a telling example. In 1897, Egypt had a population of 9.6 million, of which about 9 percent lived in Cairo. A century later, Egypt had grown sixfold to 59 million, but Cairo had grown 14-fold to about 13 million people, or 22 percent of the population. These were social changes of revolutionary dimensions.

In Europe and the United States, modern population growth and urbanization were accompanied by industrial development, providing urban jobs, even if poorly paid, for newcomers to the cities. This was less evident in Third World countries, where urban migration greatly outpaced the growth of modern industry. Third World cities displayed wealthy enclaves surrounded by slums. These cities were marked by massive unemployment, wholly inadequate housing, and little or no sewage facilities. Nonetheless, as limited as cities were, they attracted more jobs, investment, medical and educational facilities, and a wider range of opportunities than the country. The rural poor kept coming.

On the Move. Changing patterns of population growth also altered the flow of migrants around the world. In the nineteenth century, rapidly growing Europe sent huge numbers to the Americas, Australia, New Zealand, and South Africa. That flow largely stopped by the 1920s. After World War II, European emigration was replaced by a massive movement of people from Asia and Latin America, the new high-growth rate regions of the world. Pakistanis, Indians, and West Indians moved to England and the United States; Algerians and West Africans to France; and Filipinos, Koreans, and Latin Americans to the United States. Chinese continued long-established patterns of migration to Southeast Asia and beyond. Many of these migrants found themselves living in poverty, limited to the least desirable jobs, and facing various forms of racial

and cultural prejudice. Family members left behind also felt the pain of immigration, as reflected in this poem by a young Moroccan wife whose husband left for work in Europe in the 1970s:

> Germany, Belgium, France
> and Netherlands
> Where are you situated?
> Where are you?
> Where can I find you?
> I have never seen your countries, I do
>   not
> speak your language.
> I have heard it said that you are beautiful,
> I have heard it said that you are clean.
> I am afraid, afraid that my love forgets
> me in your paradise.
> I ask you to save him for me.
> One day after our wedding he left,
> with his suitcase in his hand, his eyes
>   looking ahead.
> You must not say that he is bad or
>   aggressive;
> I have seen his tears, deep in his heart,
>   when he went away.
> He looked at me with the eyes of a child;
> He gave me his small empty hand and
>   asked me:
> "What should I do?"
> I could not utter a word; my heart bled
>   for him . . .
> With you he stays one year, with me just
>   one month,
> To you he gives his health and sweat,
> To me he only comes to recuperate.
> Then he leaves again to work for you, to
>   beautify
> you as a bride, each day anew.
> And I, I wait; I am like a flower that
> withers, more each day . . .
> I ask you: give him back to me.[1]

Young and Old. Changing relationships between birthrates and death rates substantially transformed the age structure of human societies although in quite different ways. In industrialized countries, slowing birthrates (in some cases just at or below replacement levels), coupled with extended life expectancies, were creating aging populations by the end of the twentieth century. Such changes produced conflicts between generations as a growing and politically influential older population demanded medical services and retirement benefits that a smaller cohort of younger workers found it difficult to support. Struggles in the United States over Medicare and Social Security payments illustrated such conflicts.

On the whole, however, the twentieth century was an "age of the young"[2] as high birthrates in Third World regions pushed the median age of world population by 1970 to less than 22 years. This has meant tremendous problems for developing countries in attempting to provide schools, jobs, and medical care to their youthful populations. It has also contributed to political volatility in some areas and to the creation of a youth culture of global dimensions.

Debates and Controversies

Too Many People? Global population growth not only changed social life and the demographic balance among various regions of the world but also triggered fierce intellectual debate and policy disputes. One of the most contentious involved the question of "overpopulation." Was the world generating too many people? In the 1960s and early 1970s, an influential study called "The Limits of Growth" and Paul Erlich's *The Population Bomb* argued that the world's resource base was inadequate to sustain the rapidly growing population and that without sharp curbs on

further growth, impoverishment, malnutrition, famine, and global disaster awaited. Such studies prompted a variety of responses. Some economists countered that population growth actually encouraged economic growth rather than threatening it. Did not Europe and the United States, after all, industrialize during a period of rapid population growth? For others, there was a racial dimension to arguments for limiting population growth, for was it not primarily white people urging darker people to have fewer children? Mao Zedong and other leaders in developing countries for a time viewed birth control programs as a Western device to curtail the weight of Third World countries in the global arena. Still others noted that it was the enormous consumer appetites of the wealthy minority rather than the basic needs of the poor majority that threatened the health of the planet. And official Catholic policy objected to any artificial restraint of procreation on religious grounds.

Controlling Population Growth. Despite these debates, world opinion by the 1980s had largely swung to the view that limiting population growth was necessary. But how was this to be done? In all the industrialized countries, birthrates declined sharply as average income rose, education and employment opportunities for women increased, and raising a large number of children became a serious economic burden. Thus, by 1983, 12 European countries had achieved zero population growth, and several other developed nations (the United States, the Soviet Union, and Japan) had growth rates of less than 1 percent per year. This experience suggested to some that the most effective route to population control lay in modern development, with a particular focus on education and jobs for women.

But growing numbers of developing countries determined that they could not wait for

Figure 12.1   China has undertaken one of the world's most vigorous efforts at population control, urging one-child families, as this poster suggests.
Keren Su/Getty Images.

development to run its course and that more deliberate and planned efforts to reduce births were necessary. By the 1990s, the vast majority of the world's governments supported some kind of family planning. China's "one-child family" program has been the most far reaching of these efforts. By combining massive public education, easy availability of birth control devices, a system of economic incentives and punishments, and political intrusion into the most personal areas of life, China reduced its population growth rate to about 1.4 percent per year by the 1980s. Sri Lanka, Cuba, Costa Rica, Mexico, Brazil, Indonesia, and parts of India have also brought down birthrates through active family planning programs coupled with social and economic reforms. By the beginning of the twenty-first century, the world seemed poised for a historic change in favor of small families and experts began to predict eventual stabilization although at much higher levels.

These efforts at deliberately limiting population growth occasioned a great deal of conflict and controversy. In many places, they ran up against deeply ingrained cultural values favoring large families. A coercive sterilization program in India in the 1970s stimulated violent protests and the defeat of the governing party in elections of 1977. China's aggressive efforts to limit births has been much criticized for forcing women to undergo abortions for unauthorized pregnancies and for its unintended outcome of encouraging the disposal of unwanted girl babies so that couples could try again for a much-desired boy. Political pressures in the United States have pushed policymakers to deny American funding for family planning programs that involve abortion. And conflict at the more intimate level of family life also surfaced in Latin America and elsewhere when women sometimes hid birth control pills from their disapproving husbands. The echoes of the population explosion were heard in boardrooms, staterooms, and bedrooms around the world.

Economic Globalization

Economic growth has been even more explosive than population growth in the past

100 years. While world population has quadrupled, world economic production has increased 20 times.[3] Whether we use measures of economic output (like the gross domestic product of the world's countries) or trade density (like shipping tonnage) or the speed of economic transactions (since the age of the telegraph), economic growth not only has increased much faster than population growth but has increased at an increasingly faster rate. Most of the economic growth of the past 100 years has occurred in the past 50 years—the period in which population growth began to slow. So it is hardly population growth that accounts for economic growth. Higher production, distribution, and standard of living has been a result of improving technologies and immensely greater world trade, communication, and movement: the process of economic globalization.

An Industrializing World

The twentieth century saw the extension of industrial society well beyond those few places that experienced it in the nineteenth. Driven by rapid advances in science and technology, global industrialization underwrote the massive increase in human population, liberated many millions of people from ancient drudgeries, lengthened life spans by decades, and cut infant mortality sharply. But it also contributed enormously to pollution of all kinds as coal and oil were burned in enormous quantities to fuel cars, factories, and homes, particularly in the wealthier parts of the world. Historian John McNeill calculated that the twentieth century used more energy than the previous 100 centuries combined.[4] Furthermore, the expectation of continuous and rapid economic growth, unknown for most of human history, became deeply embedded in both popular and official

thinking throughout the world. Capitalist, communist, and developing countries alike pushed economic growth to the top of their national agendas as the legitimacy—and sometimes the survival—of their governments came to depend ever more heavily on economic performance.

Soviet Industrialization. The Soviet Union under communist rule experienced the first major breakthrough in twentieth-century industrialization. Building on the modest industrial development of tsarist Russia, Soviet authorities, under Stalin's leadership in the 1930s, developed a unique pattern of industrialization. Unlike Western countries, which had relied largely on the market and private enterprise, the Soviets created the first modern command economy based on state ownership and central planning. Treating the country's economy as a whole, a series of Five-Year Plans established overall goals and determined what items should be produced, in what quantities, and at what price. It was an enormous undertaking, made even more so as Stalin forced the pace of industrial growth by increasing the production targets and then urging factory managers to exceed even these high goals. The first Five-Year Plan, he demanded, had to be completed in four. Furthermore, Soviet industrialization took place largely in isolation from the rest of the world economy. Some engineers, skilled workers, and current technologies were imported from the West, but for the most part it was Soviet workers, capital, resources, and management that generated the extremely rapid economic growth that put the Soviet Union by 1948 in second place in world manufacturing output behind only the United States.

Distinctive labor policies also marked Soviet industrialization. Women were mobilized for factory work far more extensively than in the West although without much of a reduction of their domestic responsibilities. Millions of prisoners—Stalin's "enemies of the revolution"—were also conscripted from the widespread network of labor camps in a uniquely Soviet version of modern slavery or forced labor, which contributed much to mining, construction, and industrial projects in the remote reaches of the country. While the Soviet system clearly exploited its factory working class through low wages and harsh working conditions, it also celebrated urban workers as the leading group in the new social-ist society and increasingly supported them with access to education, guaranteed work, medical care, housing, pensions, and leisure opportunities.

Industrialization in European Offshoots. A further extension of industrial society took place in several countries dominated by Euro-pean immigrants—Israel, Canada, Australia, New Zealand, and South Africa. All of them used Western capital investment to develop manufacturing facilities while continuing to rely on the export of food or minerals. And each of them generated high standards of liv-ing, at least for their European populations.

Newly Industrialized Countries. Perhaps the most remarkable and surprising newcom-ers to industrialization have been the Pacific Rim countries, led by South Korea and Taiwan but including the city-states of Hong Kong and Singapore as well. Historians and other scholars have struggled to explain why these East Asian societies experienced such rapid economic growth beginning in the 1960s such that by the 1990s they had scrambled into the "club" of industrial nations. Some have emphasized their Confucian cultural tradi-tions, derived from contact with China, which emphasized deference to authority, collec-tive loyalties, and hard work. The influence of an economically successful Japan was also

important. In Korea, for example, Japanese-style group exercises frequently began the workday, and solemn ceremonies marked the launching of a new tanker or the shipment of a fleet of cars. Others have pointed to a set of favorable international circumstances. South Korea and Taiwan became bastions of an American-sponsored anticommunism in East Asia following World War II and benefited from a great deal of U.S. aid. Furthermore, a booming world economy from the mid-1950s to the mid-1970s greatly assisted an industri-alization strategy focusing on exports. Strong authoritarian governments provided social stability, low wages, and overall planning in capitalist economies that were more controlled than those of the West.

Whatever explains East Asian growth after World War II, it became clear that industrial-ization was certainly not limited to societies shaped by European culture. As the century ended, India joined China as major centers of industrial growth in the global South. Major industrial sectors likewise took shape in Tur-key, Brazil, Mexico, Indonesia, Thailand, and elsewhere, demonstrating the compatibility of many cultural traditions with modern eco-nomic life.

From Divergence to Convergence. From its beginnings in the eighteenth century, the industrial revolution benefited the industrial-izers in the West at the expense of much of the rest of the world. The fortunes of rich and poor diverged. This imbalance began to cor-rect in the late nineteenth century as Japan joined the club of industrial powers. By the late twentieth century, the East Asian economies of Taiwan and South Korea had also joined in. But China and India, together representing more than a third of humanity, had continued to diverge further by growing at a much slower pace than the West.

During the first decade of the twenty-first century, that process of divergence reversed. Like their East Asian predecessors, the two giants of Asia began to grow faster than the West. In the wake of a financial crisis in the United States and Europe in 2008, Western economies grew at a rate that barely kept up with population, while China and India marched ahead at more than 10 percent a year. Between 2005 and 2010, the economies of the emerging world grew at 41 percent. China grew 70 percent, and India grew 55 percent. In the same period, the advanced economies had grown only 5 percent. World economies were beginning to converge. The average output per person in China was still only about a fifth of what it was in the United States, but it had been a twentieth in 1990.[5] For much of the world (though still not in Africa or the Middle East), the great divergence of the past 200 years was coming to an end.

A Densely Connected World

Global industrialization vastly accelerated the economic integration of the earth's many peoples. Developments in transportation and communication technology tightened global networks. The telephone, radio, television, cassette tape recorders, movies, satellite-based communication, and most recently the Internet allowed ideas, social practices, and vast sums of money to circulate as never before. Furthermore, automobiles, passenger airplanes, superfreighters, and containerized shipping allowed far more people and goods to move far more rapidly and at less cost than ever before.

At the heart of economic globalization has been an enormous increase in international trade, in the flow of capital around the world, and in the activities of huge firms known as multinational or transnational corporations. These processes fluctuated considerably in the past century. A spurt of economic globalization, associated with the extension of European empires into Asia and Africa in the nineteenth century, dropped off sharply after 1914 as World War I and the Great Depression played havoc with international trade. In the aftermath of World War II, however, the pace of globalization picked up dramatically. Between 1947 and the early 1990s, the value of world trade increased from $57 billion to some $6 trillion annually. By the beginning of the twenty-first century, modern telecommunications made it possible to transfer capital instantly almost anywhere in

Figure 12.2 While computer technology has come to Nigeria and other parts of the developing world, enormous differences in access to this technology have added a "digital divide" to other forms of economic inequality on a global level. *AP Photo/George Osodi.*

the world.[6] Transnational corporations with facilities in many nations accounted for a great deal of this economic activity.[7] An IBM personal computer, advertised as "made in the USA," actually had 70 percent of its components manufactured abroad, while an equal 70 percent of "Japanese-made" televisions were manufactured outside of Japan. These new global corporations, with enormous financial resources, moved production sites and the jobs they generated to wherever wages and taxes were lowest and environmental regulations the least stringent. Treating the globe as a single market, they paid little attention to the impact of their activities on local communities and environments.

All this has meant a substantial shift in power from nation-states to world markets. Alongside national governments, other organizations with little loyalty to particular nations have assumed powerful roles—international banks, trade associations, producers groups such as the Organization of Petroleum Exporting Countries, world news services like CNN, and especially transnational corporations. Competition for "market share" among these huge global firms became at least as important as political and military rivalry among sovereign states. International economic organizations such as the International Monetary Fund (IMF), the World Bank, and the World Trade Organization (WTO)—all of them dominated by the wealthier industrial countries—came to play a major role in the global economy.

Germs could also travel the tightening links of the global network. A worldwide flu epidemic in 1918 killed in excess of 20 million people, more than twice the number who perished in World War I. Later in the century, AIDS was the most potent global epidemic, claiming victims on every continent

and producing more than 25 million deaths between 1981 and 2008. Man-made diseases of the natural environment such as air pollution, acid rain, global warming, and thinning of the ozone layer likewise respected no national boundaries.

A Deeply Divided World

Global industrialization and modern economic development have occurred in a highly uneven fashion. We have mentioned the economic divergence that industrialization created between the rich countries of the world—mostly in western Europe, North America, and Japan—and the poor countries of Asia, Africa, the Middle East, and Latin America. In the roughly two centuries since Europe's industrial revolution began, the economic divergence of the world's societies has been remarkable and rapid. In 1800, the average income of the richest country in the world was about two times that of the poorest; in 1900, about nine times; and in 2000, 60 times or more. During the twentieth century, the wealthiest countries, representing about 25 percent of the world's population, increased their per capita incomes sixfold, while the poorest 25 percent of the world's population increased their incomes only threefold. Thus, the gap between them grew rapidly.[8] This novel division between the rich and poor countries became one of the most prominent features of the past century, shaping the life opportunities of virtually everyone as well as structuring the political, military, and economic relationships among the nations of the world. We are only recently seeing signs that this process is beginning to reverse.

Progress for the Poor. Despite this global divide, the economies of many poor countries grew substantially, improving the lives of many millions during the course of the

Table 12.1 Global Inequality and Global Progress

	A. Wealth and Health across the World, 1994		
Region	Per Capita Gross National Product, 1994 (U.S.$)	Life Expectancy at Birth (years)	Infant Mortality Rate (per 1,000 live births)
Less developed	1,090	64	68
Africa	660	55	91
Asia	2,150	65	62
Latin America	3,290	69	43
More developed	18,130	74	9

Source: Alfonso Gonzalez and Jim Norwine, eds., *The New Third World* (Boulder, CO: Westview Press, 1998), 77.

	B. Poverty in the Third World, 1992		
Region	Population (millions)	Poor (millions)	Poverty Rate (%)
Sub-Saharan Africa	521	277	53.2
Middle East and North Africa	297	75	25.3
Latin America and the Caribbean	434	180	41.5
South Asia	1,186	509	42.9
India	880	350	39.8
East Asia	1,728	273	15.8
China	1,187	105	8.8
All Third World	4,166	1,314	31.5

Source: John Isbister, *Promises Not Kept* (Kumarian Press, 1995), 17.

Note: Poverty in part B of the table refers to "absolute poverty," "a standard of living . . . that brings with it life-threatening malnutrition and disease" (Isbister, *Promises Not Kept*, 17).

What indication of progress do these tables provide? And what kinds of inequality do they disclose? How might you explain the variations which are evident in this data?

twentieth century, especially the last half. "More progress has been made in reducing global poverty in the past five decades than in the previous five centuries," declared the UN Human Development Report in 1997. "Since 1960, the world's developing countries have cut child death rates in half, reduced malnutrition by a third, and raised school enrollments by a quarter."[9] Even in the poorest countries, average life expectancy increased by a decade or more since 1950. Some newly industrialized countries and some wealthy oil-producing countries have achieved standards of living comparable to those of the West. China's revolutionary redistribution of land in the 1940s and 1950s, coupled with its booming internationalized economy in the 1990s and first decade of the twenty-first century, lifted tens of millions of Chinese out of wretched poverty. In India since independence from colonial rule, grain production more than kept up with rapid population growth, and widespread famines largely disappeared. Since opening the economy to international markets in 1990, India has begun to regain its earlier place in world trade. By 2010, the Indian middle class numbered 300 million (a quarter of the country) and was increasing at 5 percent a year.

Failures and Instabilities. These achievements are far from the whole story, however. Africa in particular has experienced a dismal record of economic development, especially since the mid-1960s, far worse than other developing regions of the world. It has been

plagued by massive poverty, recurring famines, endemic political instability, and the
most severe outbreaks of the AIDS epidemic.
In the 1980s, per capita income in Africa,
Latin America, and the Middle East actually contracted, and living standards dropped
sharply for many people in these areas. Surging population growth in many places pushed
the number of severely impoverished and often malnourished people to well over 1 billion
people by the 1990s, close to 20 percent of the
world's population. In addition, civil war and
ethnic hostilities displaced and made homeless
tens of millions, most of them in the poorest
countries. The bitter conflict in Rwanda between the Hutu and Tutsi people made refugees of about 2.5 million people, fully a third of
the country's population. In the former Soviet
Union after the collapse of communism, a
dramatic economic contraction eroded health
care, cut male life expectancy sharply, and impoverished millions. Finally, the instabilities
of a globalized economy became apparent in
a series of acute financial crises in Mexico, Argentina, Thailand, Indonesia, and South Korea
in the late 1990s. Foreign investors quickly

pulled large amounts of capital out of these
relatively prosperous developing countries,
causing severe economic contraction, many
bankruptcies, and loss of income for millions.
When a debt crisis centered in the United
States and Europe shook global markets in
2008, the impact of the "Great Recession" that
followed was less severe in developing countries like Brazil, Russia, India, and China.

Internal Inequalities. Economic inequalities within countries grew along with the
increasing divide between rich and poor
countries. Even in the poor countries of the
Third World, some classes of people became
wealthier: large-scale farmers producing for
the international market, urban businessmen, government officials, educated professionals, and some traditional elites. In some
African countries, such people were sarcasti-
cally referred to as the *"waBenzi"* because of
the Mercedes-Benz cars in which they were
chauffeured about. Far more numerous than
these highly privileged groups were masses
of impoverished people. The hundreds of
millions who were attracted to the growing
urban centers of developing countries found

Figure 12.3 Living conditions in a favela, or shantytown, such as this one in Rio de Janeiro, are light-years away from the life of the wealthy in Brazil, among the world's most unequal societies. *Colin Paterson/Getty Images.*

themselves working sporadically or for very low wages and living in shantytowns. Millions more tried to survive on small pieces of land in rural areas, where their lives were tied ever more tightly to the fluctuations of the international economy. This was "modern poverty" occurring in societies where billboards, radios, television, newspapers, and the extravagant lifestyle of both foreign and local elites made it clear that such conditions were not the fate of everyone. More than ever before, twentieth-century poverty was relational, as growing numbers of poor people were able to compare their lives with those of the wealthy.

Debating a Mixed Record. Why have some countries prospered more than others? Historians disagree. Some point to various historical legacies, such as the slave trade and colonial rule, or to very different geographical conditions, such as rainfall, soil fertility, or natural resources, as a way of explaining sharp differences in economic performance. Others have emphasized the importance of state policies, suggesting that individual countries have the ability to shape their own destiny by pursuing a wise course of action. What constitutes wise policies is of course hotly contested. Should poorer countries seek foreign capital and involve themselves actively in international trade, or should they try to develop on the basis of their own resources, at least somewhat insulated from the world economy? Should governments actively regulate their economies and societies to foster greater equality and to protect the poor, or will economic growth, benefiting everyone in the long run, flourish better in a "free market" environment? Defenders of the global spread of markets argue that free trade has allowed the poorer countries to gain access to the technology, capital, and markets of the more wealthy. Globalization's many critics counter that it has exacerbated

the world's inequalities, heightened economic instability, impoverished millions, and subordinated the world's poor majority to the interests of its wealthy minority.

Alternative Globalizations. While debates about globalization continued, protests against the inequities of the global economic order increased. Intellectuals in the West and in developing countries alike articulated a powerful critique of the prevailing world system, focusing often on the policies of the World Bank and the IMF and on the activities of transnational corporations and the U.S. government. From the 1960s on, church leaders in Latin America, for example, developed a "theology of liberation," finding in Christian teachings the basis for action on behalf of the world's poor. They and many others argued that there were viable alternatives to a purely market-driven approach to global development and advocated policies more sensitive to workers' rights, to the environment, to corporate responsibility, to protecting the poor, and to global equality generally.[10]

Beyond small groups of intellectuals, protesters in many countries (Indonesia, Argentina, Zambia, for example) took to the streets when their governments, acting under pressure from the IMF, cut food and fuel subsidies on which the poor depended. Opposition to the North American Free Trade Agreement was among the grievances that prompted a major peasant revolt among the Mayan people of southern Mexico in 1994. Believing that the agreement would require Mexico to privatize all communally owned land, to reduce spending on schools and health care, and to cut loans to farmers producing for the internal market, the Zapatista rebels called it a "death sentence for the indigenous people of Mexico" and were harshly critical of a Mexican government that supported it. In 1999, protests in the streets of Seattle by trade unionists, religious and environmental activists, and student groups disrupted a meeting of the WTO while calling for major reforms in the relationship between wealthy and poor countries. The election of left-leaning presidents in several Latin American countries such as Venezuela, (1998), Brazil (2002), Ecuador (2002), Bolivia (2005), and Guatemala (2006) provided further evidence of resistance to unfettered market globalization.

A Diminished World

In the long run of human history, the past century will perhaps be remembered above all else as the time when humankind began to impinge dramatically on the natural environment of the planet. Human activity had altered the environment since the days of the first hunters and early farmers, sometimes with disastrous results. The collapse of early civilizations in places as far apart as Mesopotamia, the Indus River valley, and Mesoamerica owed something to the pressures of local overpopulation, deforestation, erosion, and other environmental stresses. But in the twentieth century, global modernity, combining unprecedented population growth and even more massive economic growth, encroached on—and diminished—the natural environment far more extensively than had any other form of human culture. According to environmental historian John McNeill, humankind has undertaken in the twentieth century "a gigantic uncontrolled experiment on the earth" and "has begun to play dice with the planet, without knowing all the rules of the game."[11]

Defining the Environmental Impact. Indications of this human assault on the natural order are not hard to find. Air pollution, due largely to the burning of fossil fuels, increased enormously in the growing urban areas and

industrial complexes of the world. McNeill estimated that air pollution in the twentieth century killed 25 million to 40 million people, largely through various respiratory diseases and cancer, to say nothing of chronic illness for millions more. This is a death toll approaching that of World War II. The buildup of carbon dioxide in the atmosphere began to generate "global warming" and threatened dramatic climate change in the twenty-first century, while the release of chlorofluorocarbons demonstrably thinned the ozone layer, allowing more ultraviolet radiation to reach the earth's surface, where it has caused in excess of a million additional cases of skin cancer.

Industrialization and urbanization polluted the world's waters perhaps even more than its air, creating "easily humanity's most costly pollution problem" and generating deaths in the tens of millions. The sacred Ganges River in India, where millions bathed to cleanse their souls, became heavily polluted as a growing population along its banks deposited their untreated sewage in its waters. The Rhine River in Germany was polluted by industrial rather than human waste to the point that the fish population virtually disappeared in some places. Human use of water grew ninefold in the twentieth century and involved the construction of millions of dams, wells, canals, and pipelines; an enormous increase in irrigated land; and the draining of large wetland areas. Massive Soviet irrigation for cotton production virtually destroyed the Aral Sea, diminishing its size by two-thirds and tripling its salinity by the 1990s. Conflict over water resources occasioned serious international tensions between Egypt and Sudan, between the United States and Mexico, between Israel and neighboring Arab states, and elsewhere. Globalization too has contributed to the problem of pollution. Zebra mussels,

Table 12.2   An Environmental Snapshot of the Twentieth Century

Item	Increase Factor, 1890s–1990s
World population	4
Urban proportion of world population	3
Total world urban population	13
World economy	14
Industrial output	40
Energy use	16
Coal production	7
Air pollution	~5
Carbon dioxide emissions	17
Sulfur dioxide emissions	13
Lead emissions to the atmosphere	~8
Water use	9
Marine fish catch	35
Cattle population	4
Pig population	9
Horse population	1.1
Blue whale population (Southern Ocean only)	0.0025 (99.75% decrease)
Fin whale population	0.03 (97% decrease)
Bird and mammal species	0.99 (1% decrease)
Irrigated area	5
Forest area	0.8 (20% decrease)
Cropland	2

Source: John McNeill, *Something New under the Sun* (New York: Norton, 2000), 360–61.

These figures illustrate the vast acceleration of human economic activity in the twentieth century and something of its impact on the world and its various living inhabitants.

small marine bivalves native to the Caspian Sea region, were transported to the North American Great Lakes and rivers by means of water ballast in transoceanic ships. There, they reproduced rapidly, depriving native species of essential nutrients, clogging water intake pipes, and coating tourist beaches with their sharp shells. In 2010, Asian carp that could devour all native fish began to enter into the Great Lakes despite all efforts to block them.

Human impact on the environment has not been all negative, of course. What technological ingenuity polluted it sometimes also remedied, as in the case of the smog cities of London and Pittsburgh and the cleanup of the American Great Lakes and the Rhine River in Europe. Dramatic improvements in public health and medical science enabled at least a partial human victory over certain microbes that had long plagued humankind. Smallpox was eliminated in the 1970s, and major campaigns put a dent in pneumonia, diphtheria, cholera, typhus, tuberculosis, and other disease-causing pathogens. Degenerative diseases, such as cancer and heart disease, replaced infectious diseases as the leading cause of human death in many places.

Some effects have been neutral or varied. At the level of plant life, forests and grasslands substantially contracted, while pasture and croplands doubled in area and deserts expanded. Some animals, useful to humankind, expanded their numbers dramatically—cattle, sheep, goats, pigs, and poultry—with corresponding pressures on the lands they occupied. But human breeding of favored plants and animals often meant the reduction of other species. Many others were driven to the edge of extinction. By 2000, some 24 percent of mammal species were defined as "threatened," 11 percent of bird species, 4 percent of reptile species, 3 percent of amphibian and fish species, and 10 percent of the higher-plant species.[12] If accelerating trends of species extinction continue, some experts predict that 30 to 50 percent of all terrestrial species could vanish within a century or two. Should that occur, it would rank as a "sixth extinction," similar in magnitude to five others on the planet since life began but, of course, the only one caused by the deliberate activity of a single species, *Homo sapiens.*

Environmentalism. A growing awareness of the human impact on the planet gave rise to the modern environmental movement, which began in the 1960s.[13] That movement began with the publication in 1962 of *Silent Spring* by the American biologist Rachel Carson, highlighting the chemical contamination of the environment. A number of other books followed, many of which were widely read and provided an intellectual foundation for a growing popular movement in the wealthy industrialized countries. Millions of people joined environmental or conservationist groups; the Green Party in Germany attracted substantial public support; petitions, marches, and teach-ins pushed environmental issues onto the political agenda in many countries and often resulted in legislative action to address environmental problems; non-Russian peoples within the Soviet Union cited disastrous environmental policies directed from Moscow as one reason for their desire to exit the Soviet Union; numerous civic and religious groups of ordinary people embraced environmentalism as an overriding moral and practical concern; and many people began to think about their private lifestyle choices in light of environmental perspectives. Thus, modern environmentalism took shape

first in the already developed countries where the ecological impact of industrial economies was most apparent and where wealth, leisure time, and nostalgia for a simpler past gave energy to the movement.

But environmentalist movements also emerged in a number of developing countries around issues of forests, dams, pollution, and biodiversity. Often they grew out of grassroots activism by threatened local communities. The Chikpo, or tree-hugging, movement in India was one of many intended to preserve the resources of local communities against the claims of loggers or other large commercial or government enterprises. Brazilian forest dwellers in the Amazon basin likewise took direct action to protect their environment from ranchers seeking to clear the land for pasture. Kenya's Green Belt Movement, largely a project of village women, planted millions of trees on denuded land in an effort to counter the encroachment of the desert.

Environmentalism has challenged many of the central assumptions of industrial society: that bigger and more is always better, that endless consumption is the route to a satisfying life, that the earth's resources are limitless, and that humankind stands above and apart from the rest of creation. The central issues have been those of sustainability and restraint. Does the "modern way of life"—reflected in the most developed industrial regions of Europe, Japan, and the United States—represent a viable future for the rest of the world's people or even for the minority who currently enjoy its benefits? Can a capitalist system of private profit protect the most public of spaces—the planet?

Since some environmental problems so clearly transcend national boundaries, environmentalism has also challenged the autonomy of sovereign nation-states. Attempts to work out broad international agreements on environmental questions have inevitably come up against sharp differences between the rich and poor nations. Developing countries have sometimes felt that environmental protection measures advocated by the industrialized nations would limit their own prospects for growth while locking in the current advantages of the rich countries, which have been responsible for most of the world's environmental problems. Some people in developing countries resent the West's emphasis on population control in poor countries, when each new child born in North America or Europe both consumes far more of the earth's resources and contributes much more to its pollution than a child born in Asia or Africa. They have also felt that the cost of expensive environmental protection measures should be borne disproportionately by the rich countries. The Montreal Protocol of 1987, designed to halt the depletion of the ozone layer and ratified by 184 countries, was successful in part because the richer states agreed to establish a fund of $240 million to assist developing countries to make the transition away from harmful chlorofluorocarbons. In negotiations surrounding the global warming treaty, a central issue has been which countries should limit their production of greenhouse gases and by how much. In early 2001, the United States backed out of preliminary agreements in part on the grounds that the developing countries had been largely excluded from the requirement to cut their carbon dioxide emissions. The environmental movement has thus confronted global industrialization with profound questions about both sustainability and social justice.

Political Globalization

Alongside economic globalization, two important political trends have shaped the world's many societies in the twentieth century—nationalism and democracy. Both of them, like industrialization, had their origins in the West but have been appropriated all across the world and have lost much of their earlier association with European culture.

The National Idea: Triumphant and Challenged?

The idea of the nation—the belief that some group of people share a unique and common culture, history, and territory and deserve to govern themselves independently—has become so common as to appear wholly natural and deeply rooted in human experience. Yet at the beginning of the twentieth century, much of the world's population still lived in empires, governed by foreigners. For many people, it was not the "foreignness" of their rulers that was so objectionable but their oppressive policies. Political loyalties were still primarily local, rooted in the village or clan, and where larger loyalties came into play, they were mostly religious, such as the identification with the Islamic world as a whole. Mass identification with an abstraction called the "nation" was limited largely to the West, and even there it was little more than a century old. But during the twentieth century, nationalism became a primary political loyalty in much of the rest of the world, and the sovereign nation-state became the universal political unit into which human communities were organized.

Anticolonial Nationalism. The first stage in this triumph of the nation lay in the dissolution of those empires, which had for centuries governed much of humankind. This process, described in Chapter 11, brought to an end the powerful Austrian, Ottoman, and Russian empires after World War I; the German and Japanese empires during World War II; the

Afro-Asian empires of the western European powers after the war; and the Soviet empire in the early 1990s. Here lies one of the great ironies of modern world history. While the competitive nationalisms of European states had given energy to Western empire building in the nineteenth century, the ideology of nationalism also undermined those empires by providing the leaders of anticolonial movements a set of Western-derived ideas with which to protest their domination by foreigners. Nationalism, it turned out, was a double-edged sword, both building and destroying empires.

Nationalism and Communism. Twentieth-century nationalism revealed its power not only in the end of old empires but also in confounding some of the fondest hopes of the communist movement. Blaming war and national rivalries on capitalist competition, Karl Marx and other socialist thinkers assumed that socialism would diminish narrow and antagonistic nationalisms and that revolution would lead to an international socialist commonwealth. Class solidarity among workers of every country would triumph over national loyalties, for "workers have no fatherland." Within the newly formed Soviet Union, the leadership fully expected that diverse national loyalties such as Ukrainian, Georgian, and even Russian would merge into a new soviet and socialist identity. But no such thing occurred. Soviet policies in fact inadvertently promoted national or ethnic consciousness by encouraging the use of native languages in schools and newspapers, by creating ethnically based "republics" within the Soviet Union, and by fostering Russian migration into non-Russian areas, where the newcomers were widely resented. Under Stalin's leadership, the Soviet Union drew increasingly on its Russian past. Amid the flames of World War II, it was the call to defend mother Russia rather than

the revolution and socialism that produced such heroic resistance. But defining the Soviet Union as a Russian project provoked a defensive nationalism among various non-Russian peoples, and when Gorbachev's reforms allowed this to be expressed, the Soviet Union dissolved.

Elsewhere in the communist world, nationalism also found expression. In the eastern European communist countries, many people deeply resented Russian or Soviet domination, and in Hungary (1956), Czechoslovakia (1968), and Poland (1981), massive expressions of discontent led to direct Soviet intervention or the clear threat of it. Even more startling, the two communist giants, the Soviet Union and China, had become seriously estranged by the 1960s as territorial disputes, ideological differences, and rivalry for world communist leadership drove them almost to the point of war. China and Vietnam, both communist countries, did in fact go to war briefly in 1979. National loyalties clearly trumped communist loyalties in the twentieth century.

The Failure of Alternatives. Other political alternatives to territorial nationalism also failed. Efforts to bring Egypt and Syria together in a United Arab Republic lasted only several years (1958–1961). Similar attempts to join various African countries in larger federations likewise were unable to overcome the entrenched interests of separate nation-states. The territorially divided nation of Pakistan, founded in 1947 expressly as a Muslim state, broke apart 25 years later when East Pakistan became Bangladesh. The independent nation-state thus seemed to triumph over empire, communist internationalism, and larger cultural or religious identities alike. Strangely enough, it was in Europe, tempered by the horrific excesses of nationalism in the early twentieth century, that efforts toward economic and political integration gained the most ground with the formation of the European Union, a European parliament, and a European currency.

Challenges to the National Idea: Globalization. But the triumph of the nation was far from complete, for during the twentieth century, nation-states were also undermined, eroded, and challenged. One such challenge derived from the multiple processes of economic globalization. Developing countries, many of them small and poor, found their national sovereignty challenged by the global economy in which they had to operate. They were often in a weak bargaining position when negotiating with transnational firms with resources greater than that of entire countries. Furthermore, fluctuating world market prices and rapidly changing terms of trade dramatically affected the fortunes of these countries, many of which relied on only a few exports. President Julius Nyerere of Tanzania estimated that his country had to export 38 tons of sisal (a fiber used for making rope) to buy a seven-ton truck in 1972, but in 1982 the same truck required the sale of 134 tons of sisal, as the price of that fiber dropped precipitously in relation to the price of trucks. By the 1980s and 1990s, many developing countries, heavily in debt, were compelled to accept strict monitoring of their economic policies by the World Bank or the IMF in order to qualify for further desperately needed loans. They had to abandon tariff protection for their industries, remove restrictions on foreign investment, focus heavily on exports, cut government spending on social services, and privatize state enterprises.[14] For many, the grand dreams of national independence, nurtured during the struggle against colonial rule, were punctured by an increasing dependence on international market forces over which

they had little control. Political pressures and periodic interventions by the great powers further limited the national sovereignty of developing countries.

Even industrialized countries found their national life increasingly penetrated by the global economy. When oil-producing countries sharply raised the price of that essential commodity in the 1970s, a postwar economic boom sputtered into a global recession and Americans waited in long lines for gasoline. By the 1990s, many Americans felt that the global economy hurt U.S. workers, small businesses, and local communities as competition from low-wage countries in Latin America and Asia pulled jobs abroad. Mounting protests against the regulations of the WTO included the argument that American national sovereignty was endangered by a too-willing acceptance of economic globalization.

Challenges to the National Idea: Ethnic Separatism. If globalization posed a challenge to the nation from outside, separatism in the form of movements seeking greater autonomy or independence for particular regions or peoples did so from the inside. Separatism resulted in the dismemberment of a number of nation-states in the second half of the twentieth century: India, Pakistan, Ethiopia, Yugoslavia, Czechoslovakia, and, of course, the Soviet Union, which dissolved into 15 separate states in 1991. It also contributed to civil wars or the collapse of central governments in many others: Nigeria, Iraq, Lebanon, Indonesia, Philippines, Sudan, Angola, Somalia, Rwanda, Sri Lanka, Burma, Mozambique, and Congo. Elsewhere, separatist or culturally based movements have troubled the political life of China, India, Great Britain, Spain, Canada, and the United States.

Ironically, this separatism, so threatening to existing nation-states, derived in part from the ambiguities of nationalism itself. The national idea after all had no clear answer to a fundamental question: Who precisely are the people that deserve an independent state? To what groups should self-determination apply? If the colonial territory of Nigeria in West Africa merited independence from Britain, why not the Igbo people, whose many millions inhabited its southeastern region? By the 1960s, they had come to see themselves as a separate people—a nation in the making—oppressed and discriminated against by the more numerous and culturally different northern Nigerians. Their demand for independence as the state of Biafra triggered a terrible civil war that cost several million lives in the 1960s before their military defeat and reintegration into a restructured Nigeria. Much the same logic applied to Tamils in Sri Lanka, Zulus in South Africa, Kurds in Iraq and Turkey, Welsh and Scots in Great Britain, French speakers in Canada, Croats in Yugoslavia, Tibetans in China, and many others. Thus, nationalism has cut several ways, providing a basis for unity within a state but also legitimating a proliferation of separatist movements in the name of self-determination.

The emergence of separatist movements had a wide range of causes. The disappearance of the common enemy of colonial rule or oppressive communist regimes allowed for the expression of ethnic, linguistic, religious and historical antagonisms within particular states. Rapid urbanization everywhere threw various peoples together in crowded and competitive settings, where their differences were magnified. Unequal levels of economic development within states often led to intense rivalries for economic resources and political representation. Elections were frequently contested in terms of ethnically based parties, and some political leaders were more than willing to

mobilize support on the basis of ethnic, linguistic, or religious identity. And the ideology of nationalism and "self-determination," which acquired global prestige in the twentieth century, legitimated claims for autonomy or independence. Furthermore, the very forces of globalization sometimes enabled separatist movements. Many of the new and sharply defined ethnic identities were propagated by the most modern of means—radio, tape cassettes, and Internet sites. The murderous effort to eliminate the Tutsi people of Rwanda in 1994, for example, was preceded by a carefully orchestrated campaign of hatred in local newspapers and on the radio. The complexities of the world economy offered at least the hope that even small breakaway states might find a niche in the global marketplace.

Challenges to the National Idea: World Government. A third challenge to the idea of nation-states with complete sovereignty lay in efforts to construct some form of global government able to maintain world peace and to contain the excesses of nationalism. Growing out of the devastation of World War I, the League of Nations (1919–1940) was the first such attempt, but its many weaknesses and the unwillingness of the United States to join the organization made it unable to prevent World War II. A more sustained effort in the form of the United Nations arose in 1945, supported by the victorious powers in that war. Dominated and often paralyzed by rival superpowers during the Cold War, the United Nations was unable to prevent the many conflicts of the century's second half. Nevertheless, it took the lead in eradicating smallpox, in providing relief and humanitarian assistance to refugees, and in addressing issues of children's health and welfare. Furthermore, its adoption of a Universal Declaration of Human Rights in 1948 registered a growing international consensus on a number of human rights issues, including slavery, torture, equality before the law, and the right to freedom of opinion, food, clothing, shelter, and medical care. Despite frequent violations of these rights, the UN Declaration established a standard by which the behavior of all nations could be measured. The organization also provided a forum in which Third World countries could articulate their concerns about decolonization and the inequalities of the world economy. Following the end of the Cold War, the United Nations became more actively involved in peacekeeping operations within rather than between severely divided nations, such as Cyprus, Yugoslavia, and Cambodia. By 1994, some 18 separate operations making use of 80,000 peacekeepers from 82 countries engaged the United Nations around the world. Whatever its limitations, the United Nations embodied a recognition that beyond individual states lay the interests of the world community as a whole.

Despite these challenges, the territorial nation-state has in most cases survived with some 200 of them structuring global political life at the beginning of the twenty-first century. But the triumph of the national idea in the twentieth century coincided with challenges to its dominance. Larger loyalties and networks, such as communist internationalism, regional groupings like the European Union or pan-Africanism, religious identities such as Islam, international organizations such as the United Nations, and the various processes of globalization—all these have countered the claims of the nation. So too have those smaller and often more compelling loyalties associated with ethnic, religious, or linguistic identity, such as being Igbo in Nigeria, Kurdish in Iraq, Muslim or Tibetan in China, or Basque in Spain. Together, these forces, operating both outside

and within particular countries, illustrate the fragility of nation-states despite their apparent universality and strength.

The Democratic Idea: Challenged and Triumphant?

The other global political trend of the twentieth century was democracy. Its promise was participation in the public life of nation-states through competitive elections involving ever-larger groups of people. Here, at least in theory, was an opportunity for ordinary people to shape their lives through a peaceful political process of selecting their own leaders and debating alternative policies. Based on the novel idea of the equality of citizens and their freedom to speak, write, and organize, it has meant limitations on the power of authoritarian states and traditional elites that had for centuries governed much of humankind.

Modern Democracy. While earlier forms of democracy had characterized many hunting and gathering, pastoral, or village-based agricultural societies, modern parliamentary democracy has been a recent phenomenon in world history, developing largely in the nineteenth century and limited to a small number of European and North American countries and to several British settler colonies, such as Australia, New Zealand, and South Africa. These early examples of modern democracy grew out of the ideas and practices of the European Enlightenment and the American and French revolutions and were associated with the growing influence of the "middle classes" in these modernizing societies. But they were limited democracies, and only very gradually and with much struggle did poor men, people of color, and women gain voting privileges. Not until 1945 were women in France granted the vote, while effective participation of African Americans in the United States came only in the mid-1960s and that of black Africans in South Africa in 1994.

Gains and Setbacks. Nonetheless, the progress of democracy by the early twentieth century and the victory of the most democratic countries in World War I persuaded many that democracy was the wave of the future, "a natural trend," as one observer put it.[15] But the 1920s, 1930s, and early 1940s witnessed instead the sharp contraction of democracy. In Italy, Germany, Spain, and much of eastern Europe, fascist or right-wing movements came to power in the chaos following World War I and the Great Depression and effectively eliminated the new, fragile, and often corrupt democracies. The military victories of the Nazis put an end to many others, such as those in Austria and Czechoslovakia. In Nazi thinking, democracy was associated with Germany's defeat in World War I, with the punitive Treaty of Versailles that ended the war, with political division and mediocrity in government, and with an emphasis on individualism that undermined a strong state. The triumph of communism in Russia following the revolution of 1917 likewise ended the modest democratic innovations that the tsar had recently and reluctantly established. To communists, Western-style parliamentary democracy was an illusion, benefiting only people of property while leaving the working classes and peasantry at their mercy. Nazi success in overcoming the terrible unemployment of the Great Depression in Germany and Soviet success in promoting rapid industrialization in the 1930s seemed to confirm the effectiveness of authoritarian states and to underline the weakness and fragility of the remaining democracies.

Democracy after World War II. The defeat of the Nazis and of Japanese imperialism in Asia provided an opening for a further wave of democratization following World War II. West Germany, Italy, and Japan joined or rejoined the ranks of victorious democracies. The prestige of democracy pushed Turkey, Greece, and much of Latin America in that direction as well. Furthermore, most of the colonies becoming independent after World War II—dozens of them in Africa alone—emerged, at least initially, with democratic institutions created by their departing European rulers and welcomed as a sign of equality and modernity by their new political leaders. Democratization, it seemed, was back on track.

Democracy in Decline. By the 1960s and 1970s, however, much of this democratic "progress" lay in tatters. Military takeovers in Turkey, Greece, South Korea, Indonesia, and many Latin American and African countries ended modest democratic experiments. When the army took power in the West African country of Ghana in 1966 and chased its once popular leader Kwame Nkrumah into exile, no one lifted a finger to defend the democratic system with which the country had come to independence only nine years earlier. In many places, democracy was discredited by its association with economic failure or with corruption and ethnic conflict. Military leaders claimed that only they had the discipline and resources to maintain order and ensure conditions for economic growth. Some intellectuals and political leaders in Asia and Africa argued that democracy was a Western import and a legacy of colonialism, unsuited for the needs of their developing societies. In culturally diverse nations, they claimed, it created conflict and disunity as political parties focused on particular ethnic or religious groups. And if Europeans had not begun their modernizing processes with democratic institutions, why should Asian or African countries be expected to do so? Strong states, unimpeded by the conflicting demands of democratic pressures, were necessary for the difficult transition to modern industrial societies. Finally, they argued that the individualism that underpinned Western democracy was at odds with the communal or collective values of their cultures.

The abandonment of democracy in much of the Third World led in many places to political systems even more repressive than colonial rule. Right-wing death squads, associated with conservative military governments, preyed on opposition groups in many Latin American countries. In much of Africa, massive corruption, harsh suppression of political opposition, sharp restrictions on a free press, and the enrichment of small elites seemed to betray the social promise of national liberation. The epitome of this pattern occurred in Zaire (the Congo), whose President Mobutu (1965–1997) reportedly accumulated a personal fortune in the several billions of dollars (enough to pay off his country's national debt), built himself 11 palaces, some connected by four-lane highways, and acquired a series of châteaus and estates throughout Europe.

National liberation movements leading to independence had been accompanied everywhere by the expectation of an end to oppression. While the racial oppression of colonial rule largely ended, allowing indigenous cultures to flourish, various forms of dictatorship and authoritarianism all too often restricted human freedom even more sharply. And much of this occurred with the encouragement of the Soviet Union and the United States, both of which eagerly supported dictators who took their side in the Cold War.

A major exception to this widespread abandonment of democracy in the Third World took shape in India following its independence in 1947. There, a Western-style democracy, including regular elections, multiple parties, civil liberties, and peaceful changes in government, turned India into the world's largest democratic state. The experience of that huge country suggested that democracy was not everywhere perceived as alien and that it could take root in non-Western societies.

A Resurgence of Democracy? The appeal of democracy has found further expression in the most recent wave of democratic experimentation, which, since the mid-1970s, has assumed global dimensions. Dozens of countries made a transition from highly authoritarian or military rule to multiparty systems with contested elections: Spain, Portugal, and Greece in southern Europe; most of Latin America; the Philippines, South Korea, Taiwan, and Indonesia in Asia; a number of African countries; and the former communist states of the Soviet Union and eastern Europe. In most cases, the process was relatively peaceful and was often initiated from within the old system itself under varying degrees of pressure from society.

What accounts for this revival of democracy? In many countries, economic growth, together with increasing levels of urbanization and education, created larger middle classes that sought a greater role in national life. Churches, students, and women's groups organized to demand democratic change as a means to a better life. In some Asian, African, and communist countries, ideas of human rights and democracy came increasingly to be seen as universal values, applicable to themselves, and no longer so uniquely associated with the West. The collapse of communism in the Soviet Union and of apartheid in South Africa, both of them opposed in the name of democracy, marked a failure of authoritarian politics and opened the way for democratic alternatives, while the end of the Cold War removed the incentive of the rival superpowers to support "their" dictators.

Figure 12.4 Enormous lines of voters waited to cast their ballots in South Africa's 1994 elections, the first in which Europeans and Africans voted together. Those elections marked an end to apartheid and an important element in the global resurgence of democracy in the late twentieth century. *AP Photo/Denis Farrell, file.*

The global "revolution of democracy" in the late twentieth and early twenty-first centuries put an end, at least temporarily, to any number of oppressive regimes and permitted millions of people to live in greater freedom. But how real are the changes, and how long will they last? Critics of the process have argued that much of democratic practice, even in the more established democracies, is a charade that cloaks the continuing interests of military, business, religious, or bureaucratic elites. And what happens when democratic elections bring to power those who are fundamentally opposed to continuing the democratic experiment? The experience of the past century suggests that democracy is no sure thing, that it ebbs and flows as circumstances change. Whether this most recent surge of democracy

will be more lasting and widespread than the others remains to be seen.

Cultural Globalization

If economic relationships and political institutions have been "globalized" in the past century, so too have many cultural patterns. Driven by the modern communications revolution, information, ideas, and impressions traveled rapidly, sometimes instantaneously, around the planet. People everywhere were more easily able to compare their own lives to what they learned from abroad. Such comparisons, often derived from shortwave radio broadcasts, led many Russians to realize what they were missing under Soviet communism and contributed much to the collapse of the Soviet Union. Political and cultural leaders of all kinds—Hitler, Roosevelt, Billy Graham, and Osama bin Laden—could now mobilize large numbers of people on behalf of their various causes.

Popular Culture / Global Culture

The most visible expression of cultural globalization lay in the worldwide spread of certain aspects of Western and particularly American culture. Fast food, blue jeans, and American music and movies assumed global dimensions. Basketball, an American game, became international, thanks largely to television. By the early 1990s, American films commanded almost 70 percent of the market in Europe, while McDonald's restaurants—some 20,000 of them in more than 100 countries—served 30 million customers a day.[16] Many intellectual critics decried the erosion of national cultures in an overwhelming tide of cultural imports.

Consumerism and advertising likewise took hold around the world, bringing status and temporary satisfaction to those who could afford to shop and frustration and envy to those who could not. For many millions of newly prosperous Chinese, awash in consumer goods following the reforms of the post-Maoist era, the restrained and sacrificial values of revolutionary socialism gave way to a self-serving and unabashed materialism. A popular slogan suggested that life in modern China required the "Eight Bigs": a color television, a refrigerator, a stereo, a camera, a motorcycle, a suite of furniture, a washing machine, and an electric fan. In addition, a man needed the "three highs" to attract a suitable wife: a high salary, an advanced education, and a height of more than five feet six inches. The pursuit of such a life was encouraged in the media by stories celebrating individual entrepreneurs

who took advantage of the new opportunities to become wealthy. Chinese writers and filmmakers, like their counterparts the world over, explored the tension between prosperity and mindless consumerism and asked penetrating questions about the loss of older values of simplicity, equality, family, and nature in the rush to achieve and to consume.

Other aspects of Western culture likewise spread widely, at least initially under colonial rule. French became a second language of many educated West Africans and Southeast Asians. Even more so, English assumed the role of an international language with perhaps 1.5 billion speakers by the end of the century, second only to Chinese and far more globally dispersed. Beyond these imperial languages, Spanish, Chinese, Arabic, and Russian also spread widely, even as many local languages died out. Of more than 1,000 Indian languages in Brazil in the nineteenth century, only 200 survived to the end of the twentieth century. In 1982, just 10 speakers of Achumawi survived in northern California.[17]

Christianity also spread widely in the past century, especially in sub-Saharan Africa, where it became "Africanized" in thousands of independent church movements that broke away from Western missionary "parent" churches. At the end of the twentieth century, Christianity seemed to be growing in China as well, where it had been subject to severe restrictions during Mao's lifetime. Some 82 million Chinese, about 7 percent of the population, professed some kind of Christian affiliation, most of them in "house churches" outside any official religious structure.[18] Catholicism, long dominant in Latin America, faced growing competition from evangelical Protestantism, which attracted some 20 percent of the population in Brazil and Chile by the 1990s.

Scientific ways of thinking and their technological applications represented a worldview—in some ways a new religion—that appealed to many people around the world. Such ideas bore the prestige of modernity and were widely assumed to lay behind the extraordinary success of European, American, and Japanese development. Antibiotics, high-yielding seeds, nuclear energy, the Internet, and advanced industrial techniques all became highly sought after everywhere, losing almost completely their identification with the places where they originated. International scientific meetings and publications proliferated, creating a world culture whose highly skilled practitioners viewed the world in quite similar ways, even if their political commitments differed sharply. All these people had to confront the relationship between their traditional cultures and religions and this newer scientific understanding of the world. Some African doctors, for example, sought to find common ground with traditional "medicine men," while others fiercely battled the "tyranny of superstition" that they found in the continent's "witch doctors."

Nor was cultural globalization always a one-way street. Islam came to have a place in black American culture and continued to grow rapidly in Africa, often in competition with Christianity. Buddhist meditation practices and retreat centers appealed to growing numbers of people in the West who were seeking a spiritual practice that they found lacking in mainstream Christian or Jewish culture. Restaurants featuring menus from Mexico, Thailand, India, China, and Ethiopia appeared around the world. West African rhythms found a place in American and British popular music and from there became an important element of world music. Widespread immigration from North Africa to France, from South Asia and the West Indies to Britain, and from Asia and Latin America to the United States enriched the cultures of the Western world even while generating new tensions.

Global Feminism

Among the most remarkable cultural developments of the past century were dramatic changes in the lives and the consciousness of women and in thinking about the role of women. Many millions of women all around the world joined the paid workforce; became literate; took part in communist revolutions, anticolonial movements, and democratic politics; achieved a new level of awareness about women's long subordination to men; and determined to do something about it. These changes, although highly uneven, incomplete, and frequently challenged, represent one of the most genuinely revolutionary dimensions of contemporary world history. They derived from a number of sources. Modern means of communication disseminated both Western and communist ideas about gender relations and the roles of women. So too did mass migration—from Europe to the Americas and from Asia, Africa, and Latin America to Europe and the United States more recently. Economic development and war drew women into new productive roles, such as working in munitions factories, and the spread of education afforded new opportunities and ideas to many. Novel and more widely available means of contraception—especially the birth control pill—opened new possibilities for sexual expression and separated it from reproduction, particularly for women in the West. The stimulus of other liberation movements—civil rights, antiwar, nationalist, and socialist—prompted women to act on their own issues. These deliberate efforts to address ancient inequalities between the sexes occurred on a far wider scale than the modest feminist movements of nineteenth-century Europe and America. The message of women's liberation, offered in many and conflicting variations, touched both on public life and on the most intimate private relationships of human society.

Communism and Women. It may surprise some to learn that the communists were actually in the forefront of the women's liberation movement of the past century. The Soviet Bolsheviks thought of women in terms of a few core ideas drawn from Marxist socialism: marriage should be a "free union" between consenting adults, woman attained freedom through work, housework should be socialized, and the family was an oppressive institution that would wither away. No sooner had the communists come to power in Russia than they issued a series of laws and decrees attempting to realize some of these goals. Women were to be equal to men in every legal way. They could vote and run for office. Women could marry and divorce at will. If married, they did not have to take the name of their husband. Abortion was legalized. More important, women were to be educated and drawn into the military and industrial workforce along with men.

But the idealism of the early years darkened under the shadow of civil war and economic collapse. Faced with declining population and social unrest, Stalin reset the country's priorities in the 1930s. A New Economic Policy returned some elements of capitalism. The state again favored the patriarch in property and alimony disputes. The marriage law of 1936 reversed some of the provisions of the earlier laws of 1918 and 1926. Divorce became more difficult. Abortion was no longer legal. Women were expected to maintain the home

and raise children without the support of their husbands or state social agencies.

The Chinese communist effort to emancipate women paralleled the Soviet. But with a Confucian patriarchal culture to overcome, the Chinese experiment is more astonishing. Marriage reform was one of the first priorities of the Chinese communists when they came to power in 1949. The Marriage Law of 1950 ended a number of what the communists saw as abuses of patriarchal society. Among these abuses were concubinage (by which men took secondary wives), child marriage, prohibited widow remarriage, and the unequal treatment of women regarding property and divorce. From 1950, women were to be equal to men legally and politically. After all, Mao Zedong said, "women hold up half the sky."

In fact, male resistance to women's equality proved to be as tough in China as it was in the Soviet Union. Except for Mao's wife, few women in China played any role in politics or government. As in the Soviet Union and much of the rest of the world, Chinese girls and women entered the workforce in vast numbers, but they were still expected to carry out housework and child rearing without the assistance of men.

Western Feminism. In contrast to the communist world, where the initiative for women's liberation came from party or state authorities, in the Western industrialized countries it bubbled up from a growing popular movement. This "second wave" of Western feminism exploded in the 1960s and 1970s, stimulated in part by the tension between a growing number of women in the workforce and prevailing cultural values urging them to stay at home. The women's movement found expression in many ways. Books such as Simone de Beauvoir's *The Second Sex* and widely read magazines such as *Ms* in the United States and *Emma* in Germany popularized feminist ideas. None were more influential than Betty Friedan's best-selling *The Feminine Mystique*, which laid the emotional and intellectual foundation for modern feminism, at least in the United States. "The problem," she wrote,

> lay buried, unspoken, for many years in the minds of American women. It was a strange stirring, a sense of dissatisfaction, a yearning that women suffered in the middle of the twentieth century in the United States. Each suburban wife struggled with it alone. As she made the beds, shopped for groceries, matched slipcover material, ate peanut butter sandwiches with her children, chauffeured Cub Scouts and Brownies, lay beside her husband at night—she was afraid to ask even of herself the silent question—"Is this all?"[19]

Organizations devoted to women's issues proliferated, ranging from local "consciousness-raising" groups to national bodies such as the National Organization for Women in the United States. Throughout North America and western Europe, feminists insistently raised issues about discrimination in employment and education, the legalization of abortion, violence against women, sexual harassment, lesbianism, equality in marriage, and much more. They also drew from and brought a feminist perspective to other social protests, such as civil rights, peace, and environmental movements.

Sometimes feminists operated within existing political parties and legislatures and at other times outside established channels in public demonstrations and street protests. In 1968, some American feminists provocatively challenged established values when they crowned a sheep as Miss America and disposed of bras, girdles, and false eyelashes in a "freedom trashcan." A few years later, French feminists laid a

Figure 12.5   This demonstration of French women illustrates the grassroots support for Western feminism. *Keystone-France/Getty Images.*

wreath to the "unknown wife of an unknown soldier" at the Arc de Triomphe in Paris while observing that "one man out of every two is a woman."[20] Such actions triggered a sharp backlash among those who felt that traditional family values and gender roles—and perhaps civilization itself—were under attack. The defeat of efforts by American feminists to include an equal rights amendment in the Constitution reflected this backlash.

Despite this opposition and much debate and controversy within feminist circles, the women's movement stimulated substantial change in Western life. Legislation to end harassment and discrimination on the basis of sex and to legalize abortion was enacted in many countries. Opportunities for women in higher education, the professions, and economic life generally broadened considerably. Shelters for abused women and rape crisis centers sprang up. Feminist perspectives penetrated academic life and scholarly research, and women's studies curricula surfaced in many universities. In personal life, millions of couples negotiated their marriages and raised their children differently because of the women's movement. Clearly sexual inequality persisted in the workplace, in political life, and in daily interactions among men and women. But a remarkable and quite widespread transformation of consciousness took place in the West during the past century, and the bundle of ideas that earlier defined women's proper sphere as domestic and subordinate had been sharply challenged.

Women's Movements in the Third World. Women's movements took shape as well in developing countries. But there they often enjoyed neither the state support that pushed a feminist agenda in the communist nations nor the relatively widespread popular support that Western feminists experienced in the 1960s and after. Their movements were much smaller and more elitist than those in North America and Europe. Furthermore, Third World feminists had to confront the charge that their ideas were imported from the West and were therefore illegitimate or at least tainted by association with European or American imperialism. While Western feminists could focus sharply on matters of gender inequality, those in the developing world could hardly escape matters of class, poverty, and the inequities of the world economy, for these issues clearly and directly affected women's lives. To some Third World feminists, Western concerns about nonsexist language, sexual freedom, and harassment at work seemed almost trivial compared to the daily struggles for survival endured by women in their countries.

Despite these obstacles, women in developing countries organized in various ways to address a wide range of concerns. Early in the century, it was issues of suffrage in Latin America and independence from colonial rule in Asia and Africa that drew women into political activism. Later, in many Third World countries, such as India, Nigeria, and Brazil, small groups of educated middle-class women in major cities organized marches, demonstrations, and conferences to highlight issues of violence against women, exploitation of female labor, health care, and education. In the early 1990s, such an organization in Morocco collected a million signatures on a petition to reform family law to ensure greater equality and protection for women. In Latin America and Africa, these groups were often associated with larger national movements pushing democratic reform. In Chile, Argentina, and elsewhere, mothers and grandmothers mobilized highly visible efforts to find relatives who had "disappeared" as a result of internal political repression. At the same time, local groups of lower-class women, sometimes rejecting any identification with feminism, organized around various practical economic issues, such as child care, high prices for food, wife beating, and union organizing.

Feminism on a Global Scale. By the final quarter of the twentieth century, feminism or the women's movement had clearly become an international phenomenon. A series of UN-sponsored conferences in Mexico, Denmark, Kenya, Egypt, and China brought women officials and activists together from around the world. There, they confronted a series of contentious issues: controversies between Western and Third World feminists; debates about abortion, homosexuality, and reproductive rights between conservative Islamic or Catholic countries and representatives of more secular nations; and differences between official women's groups and sometimes more radical nongovernmental organizations.

While dramatic or sweeping change in the condition of women's lives occurred nowhere, these conferences registered a remarkable change in global values. Gender equality had become an international norm and one element of political legitimacy throughout the world. Furthermore, women's perspectives came to inform other major international issues.[21] Women's rights, for example, were now viewed as human rights, making coercion, discrimination, and violence against women subject to international condemnation. Education and employment opportunities for women were now viewed as essential for population control, as they clearly induced lower birthrates. Development planning increasingly focused special attention on the needs of women, particularly in the rural areas, where they often controlled domestic food production.

All this created opposition, sometimes violent. Even governments committed to

women's rights were reluctant to make the sustained effort necessary to implement the agreements they signed. The Vatican led a coalition of conservative Catholic and Islamic governments to oppose international agreements on abortion, homosexuality, and reproductive rights, arguing that they threatened national and religious traditions. But like democracy and human rights generally, ideas about gender equality had lost some of their sharp identification with the West and became increasingly recognized as universal values.

Conclusion: Coming Together and Growing Apart

Patterns of historical development always seem clearer in retrospect than they do to participants at the time. So it is especially difficult to sum up the past century, for so much of our understanding of the past depends on what happens next—which, of course, is unknowable. This is particularly the case when we confront what is perhaps the grand issue of the century, the one question that brings together the separate stories told in this chapter and the previous one. It is the tension between global connections and global fragmentation. Has the human community been coming together or pulling apart in the past century?

On the one hand, the multiple processes of globalization continued earlier patterns and led toward an ever more densely connected world and converging human societies. Major elements of Western culture have spread around the world, while aspects of Asian culture—such as Buddhist religious practice, Chinese restaurants, and martial arts—have penetrated Western life. The sovereign nation-state has become the almost universal form of human political organization and loyalty.

Market economies have triumphed over command economies throughout the world. People everywhere have sought the benefits of industrialization and aspired toward greater social equality. The internationalization of capital, transportation, and communication networks, especially in the past half century, linked human societies together as never before. More and more people have come to understand the world as a single sphere where human and geographical divisions have ever less significance. This perception of global unity has taken strength from those remarkable pictures of a borderless Earth viewed from outer space and from the sure knowledge that pollution, global warming, epidemics, and nuclear war alike respect no boundaries and carry a profound threat to humankind as a whole.

But as the global network tightened, the past century witnessed the flourishing of new divisions, inequalities, and conflicts. The world wars, by far the most widespread and destructive conflicts in human experience, together with the Great Depression, demonstrated with a vengeance that steady progress toward an integrated world system was by no means inevitable. The disintegration of Europe's global empires created more than 100 new nations and spawned enduring conflicts such as those between Israelis and Arabs and India and Pakistan. The deep rift between the communist world and major capitalist states, as well as the North–South divide of the rich and poor nations, have structured global conflict for much of the century. The cultural assertions articulated by various "fundamentalisms"—Christian, Jewish, Hindu, and Muslim—together with countless ethnic or separatist movements have divided the human community in new and more sharply defined ways. Murderous hatreds and genocidal regimes have punctuated and disfigured the century in the Ottoman Empire, Nazi Germany, the Soviet Union, Cambodia, Yugoslavia, and Rwanda. The breakdown of government and reappearance of almost stateless societies in places like Somalia, Yemen, and Afghanistan have unleashed forces that threaten the stable and satisfied. The tension between these integrative and disintegrative dimensions of the modern world constitutes perhaps the most compelling issue of recent global history and the most pressing problem of the world to come.

For much of our human journey, we could go somewhere else. When conflicts arose or alternatives beckoned, our ancestors could pick up and start over. Fortunately, in their travels, they learned the value of learning from others. The advantages of cooperation, of living and working together, grew more obvious as they did it. Our journey has now taken us everywhere we can go. If we are to continue, we must do it together.

Suggested Readings

Bacci, Massimo Livi. *A Concise History of World Population: An Introduction to Population Processes.* London: Blackwell, 2001. One of the world's leading scholars on population history places the modern population explosion in a larger context.

Frieden, Jeffrey. *Global Capitalism: Its Fall and Rise in the Twentieth Century.* New York: Norton, 2006. A thoughtful and balanced history of economic globalization.

Gourevitch, Philip. *We Wish to Inform You That Tomorrow We Will Be Killed with Our Families: Stories from Rwanda.* New York: Picador USA, 1999. An effort to understand one of the most horrific ethnic conflicts of the twentieth century.

Guha, Ramachandra. *Environmentalism: A Global History*. New York: Longman, 2000. A world-historical account of the development of environmental movements in Western, communist, and Third World regions.

Hopkins, A. G. *Globalization in World History*. New York: Norton, 2002. An effort to cast the recent processes of globalization in a larger historical context, emphasizing the role of non-Western peoples.

Markoff, John. *Waves of Democracy*. Thousand Oaks, CA: Pine Forge Press, 1996. Traces the ups, downs, and transformations of democracy on a global basis in the twentieth century.

McNeill, J. R. *Something New under the Sun: An Environmental History of the Twentieth Century World*. New York: Norton, 2000. A prize-winning account of the human refashioning of the planet in the twentieth century.

Riley, James C. *Rising Life Expectancy: A Global History*. New York: Cambridge University Press, 2001. Explores a worldwide "health transition" that has resulted in longer lives all across the planet.

Smith, Bonnie, ed. *Global Feminisms: A Survey of Issues and Controversies*. London: Routledge, 2000. A series of essays by leading scholars that compares feminist movements and feminist thinking across the world.

Stiglitz, Joseph E. *Globalization and Its Discontents*. New York: Norton, 2003. An insider's account of the workings of the World Bank, the International Monetary Fund, and the World Trade Organization.

Notes

1. *Bulletin of the Committee of Moroccan Workers in Holland*, 1978, quoted in Hazel Johnson and Henry Bernstein, eds., *Third World Lives of Struggle* (London: Heinemann, 1982), 173–74.

2. Choi Chatterjee et al., *The Twentieth Century: A Retrospective* (Boulder, CO: Westview Press, 2002), 353.

3. International Monetary Fund, *World Economic Outlook* (May 2000), chap. 5, fig. 5.1, http://www.imf.org/external/pubs/ft/weo/2000/01/pdf/chapter5.pdf., based on Bradford J. DeLong, "Estimating World GDP, One Million B.C.–Present," http://econ161.berkeley.edu.

4. J. R. McNeill, *Something New under the Sun: An Environmental History of the Twentieth Century World* (New York: Norton, 2000), 15, 360–61.

5. Martin Wolf, "In the Grip of a Great Convergence," *Financial Times*, January 5, 2011, 9.

6. Robert Gilpin, *The Challenge of Global Capitalism* (Princeton, NJ: Princeton University Press, 2000), 20–23.

7. Susan Strange, *The Retreat of the State: The Diffusion of Power in the World Economy* (Cambridge: Cambridge University Press, 1996), 47.

8. Stephen D. Krasner, "Transforming International Regimes: What the Third World Wants and Why," *International Studies Quarterly* 25 (March 1981): 126; Nancy Birdsall, "Life Is Unfair: Inequality in the World," *Foreign Policy*, Summer 1998, 76–93; International Monetary Fund, *Globalization: Threat or Opportunity* (2001), http://www.imf.org/external/np/exr/ib/2000/041200.htm#III.

9. "A Decade to Eradicate Poverty: United Nations Development Programme," *Social Education* 61, no. 6 (October 1997): 316.

10. See, for example, Joseph E. Stiglitz, *Globalization and Its Discontents* (New York: Norton, 2002), and Jeff Faux, "The Global Alternative," *The American Prospect* 12, no. 12 (July 2–16, 2001): 15–18.

11. This section draws heavily on the concepts and data in McNeill, *Something New under the Sun*. The quotes are from pages 3 and 4.

12. *World Resources 2000–2001: People and Ecosystems: The Fraying Web of Life* (Washington, DC: World Resources Institute, 2000), 246, 248.

13. Much of this section is drawn from Ramachandra Guha, *Environmentalism: A Global History* (New York: Longman, 2000).

14. Walden Bello, "Structural Adjustment Programs: 'Success' for Whom," in Jerry Mander and Edward Goldsmith, *The Case against the Global*

Economy (San Francisco: Sierra Club Books, 1996), 286.

15. The general framework for this section derives from Samuel P. Huntington, *The Third Wave* (Norman: University of Oklahoma Press, 1991). The quote is from page 17.

16. David Reynolds, *One World Divisible: A Global History since 1945* (New York: Norton, 2000), 654–55.

17. David Crystal, "Vanishing Languages," *Civilization*, February/March 1997, 40–45.

18. David Aikman, *Jesus in Beijing* (Washington, DC: Regnery, 2003).

19. Betty Friedan, *The Feminine Mystique* (New York: Dell, 1963), 11–12.

20. Yasmine Ergas, "Feminisms of the 1970s," in *A History of Women*, ed. Francoise Thebaud (Cambridge, MA: Harvard University Press, 1994), 527–28.

21. Elisabeth Jay Friedman, "Gendering the Agenda," *Women's Studies International Forum* 26, no. 4 (2003): 313–31.

Index

Page numbers of figures (tables, charts, etc.) are italicized.